FROM GRADUATION
TO CORPORATION

THE PRACTICAL GUIDE TO CLIMBING THE
CORPORATE LADDER ONE RUNG AT A TIME

ANDY TEACH

authorHOUSE®

AuthorHouse™
1663 Liberty Drive
Bloomington, IN 47403
www.authorhouse.com
Phone: 1-800-839-8640

First edition published by AuthorHouse 12/18/2008
Second edition published by AuthorHouse 4/4/2012

ISBN: 978-1-4389-3063-3 (sc)
ISBN: 978-1-4520-3581-9 (e)

To my six young nieces—I wish you the best of
luck and success in your future careers.

Table of Contents

Important Note to the Reader

Although the author discusses a wide range of topics relating to business and career issues, neither the author nor the publisher are engaged in rendering financial, legal, tax or any other professional services to the reader. Readers are urged to conduct their own research, and to consult appropriate counselors for professional advice, before making any use of the contents. This publication is sold without warranties or guarantees of any kind by the author or the publisher, and all liability and responsibility relating to the contents of this publication and/or the use of such contents is hereby expressly disclaimed.

ACKNOWLEDGMENTS

Thank you to my family and friends for all of your support. A sincere thanks to Ann, Bob, Clay, Kate, Lisa, Ron, Van, and Vickie for taking the time during their busy schedules to help me make this book the best it can be. Thank you to AuthorHouse and special thanks to everyone reading this book—I truly hope it has made a difference in your quest to climb the corporate ladder.

PREFACE

On November 19, 1984, I began my West Coast executive career in Los Angeles, California at one of the largest television and motion picture studios in the United States. On September 14, 2007, I said my goodbyes after working for the same two bosses in the same department for twenty-three years. My bosses had decided with mixed emotions that it was time for me to leave. It's important to understand what I did right to survive and thrive for over two decades working for the same company and for the same two bosses. Yet, it's equally important to learn what I did wrong over the years that ultimately would lead to my involuntary exit.

I'm writing this book to educate young people on how to succeed in the corporate world. It contains a lot of great information for corporate veterans, too. The stories and examples that are presented here are all true and are based on my own personal experiences. It's these stories and examples that make this book unique. I didn't interview any so-called experts with Ph.D.'s. I don't try to be politically correct. In this book you'll read about the cause and effect of certain actions taken by myself, my bosses, my employees, and my co-workers over the years. I believe that you can learn from all of the examples set forth in this book. I'm brutally honest about working in the corporate world and don't try to sugarcoat anything. In fact, I'll be giving you some "tough love" to ensure that you're prepared for the challenges and rewards that lie ahead.

Over the years, there have been many times when I would interview someone for a job or had employees working for me and I wondered—what were they thinking? Then I realized—they weren't thinking! While they had a formal education, they were lacking an education in the do's and don'ts of corporate culture. It's not something that's taught in a classroom, rather it is gained from experience. And, if you're just starting out in the real world, experience is the one thing that you don't have.

Working in a corporate culture is not for everyone. You must make certain sacrifices to survive, and some people aren't willing to do that. I've had good friends say to me, "Andy, I don't know how you do it," referring to my working in a corporate environment. They used to work in a corporate culture, but they now run their own businesses. You need to work in the environment that is most comfortable for you. The corporate world is challenging, but it definitely has its rewards. The choice is yours.

My expertise is in the entertainment field, but my experiences and observations certainly pertain to any work environment. No matter which industry you choose, you will have to deal with bosses, co-workers, office politics, commuting, juggling work and family, etc. How you deal with these factors will determine the success or failure of your career.

THE "MILLENNIALS"

Over the years, I've had dozens of employees reporting to me, but in recent years I've noticed some changes, especially in some of the younger staff. They are part of a generation called the "Millennials." You've probably heard of the Baby Boomers (born between the mid-1940s and the mid-1960s) and Generation X (born between the mid-1960s and the late 1970s), but the Millennials, also known as Generation Y, are the next in line. If you were born approximately between 1980 and 2000, then you're a Millennial. You've grown up with the Internet, cell phones, text messaging, and high-definition television. You're very tech-savvy, intelligent, and have almost perfected the art of multitasking, but some of you approach work differently and have different expectations than your predecessors.

"Expectations" is an important word here, because if you've recently graduated from college, you may have certain expectations of what a job will be like and how your supervisor will treat you. But your supervisor also has expectations of how you as an employee will act. Many times the expectations of the two parties involved are very different. If the expectations are different, do you think it's more likely the supervisor will change their expectations to accommodate you or that you will change your expectations to accommodate your supervisor? It's usually the latter.

A *USA Today*[1] article by Stephanie Armour states, "More than 60% of employers say they are experiencing tension between employees from different generations, according to a survey conducted by Lee Hecht Harrison (a career management company). The survey found that more than 70% of older employees are dismissive of younger workers' abilities. And nearly half of employers say that younger employees are dismissive of the abilities of their older co-workers."

And so it seems that with every new generation comes a new generation gap. The older generation believed in paying their dues first before advancing in their careers and probably believes that newer employees should do the same. But you have grown up in a fast-moving digital world and might be a little more impatient than your elders. Many of you likely expect to move up the ladder quickly, even at the risk of moving up too quickly.

This book can help you narrow the gap between your expectations and the expectations of your employer. It can lessen the conflict that will most likely occur between you, the younger Millennial employee, and your older Generation-X or Baby-Boomer supervisor. This book is an invitation. You're invited to go inside my mind—that of a Baby-Boomer executive—and the minds of others like me in order to see things from our perspective. By understanding how your future supervisors might think, you'll have a distinct advantage when working with them.

Please consider this book the beginning of your corporate education. Unlike your college career, there's no finite end to your education in the corporate world until you retire. From the bottom rung of the corporate ladder to the top rung, there's a lot to learn and a lot of obstacles to overcome to get there. However, as you enter "the real world," you'll have an advantage over your peers by acquiring the knowledge necessary to rise to the top of your chosen field one rung at a time.

RUNG I – FINDING A CAREER

LOOK FOR A CAREER, NOT A JOB

Congratulations, you've just graduated from college! It's quite a milestone. However, don't pat yourself on the back just yet. This is just the beginning. What are you going to do now? I'm sure that you'll be looking for a job. Isn't that your goal? However, I'd like you to consider not just looking for a job but looking for a career. There's a big difference between the two. A job pays the bills, but you can take it or leave it. You may not be that enthusiastic about a job. A career, on the other hand, is something you're passionate about, something you love to do. In fact, the feeling of accomplishment you get from your career will be even more important than your title or salary because you get to do something that you truly look forward to doing every day.

THE CORPORATE WORLD IS A DIFFERENT WORLD

As a college student, you were probably used to sleeping in on some days during the week, pulling all-nighters before an exam, and partying hard at fraternity and sorority parties. Sorry, those days are over. It's time to acquire a new mindset that will prepare you to not only enter the corporate world, but to excel in it. While you were in college, you dealt with the known. After four years in school, you were very familiar with the various campus classroom facilities, dorms, students, teachers, university administration, and activities.

However, you're now venturing into the unknown. You'll be facing a new set of campus classroom facilities (your office building), dorms (your apartment), students (your co-workers), teachers (your bosses), the university administration (upper management), and activities (office lunches, parties, and seminars). You now have a clean slate and a tremendous opportunity ahead of you.

WHY A CAREER IS SO IMPORTANT

When you think ahead to how you want to live your life, how do you picture it? Do you want to live paycheck to paycheck and have to constantly endure that stress? Or, do you want to live comfortably and provide for your family and yourself? A successful career in the corporate world can do the latter. It will take a lot of hard work and sacrifice. Not everyone is willing to do that, but if you're willing to work hard, it'll pay off. Simply put, you literally can't afford to be out of work. Eventually, you'll have a mortgage, car payments, the kids' college tuition, vacations, medical bills, and other responsibilities. Wouldn't it be nice to find a career that you enjoy and that makes you financially secure? Of course it would. This is why it's so important to be able to keep a job for as long as you want to without taking a step backward.

What did my corporate career mean to me? Aside from the satisfaction I derived from doing a job well, it enabled me to purchase a house, a nice car, and to go on exotic personal vacations. I traveled around the country on business trips on an expense account. Furthermore, I have money in the bank for a rainy day. Don't get me wrong—it's not just about the material things. It's more about living a comfortable life without the stress of worrying about paying the bills. It's so important to keep your job until you're financially secure enough to retire. That's why you must constantly strive to improve yourself in the workplace.

My corporate career, which spanned more than two decades, was at one of the largest television and motion picture studios in the country. I worked in the research department. The last ten years there I was Vice-President of Network and Cable Research. I was part of a multi-billion dollar corporation. My division alone brought in approximately a billion dollars of revenue a year.

One of my main functions was to analyze the Nielsen ratings for all television shows, but primarily for those produced by my studio. A Nielsen rating generally is a number that represents a percentage of people who are watching a particular television program. This job involved working constantly with numbers. Growing up, I was always good at math and genuinely enjoyed working with statistics. I also loved watching television. I remember one weekend when I was a teenager in New Jersey, I watched television from 5 p.m. on Friday straight through to 11 p.m. on Sunday, only getting up to use the bathroom and to sleep. I believe I watched the Beatles' movie *A Hard Day's Night* three times that weekend—and this was before cable! I was lucky enough to find a career that combined two things I was passionate about: working with numbers and watching television. I received a real sense of accomplishment from my work.

It's not always easy finding what you want to do in life. Like me, at first you'll probably spend some time finding out what you don't want to do. When I was in elementary school in Englishtown, New Jersey in the early 1970s, we didn't have our own public library, so I would have to go to one in the nearest town, which was Freehold, New Jersey. Little did I know that only a few blocks away, a young man had grown up playing guitar and singing and would eventually become successful in his chosen career. His name is Bruce Springsteen. No one better represents passion about their career than Bruce Springsteen. If you've ever seen him in concert, you know what I mean. I met Bruce a couple of times in the early 1980s at a small club in Red Bank, New Jersey that was owned by the late Clarence Clemons, his saxophone player. Bruce would get up on stage unannounced at 1 or 2 in the morning and would play cover songs with the house band. I remember seeing the veins almost pop out of his neck when he sang, giving it all he had. He wasn't getting paid. He didn't have to be there. He just loved playing guitar and singing. To him, it wasn't a job, it was his life. This is a man who loves what he does.

When I was in the library, I would constantly re-read the same two large books on careers. At one point, I wanted to be an archeologist and dig up dinosaur bones. In eighth grade, I decided I wanted to be an optometrist, until I figured out that looking inside people's eyeballs all day probably wasn't a good idea. When I was in high school, I didn't do too well in Biology or Chemistry. In fact, I finished my junior year in high school with six A's, but with an F in Chemistry. That was an eye opener. So I realized that I wouldn't be pursuing a career in science, which narrowed it down to ninety-six other areas I could go into. I always did well in English and enjoyed writing. I noticed that there was a job called "copywriter" in which you could write the advertisements that you see on television or in magazines. At that point, my goal was to work in an advertising agency and utilize my creative side.

I graduated from Rutgers University with two B.A. degrees, one in Business Administration and one in Human Communications. Upon reflection, I wouldn't have taken Business Administration as a major. I did it because I thought it would look good on my résumé, which was the wrong reason to make it one of my majors. The right reason would have been if I were truly interested in this area and enjoyed learning about it. As a result, my grades were so-so. That's why it's so important to be passionate about something. You'll work harder with little motivation because you love what you do. Human Communications was more interesting to me because it dealt with mass media, especially television and advertising. My grades were better in this area as I felt this could help me more in my career and I truly enjoyed learning about this field.

I graduated from college in May 1980. Most graduates immediately started looking for a job, if they hadn't already found one. I say "most graduates" because I wasn't one of them. I realized that once I started working I would likely have a 9-to-5 life until I was sixty-five years old, so I decided to take a little detour. A fellow student and I decided to bicycle 1,300 miles from New Jersey to Florida. Yes, on a bicycle, not on a motorcycle or in a car. What was I thinking? Five days after I graduated college, we set off at 5 a.m. on a dark morning. Three weeks later we had reached our destination, which was Boca Raton, Florida, where my grandparents lived at the time.

My friend soon flew home but I stayed for a while and got my first post-college job. What kind of job did I get with my two B.A. degrees from a highly rated school? My first job was planting trees and shrubs at a tree nursery in the very hot Florida sun! It lasted three weeks before I realized that this wasn't a job I wanted, nor was it the career I wanted. I then thought that perhaps working in the corporate world in an air-conditioned office wouldn't be so bad after all. I flew back to New Jersey which, at the age of twenty-two, was my first plane trip. I had a nice homecoming, but then it was time to face the reality of looking for a career—or at least a job. I knew I wanted to work for an advertising agency in New York City, but how did I go about looking for a job? I didn't know anyone who worked at an ad agency and just sending in a résumé seemed like a hopeless situation.

NETWORKING

Networking is one of the most important factors in helping you to find a job. It begins on your first day of kindergarten, and it never ends. You've heard the saying, "It's not what you know, it's who you know." So true. Getting to know as many people as possible is critical to your future success because each person you know knows someone else. Start with your family: parents, grandparents, siblings, and in-laws. Who do they know? Ask them if they know anyone in the field you are interested in.

Meet and speak to as many people as possible. Don't necessarily wait until you're ready to look for a job. Just keep asking around. Ask your doctor or dentist if they have any patients in the field that you're interested in. Perhaps one of their patients would be willing to speak with you. If you're in a college fraternity or sorority, ask everyone there what their parents do for a living. Use your contacts to the maximum. Keep a computer record of all your contacts (with their title, email address, and phone number) as well as notes summarizing your conversations with everyone you speak to.

Another great job-search technique is the use of the "informational interview." I know many people who have used an informational interview to network with senior executives. This type of interview involves cold calling (calling someone you don't know) a person in the industry you are interested in and asking them if they have some time to speak with you about their job or field. This person might be someone in the department you want to work in or it might be a person from your college or university who works for the company. Calling alumni from your college or university is one of the most effective ways to network. If you are a student or a recent graduate, the informational interview is a perfect opportunity to ask questions in a non-threatening setting. You *do not* want to act as though you are talking with them only to find a job (although, in reality, that is what you ultimately want either from them or from someone they eventually refer you to). Your goal should be to have an intelligent conversation, come well-dressed and well-prepared with insightful questions, make a good impression, and get referrals to other people in the industry with whom you can speak. And don't forget the all-important thank-you note for their time and trouble. The person who recommended you should also get a thank-you note, letting them know how the interview went. Before you know it, you will have a great networking base and you will get the inside track on any job openings. One last thing: when you do call a referral, remember to tell them the name of the person who referred you. This gives you built-in credibility.

Another way to utilize the informational interview is to visit your parents' friends and the parents of your friends in their work environment. It doesn't matter if they work in a field you're interested in. The point is to see and experience different types of work environments and see which ones make you most comfortable. There is no pressure on you because you are most likely not speaking to them about a particular job. The key is to ask questions and make a great impression. Ask them questions such as, "What is it like to work at your company?" "What is the reputation of the younger employees who work here?" "What professional qualities lead to promotion?" "What qualities prevent people from getting promoted?" By asking these types of questions and experiencing different types of work environments, you will be better suited to find your ideal job.

When I put students in touch with some of my contacts in the entertainment industry, I like to know if my contact was helpful and how the meeting went. Try to keep your contacts informed of your career progress. When you get a job, let your contacts know and thank them for their help.

Utilizing the Internet is another great way to network. There are networking websites such as LinkedIn, which focus more on business connections and help professionals make important contacts. This particular site has well over one hundred million members and continues to grow. A great way to find people who might be in a field you're interested in is to do a company search on LinkedIn. Once you type in a company name, you will see a list of people with whom you share a common connection or group membership. Try contacting them. If the person you email or call says "no," don't give up. Keep trying until someone agrees to speak with you. There is more information about LinkedIn and other career-related websites in the WHERE TO FIND OUT ABOUT JOBS AND CAREERS section of this book.

Another great way to network is to attend networking events in your area. Professional mixers and social events provide people who work in a particular field an opportunity to gather at a restaurant or bar to meet new contacts, get reacquainted with old contacts, and network to get a job through these relationships. These mixers are often advertised online (including on LinkedIn) or in newspapers and industry publications, so watch out for them. Many websites also exist that advertise local events in various cities. When you attend these mixers, introduce yourself to as many people as possible. Ask them about *their* current situation—don't make it about you. In fact, the more you learn about them and their job, the better. Some people may get disaffected if they think you are pumping them for information or appear desperate for a job, so keep the focus on them. Always remember to bring business cards and to ask the people you speak with for their cards. If you are unemployed or a student, you should use an inexpensive service to create and print business cards (I use Vistaprint-www.vistaprint.com) with your name and basic contact information (email address, cell phone number) on it, as well as the name of your school. (If you are still in college or graduate school, many programs have pre-fabricated business card templates you can use.)

When you get a job, it's important to meet as many people as possible not just in your company but in other companies as well. After all, some day you might want to get a job at a different company and if you already have people there who know you and will give you a reference, you're ahead of the game. Over the years, I talked to contacts at competing studios as well as at all the broadcast networks and cable networks. After some initial telephone contact, I'd ask them out to lunch. Nothing substitutes for person-to-person contact. There were a few fellow researchers who like me, started out at the bottom but over the years they rose to very high positions at the networks or the studios. I asked for and received very important information from them, which my bosses appreciated.

So, how did I land my first job? I networked with the person I knew the best—my dad. My father was a vice-president of finance for a television production company, and he knew a producer at his company. This TV producer had many contacts at different advertising agencies. I met the producer and gave him an idea of what I was looking for. He immediately made a few phone calls. Soon, I had a few interviews set up in Manhattan. One of those interviews was in the media planning department at a top ten advertising agency. I interviewed there and, with the help of the producer who had called on my behalf, I got the job. This wasn't the copywriting job I wanted. In fact, media planning involves helping a client spend their advertising budget on the right advertising outlets. But my feeling was, "Hey, I got a job, which is number one, and I at least got a job at an advertising agency, which is what I wanted to do." Now that I had a foot in the door, I knew that I could eventually move to the creative side of the business.

I worked in the media planning department for the next eighteen months. After six months on the job I got a promotion from assistant media planner to media planner. This ad agency was known as a sweat shop. They paid you little for a lot of work, but it was a terrific experience and a great introduction to the corporate world. The fact that I had this job on my résumé was very helpful to me in getting my next big position.

Despite my promotion, my heart wasn't in the job. I did work with numbers, which I enjoyed, but I don't think I had the aptitude to make it a career. I wanted to be a copywriter, but I made one big mistake—I never attempted to network once I was inside the ad agency. I had a great opportunity to speak with people who were copywriters and ask for their advice, but I never did. Perhaps I was intimidated because I was a small fish in a very big pond or because I was shy. Don't make the same mistake I made. If you find a company you want to work for, get a job there, even though it may not be your ideal job. The important thing is that once you are on the inside, you should take advantage of it and make as many contacts as you can. You have a much better chance of being noticed than people who are on the outside. Eventually you will get the job you want because you are on "the inside."

After those eighteen months, I moved to another New York advertising agency that specialized in motion picture advertising. Their clients were all the major motion picture studios. One of their main responsibilities was to have graphic artists produce local newspaper advertisements, and then we would send the ads to local newspapers. These ads contained the artwork from the movie and listed all the theaters and movie times in the area.

I was officially an assistant account executive. After spending one year in a large smoke-filled room with the graphic artists and calling local newspapers every day, they asked that I take on a different role in the company, but I declined. After working for two-and-a-half years in New York City on things I didn't want to do, I felt it was time to take a chance so that I'd be able to find something I did want to do. I was no closer to being a copywriter that day than I was 30 months earlier. I'd been thinking about moving to Los Angeles to pursue a career in entertainment and, this was the catalyst I needed. I had an enormous sense of relief when I tendered my resignation.

There were a few obstacles I had to overcome. First, I had never been to Los Angeles. The only thing I knew about "L.A." was that it was supposedly laid-back. So much so that I actually thought that everyone left their job at 3 p.m. every day to hang out at the beach. Boy was I wrong! Second, I had to figure out how to get there. I decided to take two-and-a-half weeks and drove out with one of my former college roommates. It was an awesome trip. We saw Graceland (the home of Elvis Presley), the Alamo, and Carlsbad Caverns. We even hiked from the top to the bottom and back to the top of the Grand Canyon in one day (which isn't recommended!). Third, I had no apartment in L.A., so I had to decide where to live. My dad had been going to L.A. every three months on business, so I timed my cross-country trip to ensure I could stay with my dad at his hotel, the Century Plaza in Century City, for about ten days. Fortunately—and this is where networking paid off for me—I'd become good friends with someone from my first ad agency job who had moved to Los Angeles about a year earlier. He and his roommate graciously allowed me to stay with them for a few weeks. I'd bought enough time to find an apartment.

I was pretty confident about getting a good job. After all, I had my two B.A. degrees and now I had almost three years of corporate experience, so I had high expectations. I got a job but it was in a small oldies record store selling records and making minimum wage. That lasted about three months. Once again, I didn't feel I was making progress toward starting a new career. I talked to my dad again, who put me in touch with the same producer who had helped me initially because he came to Los Angeles all the time. He got me a job at a production company. No, I wasn't going to be an executive. I was going to be a messenger! That's right–my job was to drive around Los Angeles delivering packages. I could have let my ego get in the way and declined the offer because, after all, I was a college graduate with two B.A. degrees and had corporate experience. But here's a news flash: don't have the false impression that just because you graduated with honors from a top college that you'll be starting at the top. Most likely, you'll have to pay your dues, so be patient and eventually good things will happen. Sometimes you do have to take two steps back before you take a step forward.

I was a messenger for about a year. I certainly got to learn about driving in Los Angeles. Once in a while, I would run into a celebrity. However, I didn't move out to Los Angeles to have a career as a messenger. I called my dad after six months and told him that things weren't working out too well for me. He told me to stick it out for a little while longer. I did, and then I got my big corporate break.

I had taken a day off and visited my ad-agency friend at his office (remember what I said about visiting people in their work environment?). He now worked at Warner Bros. in the television research department. Once I arrived, he showed me a *Knot's Landing* research pitch *(Knot's Landing was a CBS drama that aired from 1979–93)*. This pitch highlighted the program's strong Nielsen ratings on CBS and would be used by the Warner Bros.' sales force to sell reruns of the program to local television stations. I knew nothing about television research, but when I saw that this pitch contained numbers and involved the sale of a television show, I said, "Hey, I can do this." My friend referred me to his boss, who told me that there was a research position open at another studio. I got the phone number of the person doing the hiring there and set up an interview. After interviewing with him, he invited me back for a second interview with his boss. To help my chances, I asked the TV producer who had been so helpful to me previously if he knew anyone at the television studio where I wanted to work. He knew the two presidents of the company and put in a good word for me. They called the people doing the hiring. To make a long story short, I got the job and worked there for twenty-three years! I received six promotions during this time, rising from research clerk to vice-president, as I worked my way up the corporate ladder.

The lesson here is to figure out as quickly as possible what you *don't* like doing so you can move on to something you *do* enjoy doing. Your career is out there waiting for you, and the sooner you find it, the better it'll be for you. That's why it's important to start doing your homework before you graduate. In my case, perhaps I could have tried harder to talk with people at the advertising agencies I worked for to get that copywriter position. Perhaps I wasn't hungry enough. Things happen for a reason. I'm not normally a risk taker, but I took a very big risk in leaving my family and friends behind. Sometimes you have to take risks, especially early in your career, to get what you want.

As you can see, it was a combination of taking risks, networking, and good luck that eventually landed me the career of my dreams. But it was a challenge to get to that point. It's important to use every resource you have when looking for a job. Don't be shy about asking people for help. Many people out there enjoy helping others. When people help you, they are making an investment in you and want to help you in the future.

RUNG I SUMMARY

- **Look for a career, not a job.**
- **Find something you're passionate about.**
- **Get business cards before you start networking.**
- **Network with as many people as possible, even after you get the job.**
- **Utilize cold calling to get informational interviews.**
- **Be patient–you may have to take two steps back before you move a step forward.**

RUNG II – THE JOB SEARCH AND INTERVIEW PROCESS

THE RÉSUMÉ AND COVER LETTER

I received hundreds of résumés and cover letters over the years from people who were looking for a job on my staff. Some I immediately discarded into the "circular file" (garbage can), some I put in the "maybe" pile, and some I marked down as a definite interview.

Other than your informal networking, the first thing you need to do when searching for a job is to put together a résumé and cover letter. These documents let your potential employer know why you are a great hire, so it's important to spend a lot of time creating and perfecting them in order to help you get that interview.

There are plenty of books out there teaching you how to put them together, but I want to tell you what I did and did not like to see on a résumé and cover letter.

The Reasons Why I Was More Likely to Toss Out a Résumé and Cover Letter

Typos

If you have just one typo on your résumé or cover letter, your chances of getting an interview with me would decrease (unless you have a 4.0 GPA from Harvard!). As when I go to a restaurant. I usually start out with the premise of a 20% tip, but if I'm displeased with the service, I drop the tip down to 15% or less. Similarly, one résumé typo will lower your value in the eyes of the interviewer. Typos are a sign of carelessness. If one of my employees was careless, it reflected badly on them, on me, and on our entire staff. I prided myself in the fact that my memos were error-free, as were those of my staff after I proofread them. Since we worked with numbers all the time, there was no room for error. Proof your résumé and cover letter very carefully, and then let a friend proof them.

"Out-of-Staters"

If a résumé came from out-of-state, especially if the candidate lived far away, I usually wouldn't look at it. I didn't want to feel guilty about having someone spend hundreds of dollars on airfare to come in and interview for a job they might not get. However, if your potential job is in New York City, for example, and you are within commuting distance, then being out-of-state is certainly acceptable. My advice is that if you're interested in getting a job in another city or state that's far away, book a hotel for a week there and send a cover letter to any potential employers telling them you'll be in town that week. You're much more likely to get an interview that way because the interviewer won't feel as though they are the only reason you're flying in.

International Experience

I viewed someone with a lot of international experience as a potential negative to our department. Since I worked in the U.S. entertainment industry, I wanted someone on my staff who knew what *The Brady Bunch* was all about. I wanted someone who was familiar with U.S. television and grew up with it. Of course, if you're looking for a job in a company's international division in which foreign education or international experience is a plus, play up this angle. Try to find out ahead of time what kind of experience your prospective employer is looking for.

I've lectured at several colleges and universities around the country and sometimes during these lectures, I come in contact with international students. They face different obstacles than American students. The first obstacle they face is the English language itself. Some international students have heavy accents, and unfortunately, this can hinder their employment opportunities. I recommend they take English lessons or accent-reduction courses from a local community college, watch American television, and practice English with their American-born friends. Another obstacle is that some students may be allowed to work in the U.S. only for a year on a student visa which can make it difficult for them to get a job if an employer thinks their employment will be short-lived. Furthermore, the lack of a Green Card can mean a short stay in the United States. Non-U.S. citizens need to get a sponsor, but some companies may not want to sponsor them until they have proven themselves as a worthwhile employee. If you are an international student, it may beneficial to start calling

Human Resources departments in different companies or your college career center to gather as much information as possible so there are no surprises when you're ready to graduate.

Academic Standing

I looked very closely at what college the candidate graduated from. I didn't care about their football team. I wanted to know how good their school's academic standing was. Since most people I interviewed came from Southern California, I'd look for résumés from graduates of some of the higher-rated schools there. Don't get me wrong: I did interview and hire people from other schools, but someone who graduated from a great academic school had a much better chance.

I liked to use Barron's Profiles of American Colleges guide to see how an interviewee's college/university was rated academically. Schools are generally divided into five categories: Most Competitive, Highly Competitive, Very Competitive, Competitive, and Less Competitive. I would prefer to interview candidates from the first three categories, although I did interview candidates from the others.

One word of advice: if you're attending or have graduated from a school with a very high academic standing, you should not assume that the interviewer knows about your school's high academic standing. Yes, most interviewers are familiar with the reputations of Harvard, Yale, or Princeton. However, there are many other schools with the same academic standing as Ivy League schools, but they don't have the same national prestige. I discovered this when I gave career advice lectures at certain colleges and universities. It wasn't until I looked up these schools in Barron's guide that I realized how strong they were academically. In all the years that I received résumés, including from some of these highly rated schools, I never realized how great a reputation they had. Therefore, I recommend that if your school has a really strong academic reputation, you should consider mentioning this in your cover letter or interview. Sometimes you have to be more than a job candidate; you also need to be a publicist for your school.

Party Schools

I was always wary of people who graduated from so-called "party schools." Remember, we were looking for intelligent people with an outstanding work ethic, not people who liked to drink alcohol all of the time or who majored in bong-aroma therapy. If you did attend a party school and are asked about it in the interview, just focus on the academic attributes of your college.

Generic Résumés and Cover Letters

I received so many résumés that seemed like they were a part of a mass mailing. I could tell that many people never even read the job description, because if they had, they would never have sent me their résumé. These candidates were also very general in their cover letter, and it seemed like the people who sent them just wanted to get a job somewhere, anywhere. Do yourself a favor: don't send a mass email résumé or cover letter. Since I might get fifty résumés just for an intern position, I didn't have time to look at generic résumés. Similarly, if you send a generic cover letter, you might be wasting the time of the interviewer, and your time, too. Decide exactly what you want to do and where you want to do it and tailor your résumé and cover letter specifically to the department and company for which you want to work. If you're not going to put a lot of time and effort into your résumé or cover letter, it's assumed that you won't put a lot of time and effort into your job either.

Try to avoid sending a cover letter that says, "To Whom It May Concern." If you've done your informational interviewing and networking correctly, and if you've used the Internet and your alumni networks to identify the names of persons in your target companies, you should have the name of a person to whom to send your résumé. Of course, some companies prefer you send résumés directly to their Human Resources (HR) department, but the creative job-hunter will usually first send his or her résumé to an executive whom they have already spoken to. Even when you send a résumé to HR, call the department to learn the name of the recruiter responsible for screening applicants for the position in which you are interested. It may be difficult to get this information, but try it because if you're successful, you can separate yourself from the rest of the pack.

Bright Colors

You want your résumé and cover letter to stand out from the competition, but if they're bright orange, for example, they'll stand out for the wrong reason. The best way to stand out from your competitors is through your accomplishments. Use neutral colors such as white, beige, or light brown for your résumé and/or cover letter.

Long Résumés

Since you may be just out of college, you won't have a lot of job experience, and therefore a one page résumé should suffice. If your résumé is longer than one page, give yourself the "so what?" test. If what you put down is not that impressive and someone might say to you, "so what?"–then don't include it.

Some job candidates may try to avoid putting their résumé on two pages by cramming a lot of information on one page, but this is not recommended. The overall look and format of the résumé is very important. The first thing an interviewer will judge on your résumé is its appearance and readability. It creates a negative impression if it's crowded or wordy, or if the font is too small. Use bullet points (and not too many bullets), use a common font such as Times New Roman or Arial, and have enough space between your main points.

Job Jumpers

If I saw that a candidate has jumped from job to job and has stayed at each job for a year or less, I would worry that if I hired them their tenure with me wouldn't last that long either. For recent college grads, it's a little different since most of your jobs are part-time or summer jobs, but for those who have been out of college for a while, it's important to have some stability. I realize that some Millennials want to move up the ladder quickly and sometimes this is accomplished by switching jobs quite often. However, please be aware that your prospective employer may see this as a negative.

Outdated Résumé Sections

Some résumé sections may now be obsolete. Some recruiters say that it is no longer necessary or relevant to put an objective on your résumé because the objective reflects what you want, but your prospective company is more concerned about what it wants. Besides, they already know what you want–a job with their company. My suggestion is to eliminate this section and add a "Summary of Qualifications" (Google "Summary of Qualifications" to get some examples of how this section should look) that highlights your achievements. Furthermore, it is not really necessary to include "References Available Upon Request" on your résumé. It is assumed you will have references, so bring a separate page listing your references to your interview. Consult with your college or other career center regarding these two ideas before your interview.

What Looks Good on a Résumé and Cover Letter

Your Name, Home Address, Email Address, Home Phone Number, and Cell Phone Number

I'm stating the obvious, but you need to make it very easy for someone to be able to contact you. Ask yourself if your email address is inappropriate. If your email address has the words "lazybum" or "party girl" in it, then I suggest you get another email address for your job search. If "lazybum," e.g., is your email address, the interviewer just got his/her first impression of you . . . and it's not a good one!

Internships

Having an internship on your résumé, especially if it's from a well-known company, is the equivalent of résumé gold. It means that you have experience working in the "real world" and hiring managers will be impressed by this. Even unpaid internships will pay off in the long run, so take one if it is offered. There were times when I offered recent college graduates a paid internship but it wasn't enough money for them so they turned it down. They made a big mistake because our interns were always in demand by all the other studios once they had completed their internship with us. During my college years, I worked as a camp counselor during the summers. It was a lot of fun and perhaps it showed that I had leadership skills but if I could do it over again, I would have sought out a company internship.

Specific Résumés and Cover Letters

Previously, I referred to résumés and cover letters that were too general or generic. How can you tailor your résumé or cover letter to give your potential employer a good impression and to show you are interested in and qualified for that *specific* job?

In your cover letter you can refer to how specific parts of your background qualify you for the position (by referring to the qualifications listed in the job posting), to particular projects the company is involved in, and the like. The key is to show you've done your research and that you are sending a résumé *for a reason*. Also, if you spoke to someone at the company who suggested you send in a résumé, or if you had an informational interview with an executive and made a good impression, you should refer to that person (or persons). The more you demonstrate you want the job, the better.

As for the résumé, my suggestion–especially when you are starting out and might be interested in two or more industries–is to have a résumé that targets each industry. Perhaps you have a marketing major and a finance minor. You might have had an internship in college in each of those industries. In your marketing résumé, you would put more emphasis on your marketing internship by dedicating more space to that internship. You might also list in your academic section the specific marketing courses you took, along with your marketing GPA (if your department doesn't provide a GPA for your major or minor, you can calculate it on your own).

Relevant Skills

Every job requires a certain skill set regardless of the industry. Many skills are common to multiple industries. So, even if you are applying for a job in an industry outside your major or you already have a job and are switching fields, you can sell yourself by selling your skills and by referring to those skills in your cover letter and by emphasizing them on your résumé, as discussed above.

Here's one example: Because of the area I worked in (entertainment and media research), I looked for people with experience working with numbers. Obviously, if they majored in economics or statistics, that was a plus. But, even if they worked in a bank, as long as they had some interest and experience in working with numbers in an analytical environment, they were considered.

Grade Point Average (GPA)

It certainly doesn't hurt to let prospective employers know that you're an excellent student. If your GPA is high, list it after you list the college you're attending or have graduated from. As mentioned, major and minor GPAs can also help you to target specific employers in specific industries.

If your GPA is not high and you don't include it on your résumé, you must be prepared to explain why you've omitted it. If there are specific courses in which your GPA is higher or if it is higher in your major (or in one of your majors), you can mention or list this (i.e., "GPA in Major"). Perhaps you work full-time or part-time, have to take care of a family member, or maybe you're smart but just don't like studying. Whatever the reason, you need to be prepared to answer the interviewer's questions about your GPA.

The good news is that in a Harris Interactive Poll[2] conducted on behalf of CareerBuilder.com, more than 3,000 hiring managers and Human Resources professionals were asked what their GPA requirements were for résumés. Approximately 60% replied they don't have a minimum GPA requirement, about 30% required a 3.0 or above, and 10% required a 3.5 GPA or above.

Personally, the higher a school was rated academically, the more leeway I would give the interviewee in terms of their GPA. For instance, if the interviewee went to an Ivy League school, I was fine with seeing a GPA of a 3.0 (with 4.0 being the highest) or higher. It didn't have to be a 4.0, since I knew how tough the school was. If the school was less prestigious, I would hope to see at least a 3.5 GPA, although a 3.0 or higher is generally acceptable. That's just my personal opinion and as you can see from the Harris Poll, interviewers have different expectations. There is no "Golden Rule" about this, so you should use your best judgment.

Keywords

Many hiring managers utilize computer software to search résumés electronically for certain keywords that match those in the job description. Keywords are nouns, adjectives, verbs, and phrases that tell the hiring manager what your skills and qualifications are. The more industry specific they are, the better. Hiring managers keep a database of these keywords and will choose which résumés to look at based on how many matching keywords you have on your résumé. Use as many action words as you can, not terms such as "responsible for" or "proven track record." Talk about your actual accomplishments and results, not what you're responsible for.

Some suggestions for action words are "accomplished," "achieved," "attained," "assisted," "cataloged," "compiled," "designed," "developed," "exceeded," "executed," "implemented," "initiated," "negotiated," "organized," "streamlined," and "supported."

Use keywords and phrases that are specific to certain fields, such as "accounting," "data analysis," "market research," "merchandiser," "pharmacy," "project management," "registered nurse," "strategic sales," etc. As mentioned, you must look closely at the job description, which will have many of the keywords you will need.

The more you can quantify your accomplishments, the better. If you've helped to increase sales by $50,000 or by +15%, this gives the hiring company a benchmark by which to judge you as well as to compare you with other candidates. Numbers speak louder than words.

Attached References

As previously mentioned, you may consider including an attachment listing the names, titles, email addresses, and phone numbers of your references. If a company is interested in you, this will expedite the process. I can't tell you how many times we were interested in a candidate and wasted time because we had to wait until Human Resources called the potential candidate to get their references and then HR had to call the people listed as references. We'd never hire anyone until we heard back from these people. It's important to get approval from your references ahead of time before using them as a reference. If possible, obtain written letters of recommendation from your references and bring them with you to the interview. Finally, always remember to thank those who let you use them as a reference after you are done interviewing and find a job.

Your Graduation Dates and Jobs

It's important for the reader of your résumé to be able to follow your education and career path chronologically. If I saw a résumé that didn't include dates, I'd get a little suspicious and felt that perhaps the person was trying to hide something. Many hiring managers feel the same way.

Copy, Paste, and Send as an Attachment

It is important to realize that sometimes when you email your résumé as an attachment, the recipient may not be able to open it. Since they receive so many résumés, they may not bother to ask you to resend your résumé if they have trouble opening it. To eliminate this potential problem, copy and paste your résumé into the body of the email. This gives the reader the option of referring to the email itself should there be a problem opening the attachment.

Email Signature

You might want to consider using an email signature at the bottom of your email, especially when sending an email to a potential employer or business contact. A signature gives the reader all of your contact information. You can usually find the signature option under the options menu of your email service. You may use words such as "Cordially," or "Sincerely," and then put your name underneath. You should also include your home phone number, cell phone number, email address (even though they will have it after you email them), and perhaps your LinkedIn address if your profile is complete. You may even consider including the name of your school and major.

Send a Hard Copy

Many times I had an intern position available and Human Resources sent me an email containing thirty résumés. I couldn't tell where one résumé began and where one ended. That's why I recommend that, in addition to emailing your résumé, you should follow up with a hard copy. As I've mentioned, you should try to find out the name of the person who ultimately receives your résumé and then send them the hard copy. If I had received a hard copy of a résumé from any of these applicants, they would have separated themselves from the rest of the pack. Of course, there's no guarantee that this will give you an advantage in getting an interview because there are so many other factors involved, but at least your résumé will have a better chance of being noticed.

WHERE TO FIND OUT ABOUT JOBS AND CAREERS

The Internet

Before you send out your résumé, you first need to find out where to send it. Where are the job listings that you're looking for? The Internet is a great place to start. There are many websites that list jobs and careers including:

AfterCollege (www.aftercollege.com)

CareerBuilder (www.careerbuilder.com and www.careerrookie.com)

CollegeGrad (www.collegegrad.com)

CollegeRecruiter (www.collegerecruiter.com)

craigslist (www.craigslist.org)

EntryLevelJobsite (www.entryleveljobsite.com)

Experience (www.experience.com)

Indeed (www.indeed.com)

LinkedIn (www.linkedin.com)

Monster (www.monster.com and www.college.monster.com)

SimplyHired (www.simplyhired.com)

USA.gov (www.usa.gov)

Vault (www.vault.com)

You should consider posting your résumé on at least a few of them, especially those with "college" or "grad" in the title. They are more likely to cater to college students and recent grads and therefore could have more entry-level positions listed than other job websites. Although many of these websites list jobs by individual fields and industries, you may also consider looking for an industry-specific website that lists only jobs in the field you're interested in. Even if you don't post your résumé on a particular site, please keep in mind that job-search sites often provide great career advice on résumé and cover letter writing, interviewing, and networking. Review as many sites as you can to get this information. If you know what field you want to enter and you know the names of some of the companies you may wish to work for, go to their websites. Company websites are an excellent source of information. They'll tell you exactly where to send your résumé, and hopefully, they'll have the names of some of the executives in the company. You'll most likely be sending your résumé to their HR department, especially if it's a larger company, so look for the names of the HR executives, too.

Career Center

Most schools have some type of career center or career development center whose purpose is to prepare you for the job search and interview process, and ultimately, to help you find a job. I have worked with many college career centers, and I think they are a great, yet underutilized resource. A career center can counsel you and recommend the best way of achieving your career goals. They can give you a career assessment test to help you find the right career path for you. Some have libraries with great reference books on finding your ideal career. Many provide mock interviews with their counselors to help prepare you for the real thing. Many give workshops on how to create a résumé and cover letter, where to find out about jobs, and how to interview. A lot of colleges can set up informational interviews for you with alumni or provide you with alumni listings in your chosen field. Some colleges bring in outside speakers to educate students on what the working world is really like. Although I enjoy being an author, I particularly enjoy speaking to college students to help them make the transition from college to career.

Unfortunately, many students never set foot inside their career center during their entire college career. I think these students are making a big mistake. You have nothing to lose and everything to gain. I have read or heard from students and former students who have said that they were disappointed in their career centers and didn't get much out of them. If this is the case, set up an appointment with the director of your career center and let them know why you are disappointed. I know from my experiences with career centers and counselors that these professionals are some of the most sincere people with whom I have ever dealt.

I'm a member of a great organization called NACE (National Association of Colleges and Employers). Results from NACE's nationwide *2010 Student Survey*[3] showed that students who used career center resources were more likely to get a job offer than those who did not. A total of 71% of students who received job offers used their career center vs. 29% of students who received job offers but did not use their career center. Furthermore, frequent career center users (students who used it four or more times a semester) were more likely to have job offers than those who used the career center only once a semester. The services most utilized by students in order of usage were résumé writing/reviewing, career center job listings, job-search assistance, career counseling, and internship assistance. As a student, do everything in your power to gain an edge over your competition. Utilizing your career center to the fullest gives you one more way of achieving this edge.

College Career Fairs

Many colleges and universities have at least one career fair a year where students are able to meet prospective employers. These are usually organized by the school's career center. Various companies will have a booth or table set up where you can walk up to them, ask them questions, give them your résumé, and hopefully make a lasting impression. However, try not to ask them what they do—you should know this already, having done previous research on the companies you're interested in. Remember to ask the people you've spoken with for their business cards (some companies prohibit this because their recruiters might be bombarded with emails), give them your business card, and follow up with a thank-you note. Treat a career fair like a professional job interview and dress accordingly. Even if the career fair doesn't cover a field you're interested in, consider attending anyway so you can observe how others behave and take notes on what seems to work and what doesn't. You might be surprised by how much you learn! Obviously, you should also be doing this in the career fairs you are interested in—i.e., observing how your fellow students dress, act, and interact with the recruiters. Remember, have your points outlined in advance so you can make a good impression without wasting the recruiter's time or appearing indecisive. These recruiters are also sensitive to the fact that there are other students in line who also want help.

Job Fairs

Don't limit yourself to career fairs that are sponsored by your school. Search the Internet and ask your career center for information about job fairs that are held elsewhere. The rules are the same: dress appropriately, make a great impression, bring business cards with your name and contact information on them, and send a thank-you note to potential employers after the fair.

Social Networking Sites

There are so many social networking websites available these days and many of them can be utilized to help you get a job, or at least spread the word that you're looking for a job.

Facebook

Facebook is perhaps the most utilized social networking website. It has almost one billion users worldwide and continues to grow. I have a Facebook profile, and originally joined to help promote my book. However, it ended up being a site where I caught up with old friends, some of whom I haven't heard from in 30 years.

You can search for friends already on Facebook or invite others to join. Each friend usually has access to all of the information on your

Facebook page, which includes any personal information you provide, as well as photos. You can join groups with interests similar to your own. One advantage of Facebook is that at the top of the page, it has a line that reads "What's On Your Mind?" where you can tell people what you're doing. So if you're looking for a job and you mention this on your Facebook page, when each one of your Facebook "friends" logs on to their home page, they will see that you are job searching and perhaps one or more of them can help you.

Myspace

Myspace is another social networking site, but the popularity of this website has declined and has been surpassed by Facebook as the most popular one. As its website states, "Myspace is a leading social entertainment destination powered by the passion of fans." Myspace tends to skew younger and is seen by some as being populated by the young and hip under 30. While it has grown in popularity among those over 30, it is still teen-heavy in some respects. Perhaps its music component, its reputation for being a "hook-up" site, and its being used as a venue for publicizing parties make it skew young.

YouTube

YouTube is a video sharing website on which just about anyone, from individuals to corporations, can upload their videos. There is generally a fifteen-minute limit per video. Of course, there are many music videos on the site, but members use it for different reasons. It's a great way to promote yourself. From a job search perspective, you can certainly make a video telling your audience about your qualifications. Perhaps a prospective employer will see your video and be convinced to bring you in for an interview.

Twitter

Twitter answers the question, "What's Happening?" in 140 characters or less. Not 140 words but 140 characters. Many celebrities are on Twitter and give daily updates about their lives, but most people on Twitter are non-celebrities. On Twitter you can follow people, and when you log on to your home page, you will see the updates of all the people you are following. Others who are on Twitter want to be followed because they are politicians, sports stars, or are promoting something. A Twitter update can be something like, "On my way home from work," or "Going to the concert tonight."

During my college lectures, I ask how many students use Twitter, and I'm always surprised by the lack of response. While Twitter has been growing, many college students and recent grads haven't felt the need to join. In fact, I think only about 10% of college students use Twitter. Perhaps using text messaging, email, and Facebook is enough for some. However, Twitter isn't just about following celebrities or telling people what you're doing. There is a lot of career advice on Twitter. On my Twitter profile (andyteach), I give career advice and I follow many people on Twitter who also give career advice, and have links to various career articles on the Internet. I've seen some people who list job openings every day, so these are some good reasons for those looking for a job to join Twitter.

LinkedIn

LinkedIn is a networking website for over one hundred million professionals on which you can post your résumé, make professional contacts, get or give work recommendations, have access to your contact's contacts, join groups, and search for jobs. This is not a social website, but is specifically related to careers and jobs. One of the many things I like about this website is that once you make a connection with someone, you then have access to their connections and can either ask for an introduction through your mutual connection or email a potential connection directly. And unlike a regular résumé, you also have a choice to post a photo of yourself if you so desire.

While this website is utilized more by those who have been in the workforce for a few years, I highly recommend it to college students and recent graduates. I approached LinkedIn in three steps: step 1 was to make as many contacts as possible with people I already knew; step 2 was to ask for recommendations from people I had worked with in the past; step 3 was to make contacts with people whom I didn't know previously.

However, there are some common mistakes that people make on LinkedIn:

1. **Waiting until they are unemployed before they join.** If you wait until you're out of a job (or are looking for your first job) to join LinkedIn, you'll be in a panic mode, trying to get as many contacts as

possible in a short period of time. It's best to join *before* you graduate or when you still have a job so that you can take your time posting your résumé, making contacts, and getting recommendations.

2. **Lack of a photo or having a non-professional photo.** The first thing that people notice about you is your photo. Unlike Facebook or Myspace, you are only allowed one posted photo, so make it count by using a photo in which you are dressed in business attire. A lot of people who are on LinkedIn don't have a photo (half of my contacts don't). Perhaps they're afraid that it will bring unwanted attention to them and that their bosses may suspect they're looking for a job. With so many members on LinkedIn, I think it's generally accepted that being on LinkedIn doesn't mean you're looking for a job. There are also many people who have a photo of themselves in casual dress with a swimming pool or baseball field in the background. As I said, business attire only. Another reason that some people may not have a photo posted is that LinkedIn has a 4MB photo size limit. If your camera takes photos that are larger than this, you should edit and downsize them so that they can be downloaded onto the site.

3. **Posting an incomplete résumé.** When you post your résumé on LinkedIn, you have to post it in different sections so make sure you don't leave out a section. Everything should be in reverse chronological order and don't leave out dates—employers want to follow your career path from beginning to present.

4. **Lack of a clear, specific objective.** At the top of your profile you have an opportunity to list an update. This is the perfect place to state your job objective if you wish to have one. You can also state it in the "Summary" section. Just like on any résumé, a specific job objective goes a lot further than a general job objective. Unlike a résumé, you can't keep changing your résumé objective to match a specific job since you don't know who is looking at your profile.

5. **Not using the Address Book function.** Do you already know anyone on LinkedIn? It's easy to find out. LinkedIn has a function (called Imported Contacts) that allows it to search your email address book so it can tell you which of your email contacts are already on LinkedIn. This makes it much easier for you to increase the number of LinkedIn contacts.

6. **Lack of a personal greeting when trying to get "linked in" with someone.** Personally, when I try to "link in" with someone, I always send them a personal message in addition to the auto message that says, "I'd like to add you to my professional network on LinkedIn." I think you have a better chance of getting someone to be "linked in" with you, especially someone you don't know, if you include a brief personal message.

7. **Lack of recommendations.** When potential employers look at your LinkedIn profile, they will be looking at how many recommendations you have. The more you have the better chance you have of getting noticed. Get them from supervisors, co-workers, employees, professors, and fellow students.

8. **Contacting your contact's contacts without a mutual introduction.** As I mentioned previously, one of the great things about LinkedIn is that once you are "linked in" with someone, you then have the ability to access all of their contacts, some of whom may be able to help you get a job. However, I would recommend not trying to contact your contact's contacts directly. First, ask your mutual contact if they can introduce you via email to the person you want to be "linked in" with so you're not a stranger. If your contact doesn't have the time or doesn't respond to you, then contact the person you want to be "linked in" with directly. However, don't tell them you think they can help you. A better approach would be to introduce yourself, mention who your mutual contact is, tell them your objective, let them know you admire what they're doing, and tell them you would appreciate it very much if they can take the time to speak with you about their career or interests.

9. **Not joining LinkedIn groups.** There are many LinkedIn groups you can join. All it requires is doing a search and then clicking on a link. At a minimum, you should join your college's alumni association. You should also join a group associated with your professional field. The more groups you join, the more diversified you become, and you now have something in common with many other LinkedIn members.

10. **Not using the search function.** Once you join LinkedIn, you can do a search for jobs, people, groups, and companies. Don't forget to utilize this function.

11. **Not using LinkedIn once you get a job.** Networking doesn't stop once you get a job. You should always try to increase the number of contacts you have and continue to add recommendations. There is no such thing as job security, so you should always be prepared for the next job by constantly updating your LinkedIn profile.

Studentbranding.com

This website is a resource for career and personal branding advice for college and graduate students. It features regular contributions from career experts and recent grads. In the Resources section, it lists websites that help you find the right internships and entry-level jobs as well as listing several social networking websites.

Brazencareerist.com

This is one of the top Generation-Y websites and is a personal favorite. You need to be 18–35 years old to officially join and post articles, but Baby Boomers like myself are also able to leave comments and post articles in a different section. Every day, there are several articles from members of Generation Y that discuss workplace issues, politics, marriage, and other issues directly related to Generation Y. It's always nice to hear what your peers are thinking and doing.

YOUR WEB PAGE

One quick way of hurting your chances of getting or keeping a job is to have a risqué web page on a social networking site such as Facebook or Myspace. If there are photos of you drinking alcohol, smoking pot, or striking a suggestive pose in your underwear, I can almost guarantee you that someone at the company you work for or want to work for will eventually see them. I can also guarantee you that there's a good chance it can cost you your job or an opportunity for a job. Even though there are privacy settings, you need to assume that everyone can see your profile and will act accordingly. Google yourself to see what information comes up. It's important to know what your online reputation is. If you see negative information about yourself, change it if possible. (In fact, online businesses now exist to protect your online reputation, but you need to pay for them.)

I knew one employee who had a page on a social networking site that showed her in sexy poses. She was dressed, but it didn't matter. One of the company rats—I mean employees—saw the page and told a very high-level executive about it. This executive, in turn, talked to the woman's boss about it. You can bet the boss wasn't happy to have had that conversation with the high-level executive (who just happened to be his boss) or with his employee. I'm sure that there are plenty more examples of this.

There are also many true stories of people losing their jobs because of something they wrote on Facebook or Myspace. I've heard of one employee who posted on their Facebook page that their job was boring and that they didn't like their boss. Unfortunately, they had forgotten that their boss was one of their Facebook "friends." The next day the boss called the employee into his office and basically told them that since they didn't like their job or him–there's the door.

As I've said, your reputation means everything, so please be extremely careful about what's on your web page. Keep it on the up and up and you'll give everyone at work one less reason to talk about you.

THE JOB INTERVIEW

Congratulations! You've been notified to come in for a job interview. However, there are several things to be on the lookout for. The following comes from a Harris Interactive Poll[4] conducted on behalf of CareerBuilder.com:

When asked to identify the biggest mistakes recent college graduates make during the application and interview process, employers cited the following:

- Acting bored or cocky (69%)

- Not dressing appropriately (65%)

- No knowledge of the company (59%)

- Not turning off cell phones or electronic devices (57%)

- Not asking good questions during the interview (50%)

- Asking about pay before the company considered them for the job (39%)

- Spamming employers with the same résumé and cover letter (23%)

- Failure to remove unprofessional photos and content from social networking sites, web pages, blogs, etc. (20%)

Be Flexible with Your Interview Time

If you're not presently working and are asked if you have a preferred time to interview, reply that whatever is convenient for the interviewer is fine with you. They probably have a busy schedule and will appreciate you being flexible. If the interviewer gives you a choice of morning or afternoon, take a morning appointment because it's more likely they'll have a project deadline at the end of the day, and probably won't be focusing all of their attention on you (which they should be doing).

If you have a job and don't want your present employer to know that you're interviewing, try to schedule an appointment early in the morning, during lunch, or at the end of the day. It's easier to schedule time away from your current job during these times.

Research the Company Ahead of Time

It's very important to research the company you potentially may get a job with. If you interview at a law firm, go on the Internet and read their website. What types of cases do they take on? What are the backgrounds of the law partners? If you interview at a television studio, you should know which television programs they produce. For whatever company you may be interested in working for, utilize a search engine such as Yahoo, Google, or Bing and you'll find a plethora of information. There's no excuse for not being informed, and by making the effort it shows that you are indeed interested in working for the company. Your research on the company must also involve knowing how to pronounce the name of the interviewer properly. If you're unsure of the pronunciation, call the Human Resources department or the department you're going to interview with and most likely they can help you out.

You can also read the company's press releases for the latest information about them. I've done this for informational interviews. I went to the company's website and found a number of press releases. I printed out a few of them, and in my interview, I brought up some of the information I learned which gave the interviewer the impression that I had done my homework.

Another way to research a company is to check out websites on which employees or former employees rate their companies and bosses. Some examples are eBossWatch (www.ebosswatch.com), Glassdoor (www.glassdoor.com), and Vault (www.vault.com). One word of caution: If you only see one comment about a company or boss and it's very negative, it may just be a disgruntled employee. Several negative comments about a company or boss have more credibility.

Don't Be Late

Wherever you're coming from, please allow more than enough time to get to the interview. Allow for bumper-to-bumper traffic, accidents, water main breaks, alien attacks, etc. Whatever it is, get there early or at least on time. Use MapQuest, a regular map, or a GPS system but know your route ahead of time. Consider driving there a few days before the interview as a test run to see if there are any construction or other possible delays.

If you get there too early on the day of the interview, just park and wait about fifteen minutes before the interview and then go in the building. I didn't like interviewees coming in too early because then I felt guilty about making them wait so long. But if they were a few minutes early and I was available, I'd see them early.

Don't Show Up with Wet Hair

Why not, you ask? Because if you look like you rushed out of the shower to get to the interview, it may give the impression that you don't allocate your time properly and are always rushing to get things done. An employer wants to hire someone who uses their time efficiently and can meet deadlines effortlessly.

Dress Up–First Impressions Are Everything

I've interviewed young men who came in for an interview without a jacket or tie and I wondered what they were thinking. I spent more time during the interview trying to figure out why they didn't wear a suit and tie instead of focusing on whether or not they would be a good fit for the job. This was a corporate environment and even if it wasn't, you couldn't go wrong dressing up. Men should wear a fairly conservative suit and tie. Women should wear a business suit or conservative dress/skirt.

Don't Be Nervous, Be Confident

Despite me saying this, you probably will be nervous anyway. Being nervous shows you care. However, don't ever shake someone's hand if your palm is sweaty. Get rid of any moisture on your hands by briefly (and unnoticeably) rubbing or patting your hands on your pants or dress before you shake hands. Most importantly, when you shake hands, do it firmly. When you do meet the interviewer for the first time, repeat their name (and remember it).

Turn Off Your Cell Phone/BlackBerry®/Pager/Pacemaker

Okay, I'm kidding about the pacemaker, but there's no better momentum killer than having your cell phone or pager go off right in the middle of the interview. The person interviewing you will be frustrated and you'll be embarrassed. It may be hard to recover from that, so write yourself a note the night before as a reminder to turn everything off, except your charm.

Don't Chew Gum

Chewing gum during an interview is distracting and annoying, especially if the interviewee is doing it with their mouth open. Take out your gum before the interview, or better yet just use some breath spray about five minutes before the interview is scheduled to begin.

A Smile Goes a Long Way

A smile exudes confidence and friendliness and shows that you're relaxed, even though you may not be. Believe me, I always preferred to interview a candidate who smiled as opposed to one who did not. Believe it or not, the person interviewing you can be nervous, so try and make them feel relaxed.

Here's just a quick aside. At one of my former companies, we had a summer diversity program which was designed specifically to help minorities who were in high school and college. I'd interview several candidates in succession and would choose one who'd spend about six weeks in our department over the summer. It was a great experience for the students because it was something they could put on their résumé that would be noticed by future employers. It was also a great experience for me since I got a chance to mentor young people and help them learn the basics of working in the corporate world. In fact, I was fortunate enough to be given the "You Make the Difference" Award one year from our Human Resources department.

I remember one candidate in particular. I think she was sixteen at the time, but she carried herself like she was twenty-six. I was so impressed by her, as were others who had interviewed her. Fortunately, we were able to hire her in our department for the summer. She smiled during the interview, dressed well, spoke well, and was very smart. I kept thinking that her parents had done an outstanding job raising her as she had more poise than most adults. The next summer, another department hired her and whenever I would run into people that she had worked with or for, we all said the same thing—one day she would be running a company! I don't know what she's doing now, but I'm sure she is very successful. It would have been great to have had more employees over the years like her because it would have made my job much easier.

Look Them in the Eye at All Times

Looking into the eyes of the person interviewing you at all times shows that you're interested in what they're saying. I didn't like interviewing people whose eyes wandered around my office while I was speaking with them—it showed a lack of interest and respect.

Unfortunately, I was guilty of the same thing at one point in my career. Sometimes I'd interview people and my computer would be on and I'd try to sneak a glance at my emails for a split second, but that was rude. I once took a Human Resources class in which they gave us a glass paperweight that said, *"Be Here Now."* Ever since that class, I'd put that paperweight in front of me and if I were interviewing anyone, the paperweight would remind me to give them my undivided attention.

Don't Interrupt the Person Interviewing You

Make sure they're finished speaking before you speak. You may be anxious to get your point across, but be patient—you'll have your chance. Sometimes I watch news or financial programs on which they have a panel of two or three or more people on the show and they're constantly interrupting each other to the point at which you can't even hear what any of them is saying. Don't become one of them.

Don't Say "Like" or "Dude"

I know that some young people, especially teenage girls, use the word "like" frequently as in, "We went to the mall and like, we went shopping, and like, we hung out for a while." Do yourself a favor and delete the word "like" from your vocabulary. It suggests immaturity and being inarticulate. It's extremely important to speak proper English and to not use slang. Having an accent is one thing, but if you butcher the English language you'll hurt your chances of getting a job. Oh yes, and guys, you're not off the hook–please don't call anyone "dude" in the interview.

Practice the Interview in Your Head Several Times

Write down everything you may want to ask the person interviewing you and then write down any questions that they may ask you. You don't want to be put off guard so picture the interview in your head.

Here are some possible questions the interviewer might ask you:

- Tell me about yourself (this doesn't mean telling them your life story).

- Why do you want this job?

- Why are you the best person for this job?

- Why did you choose this career?

- Why do you want to work for this company?

- Where do you want to be five years from now?

- Why did you choose your major? How has it prepared you for this position?

- Can you give me an example of a problem you had at work and how you overcame it?

- Did you ever work with someone you didn't like and what did you do about it?

- What did you like and not like about your last boss?

- Have you ever worked in a fast-paced environment?

- Do you prefer working alone or with a group?

- What salary do you want?

- What is your greatest strength and weakness?

- Why should I hire you?

Ask Questions

The interview is a give-and-take process, so it's just as important for you to ask questions as it is for you to answer them. Asking good questions will separate you from those candidates who don't. Too few and the interviewer may think that you're not really interested in the job; too many and you may annoy them. Since there's a good chance you'll be speaking first with someone in Human Resources, try to find out things such as salary and benefits so that when you meet with someone in the department in which you wish to work, you can focus on the more important issues regarding the job itself and the ability to move up the ladder.

Here are a few possible questions to ask the interviewer:

- Can you please describe a typical day on the job?

- What are the duties and responsibilities of the job?

- What kinds of projects might I expect the first few weeks and months?

- Is this a new position or did someone leave? Why did they leave?

- Does your company pay for classes and continuing education if it's relevant to the job?

- How often are performance reviews given?

- How long will it take on average for me to get a promotion to the next level?

- Has the company had any recent layoffs? If so, did your entire industry experience this?

- What is the reputation of people my age at this company?

- What makes this company better than its competition?

- What is the largest single problem facing your staff?

- What qualities and skills are you looking for in the job candidate?

- Is there a lot of team and project work?

- Who would I report to and whom do they report to?

- How much travel, if any, is involved in the position?

- What will I need to do to make you look good to your boss?

I also think it's very important to ask the interviewer to show you a copy of a typical project you'll be working on. Otherwise, everything is hypothetical. Once you can see the work with your own eyes, you can make a better determination of whether or not the job is for you. When I interviewed recent college graduates for an intern position, I'd voluntarily show them a few different examples of what they'd be working on so there'd be no surprises.

Save a good question or two for the end of the interview. Two questions I suggest asking the interviewer are: "How did you get your start?" and "What do you like about your company?" Most people enjoy talking about themselves. These questions give them the impression that you are truly interested in their career path. It also gives you some great information about how others have succeeded in your field of choice.

Interviewing the Interviewer

The interview process not only gives the person doing the hiring an idea of what your personality is like, but it can also give you an idea of what their personality is like. If the person interviewing you is your potential boss, you'll have to make the determination of whether or not you'll be able to work with this person. If you "hit it off" with them, you'll have a much better chance of having a strong working relationship once you're hired. If the person interviewing you didn't make you feel welcome, if they never smiled during the interview, or if they were "all business," you may not want to work for them. The interviewer should make the interviewee feel at home during the interview process. A former boss of mine once made an interviewee cry during the interview. I'm not sure what he said to her but my guess is that the interviewee was no longer interested in the job after that interview. Who could blame her?

Say "Thank You"

When the interview is over, thank the interviewer and tell them how much you appreciate them giving you their time. Don't forget to ask for their business card. You may then ask what the next steps are. They may just tell you that they'll be in touch. Ask them when they think they might make a final decision and if you can email or call them in a few days.

Keep a Record of All of Your Interviews

Earlier in the book I mentioned that you should keep a computer record of all of your contacts. Do the same for your interviews. Keep a record of how long the interview was, what questions were asked, how you answered them, etc. Were there any questions you forgot to ask or answers that you gave that could have been better? What were your impressions of the person interviewing you? Also, on a scale of 1-to-10 ask yourself how nervous you were and your overall assessment of how the interview went. "Practice makes perfect" so keep studying your notes and you'll improve your performance.

Follow Up with a Thank-You Note

If you decide that you're not interested in the job, email the interviewer and let them know. They'll definitely appreciate this. If you are interested, send a handwritten thank-you note, typed letter, or an email in the next day or two. Over the years, there were instances in which my staff and I would interview someone, and when it came time to decide who we'd hire, we'd always discuss whether or not they had sent us a thank-you note. If they did, it showed us that they were interested in the job. Don't get me wrong, we did hire people who didn't send us thank-you notes or letters, but sending one was a definite plus.

In addition to thanking the interviewer for their time and reiterating your enthusiasm for the job, a thank-you note also gives you an opportunity to overcome any concerns they might have had that you didn't address properly in the interview.

There is some discussion as to whether your thank-you note should be a handwritten note, a typed letter, or an email. Over the years, I have received all three types. Some executives might feel that a handwritten note shows more effort and is more personal. However, handwritten notes do have space limitations. Others might prefer something more formal, such as a typed letter. An email will arrive faster, but it might be considered less personal and as requiring too little effort. Of course, if the interviewer is making a hiring decision tomorrow, then definitely send an email. I didn't really care that much either way as long as I did receive some form of thank you.

I do have one word of caution regarding thank-you notes and emails. Please send them in a business letter format and not in a text messaging format. Do not send them from a mobile device such as a BlackBerry®. In an article from online.wsj.com[5] (*Wall Street Journal*) written by Sarah E. Needleman, the sub-head reads, "Young Job Candidates Find Too-Casual Tone of Textspeak Turns Off Hiring Managers." The article states, "Hiring managers . . . say an increasing number of job hunters are just too casual when it comes to communicating about career opportunities in cyberspace and on mobile devices. . . . [S]ome applicants are writing emails that contain shorthand language and decorative symbols, while others are sending hasty and poorly thought-out messages to and from mobile devices."

Ms. Needleman's article reiterates the differences between the different generations at work. As a Millennial, communicating in shorthand is very natural to you and members of your generation, but many of your potential supervisors may still prefer to communicate in a more formal way. If that's the case, then you should learn to communicate the way they communicate. Having said that, I suppose it's possible that once more Millennials take on supervisory roles, sending messages in a shorthand texting format could become the norm. Until then, you should play it safe and communicate the way your interviewer or supervisor does, which is most likely in a more businesslike and professional manner.

Don't Put All Your Eggs in One Basket

It's very difficult to play the waiting game, especially if you found a place where you really want to work. The best thing to do is to set up as many interviews as possible. If you want to work for one company, but you get an offer from your second choice, you may have some leverage with the first company. If they're interested in you, they might speed up their decision or risk losing you.

Some of my staff members and I had different theories about the interview process, especially for our six-month entry-level intern positions. My theory was to not rush into hiring someone until we really found someone we all liked. Unfortunately, this could prolong the hiring process and create extra work for the current staff and increase the risk of losing potential candidates. On the other hand, by being careful, you increase your odds of getting a very strong candidate who'll be an advantage on your staff. One of my former staff members liked to fill positions as quickly as possible so that we could be fully staffed. The negative side to this is that you haven't given yourself the time to really seek out the best candidates and you're more dependent on choosing from perhaps not the best talent pool.

Don't Let Rejection Slow You Down

No one wants to be rejected for a job, but if you are, don't take it personally. We all have been rejected before and you may begin to second-guess yourself. Maybe they had to hire a relative of the president of the company or maybe they were looking for someone with more experience. Who knows? If you don't get the job, you might want to ask the interviewer to tell you why. Some interviewers may not give you this information for legal reasons, but it's worth a shot.

Looking for and getting a job requires a lot of patience, hard work, and luck. Never give up. Remember that looking for a full-time job *is* a full-time job. Keep trying and you will be successful.

You Can Fool People in the Interview (But You Shouldn't Fool Yourself)

The good (and bad) news is that if you don't have it, you can fake it. Despite all of my experience interviewing people over the years, once in a while a less than desirable candidate made it through the process and got the job because they interviewed very well. That's perhaps one of the biggest drawbacks of an interview—it doesn't necessarily reflect the true abilities of the candidate. (This is why I always had Human Resources check references, but even this was no guarantee.) Please realize this: you should know your strengths and weaknesses. You might be able to interview well, but if you can't or don't want to do the job, it will very likely catch up with you.

I remember years ago I had interviewed a bubbly young woman for a position in my department. I liked her attitude, but I was a bit worried about how smart she was. I did the right thing and asked HR to check her references and to specifically ask her references if she was intelligent. I wanted to know how good her thinking process was.

Her references came back positive and said that she was smart, so I hired her. Big mistake! My initial impression was correct. This was a woman who, one week after having surgery, was bungee jumping in Las Vegas. This was also a woman who, when she was having a problem with Microsoft® Word and a co-worker joked that it was Bill Gate's fault, replied something to the effect of, "Oh, was he using this computer before me?" When told that she might have Attention Deficit Disorder (ADD), she replied, "You're right. People don't pay enough attention to me." I kid you not.

On top of this, she was out sick all the time. After several warnings, I finally fired her after one year (which I should have done after one month). It ended for her and us in the Human Resources department. The HR representative did all the talking, which made it easier on me. After telling my employee that she was terminated, her response was, "Don't I get two weeks' notice?" It had to be explained to her that terminations take effect immediately. In my twenty-seven years of corporate experience, she was the only person I had to let go.

This woman didn't try to fool us when she interviewed. In fact, she was her normal bubbly self and had a very good attitude during the interview. However, because of the demands of our department, it became clear that we made a mistake when we hired her. So were her references wrong? Maybe the demands of working in our department were a lot higher than in the other places she worked. I don't know.

By the way, speaking of references, it's very hard these days to even get a reference because of legal issues. If word gets out that you gave someone a bad reference that perhaps prevents them from getting hired somewhere, you could be potentially legally liable. I've never heard of this happening, but it's possible. Many HR departments recommend never giving a reference. Despite this, there are ways around it. If I really want to recommend someone because they did a great job working for me or in my department, I would do so. If I wanted to warn a colleague in my industry about a former employee because I believed the employee would make their life miserable, I would tell them off the record as in, "This conversation never happened." One of my former bosses once recommended an employee to a high-level executive at a competing company, and this high-level executive is still upset because the person didn't work out well. He wondered why my former boss gave this person a great recommendation. If this executive had asked me, I would've been more honest and given him the positives and negatives.

A MOCK INTERVIEW

The following is what usually happened during a typical interview I'd conduct. Let's say this is for an entry-level intern position for someone just out of college or a fairly recent graduate. My assistant would bring the candidate (let's call her Dana) into my office and I'd start with some small talk.

Andy: "Hi Dana, how are you? Would you like something to drink?"

Dana: "No, thank you."

Andy: "So please have a seat." I would then get up and close the door.

Andy: "Did you have a hard time finding the building?"

Dana: "No, it was pretty easy. I just MapQuested it."

Andy: "Good, so tell me how you found out about the job opening."

Dana: "Well, it was posted at our school and I also saw it at Monster. com. And it seems like a great opportunity."

Andy: "Well, that was my next question. What is it about the job that interests you?"

Dana: "I really want to get in the entertainment industry. I watch TV all the time and would love to study how and why people watch the shows that they do. Besides, I live pretty close to the office so this would be really convenient for me."

Her first answer is a good one (i.e., wanting to study the viewing habits of television viewers). It explains her motivation for wanting the job. However, you should never mention that this would be a good job because it's close to where you live. That's a poor reason to be interested in a job and it shows a lack of interest (or a superficial interest) in the job itself.

Andy: "So what are your favorite shows right now?"

Dana: "I love *Dancing with the Stars* and *American Idol*. I TiVo them all the time. I like a little of everything. Oh, I forgot, I also watch *Program A*, which is produced by your company. Furthermore, my boyfriend and I always watch *Survivor*."

These are really good answers. This tells me that the candidate not only watches television (you'd be surprised how many people who work in the television industry don't), but is passionate enough about them to record them. Furthermore, the candidate gets brownie points for doing her homework about the company and knows which television programs our company produces.

Also, there's no need to mention that you have a boyfriend, girlfriend, husband, or wife in the interview. It's not necessary for the interviewer to know anything about your personal life at this time so don't volunteer any personal information. The interviewer should make their hiring decision solely based on your attributes and experiences and how you conduct yourself during the interview.

Andy: "Dana, while you were in school, what were some of your favorite and least favorite classes?"

Dana: "My favorite subjects were economics, accounting, and literature. My least favorite subjects were probably logic and business law."

Andy: "And why is that?"

Dana: "Well, I really enjoy working with numbers—I've always been good with math. I love to write and to read the classics, but logic is a little too hypothetical for me and I don't plan to go into law, even though it was interesting."

For this job, the fact that she enjoys working with numbers is probably the first thing we look for in a person. For some people, they just have a knack for it and it's interesting to them; for others, it's boring and if it's one thing you can't afford to get in your job, it's bored.

Furthermore, I like the fact that Dana felt one of her least favorite subjects was still interesting to her. This is significant. One of the most important things no one ever told me when I was going to school was that if you can achieve good grades in a subject you don't like, you can improve your chances of being successful at whatever career you choose. This is because it takes a lot to motivate oneself to work hard in an area they simply aren't interested in or don't understand. How does that translate in the workplace? I've been assigned plenty of projects over the years that I didn't want to work on. I either found them too difficult or too boring, but my boss expected perfection from every project he or she assigned me. Sometimes you don't have a choice. If you perform well only on the projects you enjoy working on, your career won't last too long. That's the reality of the corporate world.

Andy: "Well, before we go any further, I just wanted to show you some examples of what we do."

At this point, I would show her numerous sheets with Nielsen ratings on them so it was clear to her that she'd be working a lot with numbers. I also think it helps her to picture the type of work she'll be doing.

Andy: "As you can see, this job involves working with numbers, and to be honest, if the person who gets this job doesn't really enjoy working with numbers, they won't enjoy the job. If you realize that each number represents something, it makes the job more interesting."

Dana: "I totally agree. When I took accounting, I knew each number represented a dollar figure and I derived satisfaction when everything balanced out. After seeing these examples, it makes me want the job even more."

Andy: "So let me ask you this, where do you see yourself in five years? What do you want to be doing?"

Many interviewers ask this type of question. The purpose is to find out what are the candidate's long-range plans. Are they really thinking of this position as a possible career builder or just a way to get in the door and then move on to something else? When I ask this question, I hope the candidate is very honest with their answer. It's a hard question to answer because many people, especially those just starting out, probably don't know where they want to be in five years.

Dana: "In five years, I'd like to be in a managerial position in the research department. My goal is to learn everything I can and do a great job and to be recognized for my accomplishments. I am very ambitious and want to constantly grow my career and get promoted when the time comes."

It's important to note that Dana mentioned that she sees herself in this department in five years. When I interviewed someone, I liked to hear that their interest was in my department, not that they wanted to eventually work in the finance or marketing departments. I've hired interns who've told me that ultimately they'd like to work somewhere else. Since it was a lower-level job, I understood that but if I were interviewing someone for a higher-level position, I wanted to hear that this department is where they wanted to be in the long term.

The reality is that it's very difficult for anyone to know where they'll be in five years but it's easier just telling the interviewer what they want to hear—that this is where you want to be, now and in the future.

Andy: "So Dana, can you tell me what your strengths and weaknesses are?"

Dana: "Well, as far as my strengths are concerned, I am extremely conscientious and detail-oriented. I love working with people and just really get satisfaction from doing a job well. As far as my weaknesses, I think my major weakness is that perhaps I take my job a little too seriously. I need to loosen up a bit, I think."

The fact that she's detail-oriented is a big plus. What I like about her answer about her weaknesses is that her weakness is really a strength. If an interviewer asks you what your weaknesses are, never say anything that would sound like a true weakness. For example, don't mention that you have trouble getting to work on time, or you have difficulty getting motivated at times, or you would rather work alone than with a team. Make your weakness sound like a positive, even though seasoned interviewers will expect this. Perhaps you always take on too much responsibility and need to learn how to delegate more. You can mention this as a negative even though it can be interpreted by the interviewer as a positive.

Andy: "Dana, I don't mean to scare you, but we work in a very fast-paced and stressful environment here. In the past, what kind of environments have you worked in?"

Dana: "In school I was the associate editor of the school newspaper and we had to meet tough deadlines every day. While it was always a little stressful, I actually enjoyed the fast pace. In fact, I would say that I thrive on it."

I think it's important to discuss with the interviewer the type of work environments you're used to. Most corporations have a fast-paced and stressful environment and any example you can give of having worked in such an environment will only increase your odds of getting the job.

Andy: "I've been talking to a few candidates, as you know, so I'd like for you to answer one last question that I consider a tiebreaker and that question is, 'Why should I hire *you?*'"

Not all interviewers are going to ask you point blank why they should hire you, but you need to be prepared to answer the question. If you aren't asked the question, you can bring it up on your own, which gives you a chance to summarize all of your good attributes.

Dana: "Andy, I know I have all the qualities that you're looking for. I have experience working with numbers, which I know is important in this job. I'm an extremely hard worker and am very detail-oriented, which is especially important when numbers and statistics are involved. As I mentioned before, I've already worked in a very fast-paced and stressful environment and I think that has prepared me well for the environment in this job. I've done a lot of research on this company and I know it creates product that's top-notch, which always makes one's job easier to enjoy. Based on our conversation today, I'm confident that we'd work together very well and I will do anything that's needed to get the job done. I always give a hundred and ten percent. Please feel free to contact any of the references that I have listed."

Dana did a great job summarizing her attributes and came across with a lot of confidence. She was able to tie in how her previous experience would be beneficial to this job. It was also smart of her to discuss the potential of the working relationship between her and the interviewer.

Andy: "Well, I don't think I have any more questions. Do you have any questions for me?"

Dana: (This would be a great time to ask the interviewer about their own career path.)

"You did a great job explaining what the position entails so I do feel very well informed about what's expected. Can you tell me when you will be filling this position?"

Andy: "I just started interviewing candidates, but ideally I'd like to hire someone in the next couple of weeks. However, it's possible the interview process may take a little longer than that."

Dana: "Would it be okay to call you or email you in a few days to find out the status of your search?"

Andy: "Absolutely, here's my business card. I appreciate you coming in and I wish you the best of luck."

Dana: "Thank you so much and I look forward to hearing from you."

This concludes the hypothetical interview. Of course, some interviews are longer, some are shorter, but I think some of the key points were illustrated here. Always remember to give the interviewer reasons why they should hire you and try to build some rapport with them in your brief time together. Just be prepared and be yourself.

THE TELEPHONE INTERVIEW

There are times when a company may prefer to conduct an interview with you on the telephone before they request that you come in person to see them. I'm not a big fan of the telephone interview because I prefer face-to-face contact. Facial expressions are very important because it gives the interviewer an idea of how interested and excited you are about the position. Obviously, the interviewer can't see your facial expressions if they speak with you on the phone. If your prospective employer wants to conduct a phone interview, here are some tips:

- Use your landline, not your cell phone, if possible. Landlines will have a much better connection, making it easier for both parties to understand each other.

- Speak from a very quiet room. Make sure you can't hear cars or trucks going by or the sound of a gardener's leaf blower. Shut off any televisions or radios inside your home. The last thing you need is for the interviewer to have trouble hearing what you're saying. You might also consider being home alone during the conversation, so that you don't get interrupted or you don't get nervous because of others who are listening to you.

- Have any research materials you may need organized in front of you. Don't put yourself in a position in which you have to quickly shuffle papers in order to answer a question.

- Stay focused. If you're sitting at a desk, don't play around with your computer or type emails. Sit straight up with your feet touching the ground as if you're sitting in front of the interviewer. Given the importance of the conversation you don't want to get too relaxed.

- Don't sit in your underwear. I'm not saying you need to put on a business suit when talking on the phone but you should dress for success, even at home, because it will reinforce the idea that you're taking the conversation seriously.

- Have any writing implements you may need at your disposal.

- Sound upbeat and positive on the phone. It's important to give the interviewer the impression that you really want the job.

THE LUNCH/DINNER INTERVIEW

There will be times when a job interview will be conducted over lunch or dinner, so it's very important to understand proper dining etiquette. I've only had one lunch interview in my career. It was very difficult because the interviewer chose a very loud restaurant, so it was very hard to hear what he was saying. Hopefully, if you have an interview in a restaurant, it will be relatively quiet.

I must admit, I am certainly not an expert in dining etiquette, but there are a few things I can pass along:

- Arrive early or on time.

- Shake the interviewer's hand firmly and smile.

- After you're seated, place the napkin on your lap before eating or drinking anything.

- Sit up straight and don't put your elbows on the table.

- Don't order anything that's messy and try not to order anything that you'll have to eat with your hands.

- Wait to eat until everyone has been served.

- Start eating with the utensil that is farthest away from your plate. The fork farthest away is a salad fork. If you have three forks, the smallest one would be a seafood fork for an appetizer. The dessert fork/spoon is usually above the plate. The spoon farthest away from your plate is a soup spoon.

- Don't eat too fast or too slow.

- Don't order alcohol.

- Keep the conversation going.

- Place your napkin beside your plate after you're done eating and place your napkin on your chair if you need to get up.

- Push your chair under the table when excusing yourself.

- Don't put salt or pepper on the food until after you've tasted it.

- Pass salt and pepper together–even if asked for only one.

- Pass all items to the right. Remember that your water glass is to the right.

- Don't chew with your mouth open.

- The interviewer will usually pay for the meal, but be prepared to pay if they don't.

HUMAN RESOURCES

The Human Resources department is important in any company. You usually must interview first with HR before you interview with the department in which you want to work. HR often acts as a screener for all other areas in the company–they examine résumés and interview potential candidates first before determining if the candidate is good enough to meet with the hiring manager. It's worth repeating that if you meet with an HR person first, ask as many questions as possible about peripheral issues such as salary, hours, and benefits so that when you meet with someone in the department in which you want to work, you can concentrate on finding out about the details of the job itself. The HR person should know more about these extraneous issues than the person you're going to interview with for the job. Of course, when you meet with the HR representative, you do want to ask questions about the job itself but they probably won't know the answers nearly as well as the person in the department in which you are interested.

The same rules apply for interviewing with HR as they do with interviewing with the hiring manager: be early or on time, dress nicely, be polite, smile, look them in the eye at all times, and ask specific questions.

Once you get a job, it's important to develop a strong relationship with HR. They can be very helpful in answering questions for you. If the job becomes difficult for you or if your boss or co-workers are causing problems for you and you have nowhere else to turn, then you'd probably set up an appointment with your HR rep. Do this if you've already discussed the situation with the person or persons making things difficult and you feel the problem can't be resolved. HR will listen to you and take everything you say very seriously. However, keep in mind that they work for the same company as you and will do everything possible to prevent a lawsuit by an employee. If you do have an issue with a boss or co-worker and you do tell HR about it, find out if your conversation will be kept confidential. Sometimes if the situation is serious, they may have to tell others in order to take action.

Here are three examples of Human Resources-related situations:

1. A circumstance in which I probably should have called HR.

2. An instance in which someone did call HR, which led to the termination of a supervisor.

3. A situation in which employees went to HR to complain about me.

First, here's an example of when I perhaps should have called HR but didn't. A few years ago one of my former companies produced a science fiction pilot for one of the television networks. (A pilot is basically the first episode of any television program that's produced for a television network. If the network likes the pilot, they'll order more episodes and it'll become a television series. If the network doesn't like the pilot, it'll never air and no one will ever hear about it again.)

We had "tested" the program, which means that we screened it for an audience and they graded the show on a scale from "poor" to "excellent." Our company conducted this testing primarily as a sales tool. If it tested well, we would send the network our results to help improve the chances of this program being picked up as a series. Keep in mind that the network also tested their pilots.

Our show tested reasonably well and I was excited about the results. I was talking to our creative executive who helped develop the show and I asked him if it was okay to call the network and tell them about our great testing results. I was stunned when our executive screamed at me over the phone and said, "Are you kidding? If you do that I'm going to come over there and shoot you in the head!" I was only trying to help our chances of getting this pilot picked up as a series, but he apparently didn't see it that way. I also knew that this time of year was extremely stressful for this executive because he had many other pilots out there being considered for series and his job was on the line. I had worked with him for a while so I gave him the benefit of the doubt. I only told my bosses about it but not HR. The next day the executive called me from out of town and apologized.

If I had reported him to HR he could have gotten into trouble, but I think because of my past history with him, I let it slide. Since he apologized to me, I felt much better about the situation and wanted to move on. Was I right in doing that? I guess it depends on the situation. I knew he wasn't really going to shoot me in the head, but it did make me feel uncomfortable. I believe that if I were thinking of going to HR, I would've spoken with this executive first. As it turns out, that was the only time he yelled at me. (By the way, the science fiction pilot did become a series, but unfortunately, only lasted one season.)

Jump ahead a few years. There was a similar situation in a different department. A supervisor had been recently hired to oversee this particular area. Apparently, they were very difficult to work for and many people left over the next few months. At some point, this supervisor had told one of their employees, "I'm going to kill you." The employee complained to management and to HR. The supervisor didn't mean that literally, but that was the straw that broke the proverbial camel's back. They were fired right after that. From my perspective, I was surprised that this person lasted that long since so many of their employees had left because of them. This is a case in which management should have seen a red flag a long time ago. I don't know if any of the former employees of this executive had complained to anyone, including HR, but when there is an exodus of employees due to the behavior of one person, HR should have been proactive and investigated the situation before it got out of hand. Again, you always have to watch what you say in front of others.

The third situation concerns myself. Unfortunately, HR had a file on me because some of my former employees complained about me. Ironically, HR never told me that these employees had come forward to criticize me. On one hand, this gave the unhappy employees a feeling of confidentiality, but on the other hand, how was I supposed to address their concerns if no one told me about them?

These employees complained about me because I micromanaged them and criticized them if I felt that they were wrong about something. Unfortunately, some people are thicker-skinned than others, or in these cases perhaps thinner-skinned. One of my former employees summed it up best when he said, "Andy, you're tough but fair." The irony is that I could have complained to HR several times about some of my bosses over the years, but I never did. I was pretty thick-skinned, and rather than go to HR, I addressed my concerns regarding my bosses with them directly. I wish my employees had done the same before they went to HR.

RUNG II SUMMARY

- For résumés/cover letters:
  - No typos.
  - Be specific.
  - Know your school's reputation.
  - Keep to one page if you're at the beginning of your career.
  - Include pertinent contact information.
  - Include a 3.0 GPA or above (overall or within major).
  - Use keywords and action words.
  - Copy and paste into email body and add as an attachment; follow up with a hard copy.
- Find job listings on Internet sites.
- Utilize your school's career center.
- Remember that looking for a full-time job *is* a full-time job.
- Promote yourself on social networking websites.
- Be very careful about what's on your web page—assume that everyone has access to it.
- Make a great impression on the Human Resources department before and after you get the job.
- For interviews:
  - Do research on the company.
  - Dress appropriately.
  - Arrive early.
  - Shut off all devices.
  - Smile and make eye contact.
  - Be enthusiastic.
  - Anticipate their questions and ask good ones.
  - Send a thank-you note.
  - Keep a computer record.

RUNG III – YOUR DECISION PROCESS: WHAT TO CONSIDER BEFORE ACCEPTING THE JOB

Before you accept a job, you need to consider several factors and answer many questions. Some of these are much more important than others. As it turns out, it's often the qualitative (or what I call the "happiness-related") criteria that will typically have the most profound and noticeable impact on your long-term career success and happiness, as opposed to the quantitative (or "show-me-the-money") criteria. Don't get me wrong, salary and benefits are important, but especially at the early stages of your career, my advice is to go "with your gut" and find the job you love at the company for which you want to work. It sounds like a cliché, but the old phrase "the money will come" is true.

QUALITATIVE ("HAPPINESS-RELATED") CRITERIA

- What is the overall environment like at the company?

- Will I get along with my prospective new boss and co-workers?

- Is there room for me to move up the ladder?

- Do I believe in the company's philosophy and products?

- Is the commute an acceptable distance?

- Will I love doing this job on a day-to-day basis?

Corporate Environment

One of the most important things you need to think about when considering a job is how well you will fit into the environment of the company. During the interview, you can see what the physical environment is like, but you need to feel comfortable working in their overall corporate environment. Obviously, different companies have different "corporate cultures." Ask the person who interviews you or ask someone you know in the company what the corporate culture is like there. You want to fit in.

Getting Along

A big consideration in working for any company is whether or not you will get along with your new bosses and co-workers. It's sometimes very hard to determine this in an interview, especially if you're interviewing with only one person. If you happen to already know someone at the company, ask them as many questions as possible about the people they work with and whether they enjoy working there. You might also ask if they know someone else you can talk to. If you don't know anyone at the company, you can contact your school's career services department to get a list of alumni who either currently work there or who have previously worked there. The point is that you want as much inside information as possible. The company (or the department in which you're applying) might be having personnel problems, there might be a boss who is hard to work for (which is possibly the reason the position is available!), or who knows what else.

I cannot stress enough how important it is for you to get along with the people you work with and for. More often than not, your relations with your co-workers and boss will affect whether you enjoy doing the job on a day-to-day basis. This is where your interpersonal skills come in. If you're a "people" person, you will have a distinct advantage in any company you work for. If you feel your "people skills" need improvement, simply acknowledging that is a great first step. My advice once you get the job is to go out of your way to be a team player, to volunteer as much as possible to help your colleagues, to make sure you go out to lunch with your co-workers, and to always be someone whom others can count on to get the job done.

Moving Up

Another key consideration in accepting a job is to find out how easy it will be to move up the corporate ladder. It's one thing to initially like the job you get, but it's another thing to feel that you're not being recognized for your accomplishments by not being promoted. Does the company have a reputation for promoting employees in a timely manner or is it difficult for people to advance in their careers there? Again, you need to do your research ahead of time to try to find out the answers to these questions.

Some people are interested in working for a particular company, but perhaps there's no opening in the department in which they want to work. They then take a position in another department to bide their time until something opens up in the area they want. (This happened a lot in the entertainment industry, where often it was more important to "break into the industry" and get a job, and then use that position as a launching board for something else.) I think this is acceptable only if you'll still give one hundred percent in the job. Otherwise, it really isn't fair to the team that you'll be working with. Also, if you don't give your all, you'll hurt your reputation.

I've seen this with a lot of interns we've had over the years. Many of them wanted to get into the company and saw it as a means to an end. After two or three months of the six-month internship, some interns decided they weren't interested in staying in the research department, so they started looking to move to another department internally or to another television studio or network. You could tell that their heart wasn't into what they were doing, and of course, my staff and I suffered the consequences. I actually didn't mind if our interns wanted to speak with other departments regarding future opportunities since there was a good chance they weren't going to stay in research anyway, but if you worked for me, I expected one hundred percent out of you during the six months you were with me.

Believing in the Company

Another "qualitative" consideration is whether you will feel comfortable being a company cheerleader, touting their products and philosophy. Do you truly believe in their product or service? If so, this will make it much easier for you to enjoy what you're doing. When I worked at the television studio, there were many television programs that we produced that I enjoyed watching and some of them became my favorite television programs at the time. This made it much easier for me to enjoy my job. If you don't believe in the company's philosophy, but they're willing to pay you a large salary, think twice before you accept the job. It is much more important to enjoy what you're doing and to feel comfortable representing your company because you truly believe in it, than to make a lot of money at a company where you may be at odds with its overall methods and philosophy . . . and people.

Commuting

Back in 1980, I was excited to get my first real job. What I didn't realize is that commuting can be a job all by itself. My dad had commuted from New Jersey to Manhattan for many years, and because my first job was in Manhattan, I would commute with him. From the time we left our door to the time I walked into my office in midtown Manhattan, it was a two-hour journey. That's right, two hours commuting each way, every day! I felt like my day was over before it even began. I occasionally napped on the bus and I did enjoy seeing that beautiful New York skyline every day, but wasn't there a better way? I always had to keep in mind that I was just starting out and I needed to sacrifice so that one day it would all pay off.

As I've said, the most important factor in finding a job is to find one you really enjoy doing. If you live far away from your job, the long commute will take away from your enjoyment. Commuting is not a fun thing. Of course, it may be cheaper to live far away because perhaps you can't afford to live closer to the office. You may consider getting a roommate or two to help reduce your rent. However, if you do have to commute, you can use it to your advantage. If you drive to work, perhaps you can carpool so on the days you don't drive, you can go through emails on your laptop or communication device. If you take mass transportation, you can do the same. Think of your car, train, or bus as a second office. If you can get some work done before you arrive at the office, this will reduce some anxiety and stress.

You have a lot to consider when accepting a job but I think there is one question that you need to ask yourself that is more important than any other. That question is, "Will I love going to work and doing this job on a daily basis?" If the answer is yes, then you may be about to embark on the beginning of a very illustrious and rewarding career.

QUANTITATIVE ("SHOW-ME-THE-MONEY") CRITERIA

- Am I happy with the salary?

- Are the benefits (health insurance, life insurance, 401(k), vacation, bonuses, profit sharing, stock options, etc.) desirable?

While the work itself should be the primary factor you consider before accepting a job, the salary and benefits you receive are important, too. My advice on benefits is based on my own personal experiences, but every company is different. It's best to consult with your family, friends, co-workers, the HR department, and perhaps a financial advisor before signing up for any insurance or 401(k) plans.

Salary

You may have a rough idea of what you think you're worth, but don't be surprised if a company offers you less. You may have done well in school, and armed with your bachelor's or master's degree, you may feel you deserve much more than they offer you. If possible, try to find out the salary range of the position you are vying for, not just at your company but at other companies in the same field as well. This will be very difficult to do unless the salary ranges are posted on the job websites or unless you know someone who is already working at an entry-level position in your field. You may be able to get a salary range on websites such as Glassdoor (www.glassdoor.com), PayScale (www.payscale.com), Salary (www.salary.com), and SalaryList (www.salarylist.com) that give out such information. Every little bit of information helps.

If the salary offer is less than you want, don't necessarily turn it down. Remember, the key is to get a foot in the door of the company and department you want to work for. You need to think in terms of the long run and see the big picture. Don't be shortsighted.

Never take a job just because it pays well. The #1 reason to accept a job is because you are going to enjoy the work that you're doing. If you work at a company where you enjoy the work, the promotions and raises will come because your enthusiasm and accomplishments will be recognized. I don't care if you earn a million dollars a year. If you don't enjoy the work or the people you work with, you will be miserable.

When I got the offer for my first job out of college as an assistant media planner at the tenth largest advertising agency in the world, the starting salary was $8,000. That's $8,000 a year, not a month! I was so happy simply to have a job at an ad agency that I accepted the low pay. On top of that, as I mentioned earlier, I had a two-hour commute every day. So was it worth it to accept a lower salary than I thought I deserved? Well, considering that a big factor in my getting the job at the television studio several years later was the fact that I had this advertising agency experience on my résumé, I'd have to say the answer was a resounding yes!

Health Insurance

When you ask people why they want a job at a particular company, many times they'll reply, "Because they have good health insurance." Obviously, health insurance is a major consideration. Hopefully, you won't need to use your health insurance benefits too often, but if you or your family requires medical or dental care, insurance can alleviate much of the financial burden.

You may have a choice of joining an HMO (Health Maintenance Organization) or a PPO (Participating Provider Option). The HMO is usually cheaper, but you must use the doctors in their network. The PPO is typically more expensive, but you usually have greater flexibility in choosing your doctors. As I said, discuss your options with others who know your situation to see which choice is best for you.

Many companies, especially large companies, usually have some type of health insurance. A certain amount of money (the premium) is usually deducted from your paycheck to pay a portion of the insurance. For medical insurance this could add up to several hundred dollars per year per person. Dental insurance is typically much less expensive.

In addition, medical insurance usually has a deductible, which is an amount you have to pay 100% out of your pocket. You're usually given a choice of different deductible amounts, which affects the cost of your policy. After the deductible is met, the company will pay a certain percentage (80% in my case) of the remaining medical expense. I always chose a $500 a year deductible, so basically if my medical expenses for the year were $2,000, I would pay the first $500 myself and the company would pay 80% of the remaining $1,500, which would come to $1,200. This means that I would have to cover the $300 difference between the $1,200 and $1,500 in addition to the deductible of $500 for a total of $800 out of my pocket. The higher the deductible, the lower the amount you'll typically have deducted from each paycheck to pay for participation in the health insurance plan, but with the higher deductible you'll pay more up front as you incur medical expenses through the plan. If you're the type who never gets sick, you may be better off paying less toward your coverage each month and having the higher deductible. Of course, you're taking a risk because no one can predict how your health will be in the future or if you'll be in some type of accident.

Please keep in mind that some companies may not give you a choice of how much your deductible may be. You may not even have much flexibility in terms of what type of insurance you can purchase. That's why it's so important to ask questions about health insurance before you accept the job.

Life Insurance

The purpose of having life insurance is to provide financially for your loved ones (your beneficiaries) in the event of your death. Some companies will pay 100% for your life insurance, while others require that you pay a certain amount (the premium). If life insurance is free at your company, then consider this a nice perk.

Who needs life insurance? Well, that depends on several factors including your age, your health, your wealth, and the size of your family. If you're just out of college and don't have a lot of assets and you're single, you might not need the added expense of life insurance at this point in your life, unless you'd like to provide for your parents or siblings. Once you get married and have children, you might want to reconsider. Please note that there are different types of life insurance policies, so it is best to speak with your HR department or financial advisor to choose the one that's best for you.

401(k) Plan

One of the most important benefits at any company is the 401(k) plan, which is a retirement plan. If you are at least twenty-one years old and have been with a company for at least a year, you might be eligible to contribute to your 401(k) plan if your company has one (which many do).

So you just got out of college and retirement is the last thing you are thinking about—right? Wrong! In my opinion, the 401(k) plan is one of the greatest inventions in the history of the world. You're basically getting free money from your company, which invests in your future. You deduct a certain amount from each paycheck up to a maximum that the U.S. government mandates. Your company might match up to 100% of your contributions up to a certain percentage. So, for example, in my situation at one of my former companies, I chose to take out 8%

of my earnings each paycheck for my 401(k). My company matched and contributed 100% of the first 3% that I invested. It then matched 50% of the next 3% of my investment. What this meant is that the company matched a significant portion of the first 6% of my annual 401(k) investment. In order to be "fully vested" in your 401(k) plan, the company will usually require that you are an employee for a certain amount of time, usually a few years, as an incentive for you to stay with the company. By staying that long, you will get 100% of the company's matching contribution.

Most companies give you at least some choices as to how to invest the money. Many choices involve investing in mutual funds in the stock market and some companies will give you a choice of owning company stock. If you do have the choice of investing in company stock, learn from the mistakes of the Enron employees as well as employees of other failed companies. They invested most of their money in company stock only to have their company go belly up. They lost everything. Limit your company stock investment to a small percentage of your total portfolio. The best bet is to check with a financial advisor on any investments.

You may also have the choice of investing in money market funds, bonds, bond funds, as well as international funds. The key is diversification. Don't put all your money in one or two funds, if possible. Spread things out. Keep in mind that you cannot withdraw your 401(k) plan money (without penalties) until you are 59 ½ years old, so plan for the long run. If you're young, you can afford to invest in riskier investments because even if they're bad investments, you have plenty of time to make up for your losses.

One of the great benefits of the 401(k) plan is that the profits and dividends you receive are tax deferred. You will not get taxed on your 401(k) plan money until you start to withdraw your money, which is decades away. Furthermore, a 401(k) plan reduces the amount of income taxes that you have to pay the IRS (Internal Revenue Service) each year. For example, if you earn $75,000 a year and $7,000 of that goes toward your 401(k) plan, the government will tax you on $68,000, not on $75,000.

One more word of advice: don't panic if the economy experiences a downturn, as we've recently experienced. Since you can't even touch your 401(k) plan without penalty for several decades, you have an extremely long time horizon on these investments. The economy and the stock market will go through several cycles during that time—some good, some bad. In the meantime, your stocks and mutual funds will be reinvesting dividends. Once you're within 5 or 10 years of retirement age, you can devise a plan to start withdrawing your money.

I don't care if you can afford to invest in your 401(k) plan or not. I don't care if you have to live in your car to afford investing in your 401(k) plan. If your company has any type of matching contribution plan, take advantage of it and participate in your company's 401(k) plan!

Vacation

Although vacations obviously promote health and happiness, a company's willingness to pay you for time you don't work is, in fact, a financial benefit. Most companies offer two weeks of vacation for the first year, plus a floating holiday or two that you can take whenever you'd like. After about three to six years with the company, you may receive three weeks of vacation a year. After anywhere from seven to ten years with the company, you may receive four weeks of vacation a year. Since you're new to the company, don't dwell too much on their vacation policy—your focus should be on the days that you work, not the days you don't work.

Bonuses

Not all companies give out bonuses, but many do. Receiving a bonus is a great perk and is usually related directly to how profitable your company is during their fiscal year. A bonus is a great motivation to do a great job as well as to help others do a great job because in the end all employees have to be working on all cylinders in order for a company to be successful. I tried not to get too used to my bonus because if you count on one and don't get one, you'll be severely disappointed and your morale may suffer. I was very fortunate because once I started to receive a bonus, it would either stay the same or increase each year—but of course there's never a guarantee.

In many companies, bonuses are reserved for upper management, perhaps at director or vice-president levels and above. Sometimes it's up to the discretion of the department heads to distribute bonuses to whomever they want. One of my former bosses was nice enough to give everyone in our department a bonus, from interns and assistants up to the senior vice-president level. Technically, many of the employees in our department weren't eligible for a bonus but our boss made an exception, which made a lot of people who weren't expecting one very happy.

Profit Sharing

Another great perk in the corporate world is profit sharing. Basically, the company gives you a percent of your salary that goes directly into your 401(k) plan. Again, this is free money that is set aside for your retirement. Profit sharing is usually reserved for management, so it's another good incentive to stay put at a job.

Stock Options

Some companies give their employees, especially higher-level employees, stock options as a benefit. When you join the company, they might give you a certain amount of shares in their company stock in addition to your salary. However, strict guidelines exist concerning stock options. The company will determine what price you can buy the stock at (the strike price) and how long you need to wait before you can sell it. The hope is that by the time you are allowed to sell the stock, the price has gone up and you have made a profit.

FINANCIAL ADVICE

Since we've been discussing some of the financial benefits of a job and a career, I'm going to give you some financial advice. First, let me make this perfectly clear: I am not a financial advisor and have no degrees or certificates in this field. However, my advice is just common sense and you can take it or leave it.

- Read financial books.

- Watch a financial news cable network.

- Pay off credit card debt starting with the highest percentage interest cards.

- Have enough funds available in easily accessible accounts (like savings accounts or money market funds) to pay your expenses for six months in case you are unexpectedly laid off from your job.

- Diversify your investments.

- Live below your means.

RUNG III SUMMARY

- When considering a job, look at qualitative criteria such as the environment, the type of people you'll be working with, the ability to move up the ladder, the company's products and services, and commuting.

- Also look at quantitative criteria like salary, health insurance, life insurance, 401(k) plan, vacation, and sick days.

- Utilize websites such as glassdoor.com and salary.com to gather as much information as possible.

- Become responsible for your financial future:

  - Read financial books.

  - Watch financial news.

  - Diversify your investments.

  - Pay off your highest percentage interest credit cards first.

  - Keep six months of expenses saved up in an emergency fund.

  - Live below your means, even as you earn more money.

RUNG IV – THE BEGINNING
OF YOUR CAREER

Congratulations, you've found a job! It may not be your ideal job, but you really won't know until you work there for a while. Of course, you're a little bit nervous, but guess what, so are your future colleagues. After all, there's a team dynamic already in place and you're being added into the mix. You're the unknown to them. You'll most likely start in the Human Resources department filling out paperwork. They will then most likely give you a pamphlet or guidebook with the rules, regulations, and requirements of the company. Please read it. When you go to HR, have a smile on your face and be very nice to whomever you're speaking with. Remember, it's very important to make a good first impression.

At some point, you'll report to your department and you'll be introduced to many people. It'll be difficult to remember everyone's name so try to get a staff list before you're introduced. Your boss should make sure that you have any supplies you many need, and hopefully, your computer is already set up with your ID and password. If not, call your IT (Information Technology) department immediately.

Your first day, first week, first month, and first year are a learning process. If it seems overwhelming at first, don't worry, things take time. When an intern started in our department, I'd always tell them on the first day that their first two weeks will seem overwhelming to them because there's so much training involved and that this was normal. I told them not to worry and that after two weeks it'll start making sense to them. I think by telling them that it alleviated some of their tension and stress.

There's one more important thing you should think about even before you start your first day. Always remember that from the moment you walk in the door at work, you are being judged. You are being judged by how you look, how you talk, how you write, and how you act. This judgment takes place on a daily basis, so you should never let your guard down. That's why it's so important to always think about and protect your work reputation. Your reputation should mean more to you than any paycheck or title. If you take pride in your work and yourself, your reputation will be stellar.

This will sound crazy but think ahead about forty years from now. How do you want people to remember your career? What kind of reputation will you have? What will be your legacy? Will people remember you as the person who worked hard, who was easy to work with, the one with a good sense of humor who treated everyone with respect? Were you the one that people wanted to work for because you were a mentor? Or will you be known as the one who always complained, the one who was hard to get along with, the one who always came to work late? You are the one person who can control your reputation more than anyone else.

When I was leaving the television studio after twenty-three years, it was great to hear my fellow employees tell me that they'd miss me and miss working with me. They told me that I'd done a great job, and some of them remembered some of my humorous encounters with other executives over the years. I'd always tried to inject some humor in meetings, and I enjoyed the fact that my co-workers remembered some of these moments and got a kick out of them. I left the company with a pretty good reputation, and in the end, that's really what matters most.

DON'T JUDGE THE JOB BY YOUR FIRST DAY

On your first day on the job, you may be disillusioned right away by the work or the people. You might feel that you've made a mistake. Give it a chance. You're new, and you're nervous. First impressions are not always the correct ones, especially when you're in a new environment with new challenges. Despite this, sometimes people do go with their gut.

One of my former bosses told me a funny story about someone his old department hired about thirty years ago. It was the employee's first day and the employee went to lunch. It was late afternoon and everyone wondered what had happened to this guy since he hadn't yet come back from lunch. They went to his desk and found a note that the employee had written before he left. It read quite simply–"This job is f--ked." I guess that kind of summed up the employee's feelings about the job. He felt that he'd made a mistake and didn't want to take the time or effort to rectify the situation. Perhaps he was a bad fit, who knows. One thing is for sure. Since he still hasn't come back from lunch thirty years later, he probably holds the record for the longest lunch ever. And I thought my two hour lunches were long!

There's one thing I remember about my first day at one of my former jobs, and it isn't a good memory. Of course, this was many years ago, but I still remember it well. It was the end of my first day, which was a long one. Of course, I was trying to acclimate to my new situation. It was a lot to take in, and it was a little overwhelming. Most people in my department had gone home, and I wanted to know if it was okay to go home for the day. My boss had left and his boss had left too, so I knocked at the door of the big boss. He was in a meeting with someone, but I didn't know the protocol. Perhaps I could've just left the office, but I asked him if it was okay to leave. I was expecting a "How was your first day?" or "Yes, of course, go home, we'll see you tomorrow." Instead, the big boss acted disappointed that I was leaving. That didn't make me feel too good and it certainly didn't give me a good first impression of the big boss.

As it gets closer to lunch, you should ask your boss or co-workers when is a good time to go to lunch, as well as what time you should return. Ask someone if there are any good cafés or restaurants in the area. Hopefully, someone will ask you to go to lunch, but don't be disappointed if they don't. Eventually, when you're accepted as part of the department, you'll get invites all the time. In the meantime, you should take it upon yourself to ask your fellow employees out to lunch and don't be afraid to ask them about their experiences at work.

If someone is nice enough to take you out to lunch, meaning that they're paying for your lunch, don't order the most expensive thing on the menu. If you do, that may be the last time that person takes you out to lunch. Years ago, one of my former bosses took me and another employee out to lunch. The other employee ordered the steak tartar, which was pretty expensive. This employee turned out to be a great employee, and my former boss would still take him out for lunch from time to time despite his high-priced tastes. However, many bosses wouldn't be as understanding as my former boss was so just be safe and don't order the filet mignon or lobster.

AT THE END OF THE DAY, DON'T JUST GET UP AND LEAVE

Stop by your supervisor and ask them if there's anything else they need from you before you leave for the day. Most of the time, they'll tell you that they don't need anything and you can go home. However, if they ask you to stay, don't act disappointed–act enthusiastic instead. It always bothered me when new employees just got up and left and passed my office without saying a word. All they had to do is say "Good night" on their way out. A quick acknowledgment can go a long way.

DON'T BE LATE

I wrote the following guest blog for the Gen-Y website, brazencareerist.com. It hopefully explains why you shouldn't be late on your first day or on any other day.

"I read a comment recently from a member of Generation Y that basically asked the question, 'What's the big deal if I come to work at 9:15 a.m., instead of 9 o'clock?' I'm in no way suggesting that this attitude represents an entire generation. In fact, I've observed many Gen Xers and Baby Boomers coming in late so this question really pertains to every generation, not just Generation Y. However, this question does illustrate a lack of understanding of the importance of being on time in the workplace. I do understand that in certain work environments, it's not a big deal if employees come in a little late but my comments are more focused on a company with a corporate culture. These are just a few reasons why you shouldn't be late to work.

9:15 a.m. soon turns into 9:25 a.m. which soon turns into 9:35 a.m., and, well you get my point. If you give someone an inch, they will take a yard. Let's face it, if you come in a few minutes late and you can get away with it, you might try coming in even later the next day and before you know it, you start arriving at work during lunch. On one hand, your work days will be shorter but on the other hand, your job tenure may be shorter, too.

If you're constantly allowed to come in late to work, then everyone else will want to, too. Every workplace requires rules and guidelines because it's important that all members of the team are on the same page and follow those same rules and guidelines. What makes you so special? If the boss allows one employee to come in late, they have to let everyone else come in late and without any set time to begin the work day, mornings could become quite chaotic. "Where's John?" "Oh, he's late." "Where's Sherry?" "Oh, she's late." "What time do you expect them?" "Well, there is no time really, they just get here when they want." If someone consistently bends or breaks the rules, it becomes more about them and less about the team.

Why tick the boss off first thing in the morning? When you come in late, you will most likely put the boss in a foul mood first thing in the morning. If you're going to tick the boss off, at least try to do it toward the end of the day. I had an employee who was habitually late and I was annoyed first thing in the morning many times. This hurt our relationship over time and if it's one relationship you don't want to hurt, it's your relationship with your boss.

You may unknowingly be preventing your co-workers or boss from getting their job done. You may not realize that your co-workers or boss may be waiting for you first thing in the morning to complete a project. Perhaps they have a question or need help on something that was discussed the previous day but they can't proceed without your help. I had a boss who was always late. While it was his prerogative, his tardiness prevented me from completing projects that in the end would make him look good. Unfortunately, I was not in a position to ask him to come in on time since he may have had a legitimate reason, such as a breakfast meeting, for example.

It's just plain rude to keep people waiting. When you are late for something, whether it's for work, to a meeting, or for a doctor's appointment, and you're keeping people waiting, you're basically saying that your time is more valuable than theirs. It isn't. How do you like it when other people keep you waiting and it prevents you from working on something you need to complete?

If you habitually come in late, just set your alarm clock to go off a few minutes earlier and you should be on time for work. In fact, you may even consider coming in a few minutes early to catch up on emails and phone calls. Well, I'd like to write some more on this topic but I'm late for a meeting. No big deal, I'm sure they'll wait for me!"

As I said, you should set your alarm to go off earlier than you think is necessary. After you set your alarm clock, set your cell phone alarm, too, as a backup. Have the clothes and shoes that you're going to wear on your first day already laid out. Check out the weather report the night before you go to work. If the weather is going to be bad the next morning, leave yourself enough extra time to get to work. Listen to the traffic report every morning. Has your car been serviced lately? You don't want to have to use the old "My car broke down" excuse. Arriving early to work is much better than arriving late.

As I mentioned, I once had an employee who was consistently late to work and to meetings. Once at a big convention, he walked in late to a sales meeting with many executives present. The head of our sales department stopped in mid-sentence and made a half-joking comment about him coming late to the meeting. As his supervisor, I was embarrassed. What made matters worse is that this employee really didn't even need to be at the convention. This was a perk given to him by our boss.

I found it very selfish on his part to act this way. I had a plan every day that sometimes started with a morning meeting, but we couldn't start without this employee. This was frustrating to me. I had several talks with this employee about his tardiness. The employee said that he would try to be punctual but then would be late next time. I complained to my bosses and they agreed with me, but there wasn't much that they were willing to do about it. In some ways, it became expected behavior and may have been overlooked because he was a very good worker. I don't think my employee purposely was trying to slow down the process—I just think he had a bad habit that was hard to break. I didn't mind if someone came in five to ten minutes late once in a while, because there certainly are things out of our control such as traffic accidents and flat tires. As I mentioned before, if someone is consistently late, it's a great way to make your boss mad. Why put your boss in a bad mood first thing in the morning if you can prevent it? Oh yes, after I left the company, the employee's boss had to talk with him about his tardiness. I guess some things never change.

Having said all of this, guess what? I was guilty of being consistently late, too! It didn't start out that way. In fact, when I started my career at the television studio, I *had* to be at work at 7 a.m. every morning—and that was with a forty-five minute commute. My supervisors gave me a lot of responsibility early on. I was the first one in the office every morning and was also the one with the least experience.

After only two weeks on the job, I was given the awesome and scary responsibility of calling the two presidents of the company on the phone with the Nielsen ratings for the prime time programs that had aired the night before on ABC, CBS, and NBC (there were only three major networks back then). I had to call them at 7:15 a.m. each morning. While I was a bit intimidated by this responsibility, it forced me to become a ratings expert in a short amount of time because I had to know what I was talking about when speaking with the top two executives of the company. I did my homework and knew that this exposure to upper management was an honor and probably very rare for someone who was at the bottom of the ladder. Over the years, automated phone ratings hotlines and emails replaced the need to speak to management by phone, but I'll never forget the great opportunity I had.

Now, can you imagine if I came to work late and made the presidents of the company wait for my phone call? What if I was consistently late? How long do you think it would've been before they replaced me? Being late for work was never an option for me. There was too much on the line. In fact, whether it's work, a lunch, a date, or a doctor's appointment, I've always been early or on time because I think it's rude to make someone wait and I would hope that they'd have the same respect for my time as I had for theirs.

In recent years, I had a staff that was large enough to handle things first thing in the morning so I didn't really need to be at work at 9 a.m. I would roll in anywhere from 9:15 a.m. to 9:40 a.m. but would always stay late to make up for it. Since one of my bosses also came in late, perhaps unconsciously I figured that if it was okay for him, it would be okay for me. It wasn't. Here I was, complaining that my boss would hold my projects up because I had to wait for him to come to work, and yet I wasn't even thinking of the consequences that my being late to work had on my staff. Perhaps my tardy employee thought the same thing about me that I thought about my boss—if it was okay for the boss to be late, then it must be okay for the employee. Again, it wasn't.

DON'T BE SHY

I've found over the years that the people who gravitated to our research department were generally quiet, reserved, and shy. This often isn't a good thing. In the corporate world, people like to see go-getters and those who are aggressive and can communicate well with others. In a meeting, this means that management wants to see team members participate and not just sit there listening all of the time.

When I first started in the business, I remember having a few informational interviews with some important executives and I felt a bit intimidated. I recall not saying a lot but mostly just listening. As I have mentioned previously, I got a job as an assistant media planner in New York at a top ad agency. However, despite my contacts, I almost didn't get the job. Why not? I was told that I came across as being too reserved. Thankfully, the same person who said that after my interview with him called me into his office six months later to congratulate me on a job well done and gave me a promotion.

Over the years, I'd become more outgoing at work. As you can see, being quiet or reserved is seen by many as a negative in the corporate world, so if you're a shy person, you should work at being more aggressive and outgoing at work. You can accomplish this simply by talking to people more. If you don't feel comfortable speaking to people all the time, don't worry, after a while it'll seem natural to you.

GETTING A GOOD NIGHT'S SLEEP

I can't stress enough how important it is to be well rested when you go to work. If you don't sleep well, then you're tired, grouchy, irritable, and inattentive. You'll increase your chances of making mistakes at work when you're tired. This isn't the condition you want to be in when trying to meet deadlines or when participating in important meetings. Unfortunately for me, getting a good night's sleep was very difficult. I thought about work so much at times that it literally kept me up at night. Actually, I'm not sure if I was up because I was thinking about work or I was thinking about work because I was up. Fortunately for me, I was able to drink caffeinated drinks the next day, which helped me keep my energy level up, but I obviously would have preferred to have had a good night's sleep. You may have to go to sleep before those late night talk shows go on the air, but that's what DVRs (Digital Video Recorders) are for.

BE A GOOD STUDENT

Always remember that from the day you begin your career to the day you retire, you're constantly learning. Sometimes your learning is obvious, such as when a supervisor or co-worker meets with you to specifically explain something. However, most of the time, your learning comes from simply observing and doing. It's crucial to listen carefully at any meeting you attend or to any phone conversation you have. If you present an idea to someone and they say, "That's a good thought, but here's a better way," pay attention to their explanation.

A great way to learn is to ask questions. A former boss used to tell me that the person who is asking questions is the person in power. You don't want to ask too many questions because it may be annoying and it may show that your knowledge of things is too limited, but the best way to learn is to ask questions. If you think your question may be classified as a stupid question, then think about what you're asking before you ask it.

ALWAYS SAY "THANK YOU"

When you first start out, you'll most likely be doing things for others much more than they'll be doing things for you. You'll be working on projects for your boss and with your co-workers. Hopefully, whomever you're working for will take the time to say or email a quick "thank you." However, if you don't get a "thank you," don't despair. Sometimes people are just too busy to say "thank you," but it doesn't necessarily mean they don't appreciate your work. Regardless of who does or does not thank you, you should get in the habit of thanking people who help you in some manner, especially your supervisors or co-workers. Regardless of how high up you climb the corporate ladder, you should never stop saying "thank you."

I remember once asking a colleague in another department for some information that I needed for a project. After he supplied the information to me, I heard through the grapevine that he wasn't happy because I didn't thank him. At the time, I thought that he was perhaps a little too sensitive. After that, I always made it a point to thank him for any information he gave me, which made our work relationship much stronger. This brief example illustrates how important it is for people to feel appreciated.

I recall another thank-you faux pas I inadvertently made, but this was even more important because it involved my boss. I was on a business trip to New York. We had received our bonuses while I was away, and I was told the amount of the bonus over the phone. Because I was on the road and wanted to thank our big boss as soon as possible, I sent him an email telling him how much I appreciated the bonus and his help in getting it. When I got back to the office, I was informed by my direct supervisor that our boss wasn't happy because I didn't thank him for the bonus. I informed my direct supervisor that I had indeed sent our boss a thank-you email, to which he replied, "Yes, but it wasn't a handwritten note." I was somewhat surprised! It just goes to show that thanking someone with a handwritten note is very important to some people regardless of the circumstance.

GIVE COMPLIMENTS

You can build strong relationships at work by complimenting others. Perhaps it's the way they handled a tough situation or the fact that they came up with a great idea, but compliments can go a long way. You should always compliment someone because you truly think highly of them, not because you think it will get you somewhere. There is no better compliment than a sincere compliment. The best compliments at work are work-related. If your co-workers or supervisors do something that impresses you, don't be afraid to tell them. They will appreciate it because everyone likes to hear that they are smart or doing a great job.

GET TO KNOW THE ASSISTANTS

Be nice to as many assistants in the company as possible. Assistants can be very powerful because they can control who gets to speak with their bosses and when. If you need to speak to an executive quickly, it makes a big difference whether or not the executive's assistant knows you or not. If the assistant knows you by name and likes and respects you, you'll have a big advantage in being able to get in contact with their boss and you may even move up to the front of the priority list.

NEVER SAY "IT'S NOT MY JOB"

I never liked it when I'd ask someone for information and they'd reply, "Sorry, it's not my job." You should never tell someone that it's not your job or that you can't help them. Instead, see if you can at least steer them in the right direction. When people called me for something that I wasn't responsible for, I'd usually tell them the name of the person who could help them and I'd give the person who was calling the phone number of the person who could help them. If you called the wrong person, wouldn't you want them to go a little out of their way to help you?

TAKE CLASSES/CONTINUING EDUCATION

Many companies give you the opportunity to take classes free of charge during the year. These classes can be about how to deal with a tough boss, how to give and receive feedback, how to deal with change, how to manage people, how to work more efficiently, etc. Usually, the classes can be anywhere from a half day to two days. With your supervisor's permission, you should try to attend as many classes as possible. Even if you retain just a small percentage of what you learned, you'll still be improving yourself. I took several management classes over the years, and while I didn't retain everything I learned, the classes were still helpful.

Furthermore, many companies will pay for you to continue your formal education. I've had employees who worked full-time, but they went to school once or twice a week at night to earn an advanced degree. The company paid for it because their area of study was related to their job. Of course, if your company pays for your further education, once you earn your degree it wouldn't be wise to seek a job at another company. This is an instance where loyalty should come into play. The company is making an investment in you, and in return you should continue to make an investment in the company.

KEEP INFORMED ABOUT THE LATEST TECHNOLOGY

It's critical that you keep up with the latest technological advances. What was new and innovative six months ago is old news today. This could mean getting the latest and greatest version of the BlackBerry® or iPhone. Perhaps more importantly, it means keeping up with the latest advances in your industry. Does your company have a strong online presence? Is it bringing in revenue through the Internet? If so, you need to be well informed about these types of things. Sometimes it can be as simple as learning specific computer programs that can help you in your job.

If you're a Millennial, you are probably already more technologically advanced than most people you work with or for. Since you have this technological knowledge, you may find yourself changing from a student at work to a teacher at work. Some members of the older generation may come to you for help when it comes to technology. This is a great opportunity because it helps you come across as a team player as well as someone who's knowledgeable about an important work component. If you can take the time to teach your older co-workers and bosses something that will make their jobs easier, they will certainly appreciate it and will see you more in a leadership position as your career progresses.

If I had learned as many computer programs as I should have, there's a strong possibility that I'd still be at the television studio. Many years ago when I first started my career, I was very hands-on when dealing with computers. However, over the years, I was fortunate enough to have a staff that would pull information for me off the computer. After a while, I stopped learning the specific computer functions that were necessary to get the projects done since my staff could do it and I could focus more on "big picture" items. One of my younger colleagues was also moving up the ladder like me, but he never stopped pulling his own information from the computer. Part of me thought that as a vice-president, he should've let his staff do more of the pulling of the information but he was smart enough not to rely on his staff for any information that he could access himself.

What was the difference between us? I put more stress on and created additional work for my staff because I totally relied on them to pull information that I needed while my colleague was able to alleviate stress and decrease the workload for his staff by being self-sufficient. If I had been able to access the information off the computer myself, I probably would have been even faster at work because many times I'd sit there waiting for my staff to pull data. Ultimately, I would have been able to micromanage less, which would have created a more harmonious working relationship with my staff. By hovering over them less and giving them more independence, I think they would have felt that I had confidence in them—which they would have appreciated.

READ INDUSTRY MAGAZINES/NEWSPAPER ARTICLES

Whatever industry you work in, it's constantly changing. It's vital to continually be informed about what's going on in your industry. Most industries have trade magazines that pertain to that particular industry. It can be about entertainment, finance, medicine, law, engineering, computers, etc. If you're a new employee, it's likely that you may be able to read a trade magazine only after someone higher up than you finishes reading it. If you're really fortunate, you'll have your own subscription that the company will pay for. Some magazines will be hard copies, others will be online. Of course, if they're online, you can access them whenever you wish and won't have to wait for another employee to pass them on to you. It's important to read these trade magazines and articles first thing in the morning since many of them contain topical information. By reading these magazines and articles, you'll not only learn new information that can be helpful at your job, but you'll also look informed to your bosses. The main thing here is to always be informed.

TAKE CREDIT FOR YOUR ACCOMPLISHMENTS

One of my rules has always been to take credit for my ideas and not to take credit for other people's ideas. Unfortunately, not everyone abides by this rule.

During my first corporate job working for my first boss, I came up with an idea for one of our clients. The client was a New York metropolitan area hot dog maker and since I spent every summer at the New Jersey shore, I knew that airplane banner advertising was big at the beach. I thought that since hot dogs and the Jersey Shore go together, why not advertise the hot dogs on banners pulled by airplanes that would be seen by thousands of people? My idea went to upper management. They liked it so much, it became a reality.

I was very proud of my idea, but I then heard from my boss's boss that my direct boss was taking credit for my idea. I now faced a dilemma. Since I was the new guy on the block and this was my first real job, do I remain quiet and not stir the pot? Do I let my boss take credit for my idea and not risk ticking him off? My other option was to take credit for my idea by letting people know it was my idea, but this might have angered my boss. It could have also given me a reputation for being someone who wasn't a team player.

Even though I was new, I did have an ego and I felt that I should be recognized for my idea. It meant enough to me that I was ready to face the consequences. Sometimes you have to pick your battles, and I decided that this was one battle I wanted to fight. I told my boss's boss that the airplane banner advertising was in fact my idea, not that of my direct boss. Fortunately, my direct boss came to me and actually apologized for taking credit for the idea. If you face a similar situation, you may not be so lucky. Since there's so much at stake when people try to keep their careers going, sometimes a person will try to elevate themselves by taking credit for others' ideas so that they'll look stronger in the eyes of their boss. My feeling is that if a boss takes credit for their employee's ideas, then they shouldn't be the boss.

A good way to prevent this from happening is to constantly promote yourself and your ideas. If you have a great idea, send it in an email and save a hard copy of the email. If someone responds to your email with a "Hey, that's a great idea," save that email. Keep a hard copy file of all of your ideas so if one day someone else attempts to take credit for your idea, you have a paper trail and no one can dispute it. Once you save a variety of ideas and compliments from others, you have something to present to your management when your review comes up, which can only help you move up the ladder.

LEARN FROM YOUR MISTAKES AND THOSE OF OTHERS

Everyone makes mistakes. The key to work and to life is to learn from them and to make sure you don't repeat them. At work, I used to quote an old saying, "Those who do not learn from history are doomed to repeat it." When you make an error, ask yourself why you made it and then make a mental note not to repeat it. It's also important to observe your co-workers and bosses because they'll make mistakes, too. Find out what they did wrong and make sure you don't follow in their footsteps. Your career is an ongoing learning process, so if you're constantly thinking about ways to improve yourself and you're willing to study and learn from others, you'll greatly improve your chances of success in the corporate world.

CONSTRUCTIVE CRITICISM

There's nothing worse than being criticized at work. It implies that you've done something wrong. When you're reprimanded you have two choices: you can either fight it or accept it. During my career, I've been criticized many times. If it was constructive criticism, I would take a step back and really try and listen to what my boss was saying and try to learn from it. If my boss was criticizing me just for the sake of it, I would listen to them, but underneath I would be a little resentful and sometimes I'd even argue.

My employees had one of two reactions when I criticized them. They'd either accept and acknowledge what I was saying and would try to improve next time or they'd go on the defensive and try to fight me on the point. From a manager's perspective, I didn't like it when they went on the defensive. I really wanted them to listen to what I was saying and accept my criticism. Some employees get very upset when they're being chastised, even if the criticism is legitimate.

I never was critical just for the sake of being critical. I always had a reason to criticize an employee when I did so. The best thing to do if someone criticizes you is to ask yourself if their point is valid. If so, you should accept it and try to improve. If you disagree with the criticism, it's okay to defend yourself but try to do it with a positive and conciliatory attitude, which is not always easy to do.

I once had given a twenty-something employee their yearly review, and although overall I gave them a positive review, a year later this person was still dwelling on some of my criticisms. At the time, I felt that this employee was just being too sensitive. However, as I was writing this book, another theory occurred to me. Many Millennials are brought up with a lot of praise given to them by their parents, teachers, and sports coaches. Some of them are given kudos for just participating in various activities, regardless of whether or not they were successful in their endeavor. Many Millennials received sports or school trophies for just participating (hence, they are also known as the Trophy Generation), while my generation had to actually win something to get a trophy. I earned many first-place trophies in my time. Granted, they were for bowling, but that counts!

While I certainly can't stereotype an entire generation, I do believe that some members of Generation Y have grown up without a lot of criticism, so when they are exposed to it at work, they may be a bit surprised and disappointed. If you do fall into this category, you should know that it's perfectly normal to be criticized at work. If you are, don't take it personally. It's important to note that when your boss gives you criticism so that you will improve in certain areas, they also are paying close attention to how you react to their criticism, so don't be on the defensive.

ACKNOWLEDGE PEOPLE

When you see people walking down the hall toward you, what do you do? Do you say "hello" or ignore them? It's very important to acknowledge people at work when you see them. It doesn't take a lot of effort and it can go a long way toward building strong relationships.

I remember a few years ago I was at a mall near my office after work and I saw the president of our company in the distance walking toward me. As soon as his eyes met mine, he put his head down and stared straight at the ground. Just as he was about to walk past me I said "hello" to him and he looked up. We spoke for a minute and then we moved on. I found his behavior to be very strange. I asked myself why he tried to avoid me. Did he feel uncomfortable speaking to a lower-level employee? After all, he knew me, and from what I could tell from work, he liked me. It made me feel unimportant, especially since I had worked very hard for him and our company. I realize that some people feel awkward when they see work people in a non-work situation. However, he was the president and should've been able to acknowledge me, no matter who I was, especially since he knew me.

One of my former bosses would always complain that when some of the younger employees would see him in the hallway, they'd never acknowledge him. He felt that they should be the first ones to say hello, not him. I explained to him that some of them were shy and maybe felt a little intimidated by him. I'm sure that the younger employees probably felt that he, as the boss, should be the first to say hello. Remember at the beginning of the book when I mentioned that there can be a gap of expectations between the Millennials and their supervisors? This was a perfect example. The older generation (our boss) expected the younger employees to say "hello" first, while the younger generation perhaps felt that the boss should be the first to say "hello." Since there were differing expectations, the end result was that no one said "hello." The solution is quite simple. Just say "hello" to anyone you see or walk by in the hallway.

RUNG IV SUMMARY

- Always think about your work reputation.
- Don't judge the job by the first day or week. Your first impression may be wrong.
- Check in with your supervisor before you leave for the day. Be prepared to stay late, if necessary.
- Don't be late. Allow time for bad weather, road construction, and accidents.
- Get a good night's sleep.
- Ask questions. This is the best way to learn.
- Always thank people for their help.
- Get to know the assistants. They can give you quick access to their supervisors if you need information from them.
- Never say "it's not your job." Find out whose job it is and pass on that information.
- Take classes and stay informed about the latest technology in your field.
- Read industry websites and trade magazines.
- Take credit for your accomplishments. Send out your ideas in an email so there's no doubt about who came up with the idea.
- Learn from your mistakes and from the mistakes of others. "Those who do not learn from history are doomed to repeat it."
- Don't be afraid of constructive criticism and don't take it personally.
- Acknowledge people. Saying "hello" or smiling goes a long way.

RUNG V – YOUR WORK ATTITUDE

THE FACTORY WORKER MENTALITY

It is crucial to remember that your work attitude is just as important as your work aptitude. There are many people who just want to work the official hours of the company and not a minute more. If the hours are 9 a.m. to 6 p.m., you'll see them on the elevator at 9 a.m. coming to work and then again at 6 p.m. going home. It's rare that you see them coming in early or staying late. I call it the factory worker mentality (this is nothing against factory workers but speaks more to people who have an "on the clock" mentality). Their attitude is, "You got me from 9 to 6 with an hour for lunch, and that's it." If you're one of these people, it's unlikely that you'll rise up the corporate ladder. Yes, you could keep your job for many years and earn your three to four percent raise every year and maybe you're okay with that. However, if you want to be a successful manager or executive, you need to be willing to work beyond the official work hours of the company. I can't tell you how many times I had to work late or on weekends, but it never bothered me because my attitude was always, "I'll do whatever it takes to get the job done."

I once read a magazine article that surveyed many CEOs (Chief Executive Officers) around the country. One of the things they had in common was that almost all of them woke up very early every day. I'm talking 5 a.m. or 6 a.m. Many of them would work out first thing in the morning and read emails as they were working out–every minute of their time was put to use. I knew top executives at one of my former companies who were at the gym by 5 a.m. or 5:30 a.m. Personally, I'm not an early morning person and couldn't function by rising at the crack of dawn, but one thing is for sure, none of these CEOs had a factory worker mentality.

Some people with a factory worker mentality may have a lazy streak. This advice is for them: don't get caught sleeping on the job– literally. In one of the office buildings I used to work in, there was a large lobby and in one section there was a group of leather chairs and sofas. I'd see employees taking a nap there during lunchtime, including an employee from my department. The employees I'd see napping were never executives. They were rank-and-file employees. Perhaps they didn't realize that their building wasn't a hotel, it was a place of work. If you're very tired, drink a caffeinated drink or two to keep you awake as I used to do. If anyone sees you sleeping on the job, you'll be labeled as being lazy and you certainly won't be seen as management material. In my entire corporate career, I never took a nap during the day during the work week. Neither should you. If you need to, start going to bed earlier—there's no excuse for sleeping on the job.

STAYING LATE

In most corporate jobs, you'll be required to stay late after work in order to complete certain projects. Sometimes it's just unavoidable and it's always best to expect that you'll need to work overtime now and then. Some companies will pay you for overtime, some won't. It's helpful to have a good attitude about it. If your boss asks you to stay late, even if it's without much notice, you should gladly do it. On the other hand, it's probably not a good idea to tell your boss you can't stay late because you have a Pilates or yoga class. Some Millennials (and others) may have a conflict between their Baby-Boomer boss's "work-late" mentality versus their need for a work-life balance. However, your boss will appreciate you much more if you're the employee who can roll up your sleeves and work late. You'll be seen as a team player who will do what it takes to get the job done.

Of course, staying late can be avoided if you work efficiently during the day. If need be, take a shorter lunch if you have a large project to tackle because this could prevent you from having to stay late unnecessarily.

I once had a boss who would keep our department late from time to time simply to show his boss that we were working hard. It was totally unnecessary for us to be at work late since we had already completed our work, but this was totally for show. He saw it as a badge of honor. This boss would also point out to me on occasion that one of my employees would always be working late and that I should do the same. I had to remind my boss that this employee was working late because he would come in late and because he wasn't very fast in getting his work done.

I also had to remind the boss of all the times I did stay late and of all the weekends I had worked.

My feeling is that people shouldn't have to stay late just for the sake of staying late. If you get your work done on time, then you should be able to go home on time. After all, you'll be back the next day to complete any unfinished business. Having said that, you also don't want to get a reputation for leaving on time every day. Management prefers employees who go the extra mile and work late. Even when I had completed my work by the end of the day, I'd usually stay fifteen or twenty minutes late. This would enable me to avoid getting into a full elevator and to avoid the long line of cars waiting to get out of the parking garage. Furthermore, by leaving a little later, you can avoid some of the traffic on the highway or freeway. Take those extra fifteen or twenty minutes to catch up on emails. You can also use the time to chat with your boss, which in a subtle way is letting them know that you're working late. If you don't want to be criticized for not staying late, your best bet is to wait until your boss leaves for the day and then you can leave.

"JUST DO IT"

One reason that I buy Nike® products is because I love their "Just Do It"® slogan. There were many times when I had given an employee a project and they weren't particularly enthusiastic about completing the project quickly. I wanted to shout out, "*Just do it!*" I never did that, but it was tempting. There will certainly be projects that you may not be interested in working on, and there may even be days where you don't particularly feel like working at all. Unfortunately, you are getting paid to do a job. If you are unwilling to do certain things, you can easily be replaced by someone who does want to do the job. Bosses do not want to hear excuses. In fact, one of my former bosses had a great saying that I think represents what the workplace is all about. He used to say, "All I care about is results."

The key is to somehow find a way to motivate yourself to do something you don't want to do. Sometimes you may put off working on a project until the last possible minute because it may not interest you or you may not understand how to go about completing it. If you find yourself in this position, say to yourself, "Just do it." Say that to yourself *before* your boss says it to you out loud. Remember, if you can work just as hard on these types of projects as the ones you do enjoy working on, you'll have a much better chance of moving up the corporate ladder.

DISCIPLINE YOURSELF

If you look up the word "discipline" in the dictionary, you will find that the word has several possible meanings, including the following: (1) "Training that corrects, molds, or perfects the mental faculties or moral character" and (2) "Orderly or prescribed conduct or pattern of behavior." In other words, it's up to you to figure out a regimen that you can stick to each day. It starts with figuring out what time you need to get up each morning so that you have plenty of time to work out, take a shower, and commute to work and still arrive early or on time. Once you arrive at work, you need to have a regimen that optimizes your performance every day. The key is to be consistent and to constantly remind yourself of the things that need to be done.

Disciplining yourself can involve utilizing a combination of physical and mental abilities. On the physical side, if you do exercise, you should try and do it at the same time every day. This way, your body will get in a rhythm. If you don't feel like exercising on a particular day, you may need to psyche yourself up in order to exercise that day. Of course, this involves discipline of the mind as well as of the body. All you need to do is to remind yourself of all of the benefits of exercising (improving your health, losing weight, feeling better about yourself, etc.) and you'll be more likely to exercise consistently.

At work, you may need to push yourself mentally from time to time. If you face a roadblock on a particular project, you need to challenge yourself to overcome that roadblock so that you can continue on your path. You need to ask yourself why you're having difficulty with a particular project and then come up with ways to move the roadblock aside. Again, you need to psych yourself up to work on these projects by always reminding yourself that this is your job and that you'll be rewarded for doing a good job.

BE A PERFECTIONIST

You can't be a perfectionist unless you strive to be a perfectionist. If you strive to be a perfectionist, you'll increase your chances of achieving excellence. One of my goals was to always send out emails and reports free of errors. Why? Because many people will assume that if they find one error, they will probably find more, and they may end up questioning your accuracy and credibility, which is something you don't want them to do. I'd always proofread my emails at least once but usually more than once. Guess what? In my quarter-century of working in the corporate world, my error rate was near zero. Of course, no one can be one hundred percent perfect all the time, but you won't get close to perfection if you're careless.

You should be your own harshest critic. No one should be tougher on you than you. If you are tough on yourself, you'll beat others to the punch. Personally, I always preferred to criticize myself rather than have someone else do it to me. Can you be too much of a perfectionist? Perhaps, but as long as you do everything to the absolute best of your abilities, you should be successful.

BE A TEAM PLAYER

No matter what company you work for or what department you work in, everything that gets done is a result of a team effort. You depend on other people and they depend on you. Working together as a team helps improve morale and contributes to camaraderie among the team members.

Millennials are known for valuing teamwork. Therefore, I would suggest that when possible, ask your boss to assign you projects on which you can work directly with someone else in your department. If your team does a great job, your supervisor will be more likely to assign you more team projects in the future. Furthermore, working on a project as a team is usually more fun than working on a project alone.

A great idea is great only if someone executes it. Only then can it become a reality. When a project is assigned to your department, your boss may come up with some ideas on how best to go about completing the project. However, your boss needs you and your co-workers to do the research necessary to execute their ideas. Once that's done, you may require the department assistant (if you have one) to put the project in presentation form, and of course, you then may need to work with the assistant to explain how the presentation should look. After that, you or your co-workers will need to proof the presentation to make sure there are no typos or other mistakes. Working together is a give-and-take process, but in the end, the department that works best together has the most success together.

MULTITASK AND KEEP A LIST

One of the keys to success on any job is having the ability to multitask. You must be able to work on different projects simultaneously. This means that you need to be flexible enough to change priorities at any given moment. It's rare that you'll be in the ideal situation of having the luxury of working on one project at a time. Actually, you'll never have the luxury of being able to work on one project at a time. You must be able to switch gears at a moment's notice. It can be very frustrating when you're working for a few days or even weeks on a project, you're in your groove, and then someone decides that the project can wait and you have to put it aside for a new priority. You can't take it personally or feel bad. You need to just move on to the next priority and do a great job.

Many Millennials should have an advantage when it comes to multitasking. After all, it seems like you can effortlessly instant message someone from your computer while talking on your cell phone and watching television. Despite this, it's easy to get overwhelmed when you're working on many different projects at once. Throw in some personal tasks and errands you want to do and you'll experience a lot of stress.

I always found that one way to reduce my stress in a busy time was to write down everything I had to do. I was known as "the man of lists" by some, but it really helped me organize things in my head. I felt like I had a handle on the situation when I could actually see what lay ahead of me on paper (or on my computer). When my to-do list of things decreased, I felt less stress and more in control. As long as I had that list, there was little chance of me forgetting to do something important.

In order to multitask, it's important to be able to focus on the mission at hand. Concentration at work is critical. This means getting rid of distractions in your office. I've seen plenty of people who had a television set on in their office or they were listening to the radio. Some employees listen to their iPods while they work. I don't see how these people can concentrate one hundred percent with these distractions. Yes, watching TV or listening to tunes does make the day more enjoyable, but it may also contribute to you making mistakes on a project. Please be aware that some bosses may think of you in a negative way because you are listening to the radio or watching television at work. They might assume that your focus is not on work.

If you're like me, when I'm driving and I get lost, the first thing I do is shut off the radio. Why? Because the radio is distracting and when the radio goes off, it means it's time to get down to business and concentrate. The same holds true for work.

FOLLOW UP

No matter where you work, you'll come to depend on other employees to make your job easier. In order to complete a project on time, you'll usually need to get information from someone else. Perhaps you emailed them requesting some information or perhaps you spoke with them on the phone or left a voicemail but you haven't heard back from them. What do you do? You must follow up with them. Don't take it personally if they haven't gotten back to you. Keep in mind that they're probably very busy and you aren't their first priority. If you need information back in a timely manner and you requested it in email form, you can check off the "Return Receipt" box in your email which tells you if and when the recipient opened your email. At least you'll know if they've seen your email or not.

If you've left a voice message, I think the best thing to do is to call them again or even stop by their office (assuming they're in the same building as you; this also applies if they haven't responded to your email). In a nice way, you can say something like, "Hi, I don't know if you got my message, but I'm trying to find out information about X and would appreciate any help you can give me." What you don't want to say is, "Because you didn't respond to my request, I'm now scrambling to get this project done and I'm going to look bad to my boss."

WORK VS. FAMILY

One of the keys to success in the corporate world—or any working world, for that matter—is to achieve the right balance between work and family. Unfortunately, there's no magic formula for this. Everyone has a unique situation. If you're single and live alone, you may have fewer distractions and responsibilities than someone who is married with children. If you're married and have kids, you may need time off once in a while for doctor's appointments, school plays, soccer practice, and whatever else comes up. On the one hand, you hopefully realize how important it is to your boss and co-workers to take the least amount of time off from work as possible. You may also realize how important it is to get that paycheck every week or two and you don't want to jeopardize that. On the other hand, you have family obligations and your family at home will most certainly take precedence over your "family" at work. So what do you do?

The best thing you can do is to communicate with your family as well as the people at work. Find out what everyone's expectations are. You may be fortunate to work with a group of people who are in a similar situation. In this case, everyone will pitch in for each other when the situation dictates. Or, you may have a very understanding family who knows how important it is for you to do well at your job and career. While they might not like the fact that you always come home late from work, they know that it'll all pay off in the end.

Of course, you may have a boss and co-workers who think that you need to make work your first priority. Your single co-workers might think it's unfair that they're constantly pitching in for you while you're meeting your family obligations and they're stuck doing their job and yours. The corporate world can be very demanding and you may have to make some sacrifices. If you do need to take time off for family issues, volunteer to come in early or work overtime to make up for the time you lost at work. Your boss and fellow employees will appreciate this.

One of my former employees was married and had a child. The child had some medical issues. This employee and his wife would always go to the child's doctor's appointments together. His wife didn't work, and therefore, my employee was the sole breadwinner of his family. He would take a decent amount of time off from work sometimes to attend these doctor appointments. Of course, when he was away, his work was not getting done, which put more pressure on me and others in our department. I asked him why it was necessary for him to attend all of these appointments since his wife was already going. He replied that he needed to be there to support and help his wife.

This employee never fully explained to me what the medical issues were with his child and why his wife couldn't attend the doctor's appointments alone. This put us both in a very difficult and sensitive situation. On the one hand, I tried to be understanding and allowed him to handle what needed to be handled. He and his wife even sent me a thank-you note at one point. On the other hand, I was very frustrated. From my point of view, since he was the sole wage earner in the family, I would've thought that he'd do everything in his power to leave work as little as possible. He could've even been jeopardizing his job with all of his time off, and without his paycheck and company health insurance, his family would truly suffer. Again, I didn't know what the medical condition of his child was and how serious or not it was. He certainly was a loyal husband and father and you couldn't blame him for that. There was no right or wrong way to handle this situation.

I did express my sentiments to him at the time. A couple of years later he went to work for another company, where apparently he had the same issues. His new boss had also spoken with him about taking time off, but he seemed to have continued with the same habits. Perhaps if he had explained to me (or to his new boss) in more detail what his situation was, it might have been easier and less frustrating for all of us. Again, the lesson here is to always communicate with your boss as much as possible.

INITIATE/ANTICIPATE/RECIPROCATE/COOPERATE

Initiate

One of my former bosses used to have some good advice: always come up with three ideas a week that no one asked for. Now, I don't necessarily agree that the number of ideas you need to come up with is three per week, but the point is to initiate. I believe that 90% of the people at work are executors and only 10% are initiators. It's the 10% who move up the ladder the fastest. If you initiate, you can prove to management that you're a thinker, not just an executor. However, the complaint I heard most often from employees was that they're so busy just executing, they didn't have the time to initiate. "I'm so overwhelmed as it is, I have to work overtime–how can I possibly have the time to come up with new ideas?" Again, you have to ask yourself whether you want to move up the ladder or not. If you do, I guarantee you that you'll somehow find the time to initiate.

What supervisors are looking for are new ideas and new ways of doing things. They don't care how busy you are. It's not as hard as you think. If your goal is to enjoy and love your job, then initiating gives you more satisfaction in your job. Initiation could involve finding a way for your department to save money or perhaps disseminating information in a different manner. It could be just forwarding a newspaper article that affects your company. When you initiate you impress people, and when you impress people they'll remember you when it comes time for a promotion.

Of course, if you initiate, you'll probably be rejected more than once. If so, don't let it stop you. It's great if you're known as the person who comes up with new ideas, even if most of them are turned down. The more ideas you come up with, the greater your chances of having some of them accepted and executed.

Some of my best ideas were never accepted. Years ago, I sent a memo to the president of our division with an idea to simulcast one of our television game shows on radio. There were a lot of people who were driving home from work who may not be home in time every night to see this game show on television. If you gave them the opportunity to listen to the show on radio and play along while they were driving, it would keep their interest in the show intact. The president thought it was a good idea, but it never got off the ground. I still think this is a good idea to this day.

Another idea I had involved television programming on Saturday nights. Saturday night used to be a great night of television. The networks used to provide programming that appealed to an older audience, with classics like *All in the Family, Mary Tyler Moore, The Love Boat* and hits like *Golden Girls, Dr. Quinn, Medicine Woman,* and *Walker, Texas Ranger.* Today, it's all repeats and reality programming on Saturday night.

My idea was to air a live variety show (similar to *The Ed Sullivan Show*) on Saturday nights from a Las Vegas casino. The goal would be to target viewers over 50 years old, which was counterintuitive since most advertisers targeted 18–49 year olds. I felt that the show would be a great advertisement for the casino and that older viewers would benefit because they would finally have a broadcast television show that would cater to them.

I told my idea to some of the top people in the company. They immediately said "no." I then started telling others in the company. The head of one of our key departments really liked the idea. To this day, nothing further has happened, but the point is to let people know about your ideas and to never give up on them. (By the way, this idea might have been risky since gambling is involved, but hey, making a television show is a gamble anyway!).

I've also had a lot of ideas that my bosses liked and executed. One of the television programs that my company distributed was a comedy that was produced a few years ago. It originally aired on cable and attracted a decent but not exceptionally large audience. We then sold the reruns of the program to various television stations and to one basic cable network. Unfortunately, the show didn't perform as well as we would have liked. It was then time to sell the show once again to a basic cable network since the original deal had expired. We knew that it would be a tough sell given its recent lack of performance so we had to approach things differently.

My idea was to focus on the guest stars of the show. Over 150 guest stars had appeared on the show. I did my research and divided these stars into four different categories: Oscar winners and nominees, Emmy® winners and nominees, Golden Globe® winners and nominees, and People's Choice winners and nominees. My thought was that you can have different theme weeks for each category. For example, around the time of the Academy Awards®, you could feature the episodes with the Oscar winners and nominees. Furthermore, you could have a lot of fun online showing the photos of these stars then and now in addition to some great trivia questions. Basically, we would present this show as a pop culture icon.

Everyone went along with this idea and part of the research pitch talked about the guest stars and the potential theme weeks and interactive possibilities. Basically, I thought out of the box and that's what management was looking for.

Here's another form of initiation: A few years ago, our division moved to a new location about five miles away. Moving is a great time to go through all of your files and delete or throw out the unwanted or unnecessary ones. Our department had a research library filled with file cabinets and shelves of files going back thirty years. We were given the news that our research library location in the new building had only about half of the space as the library in our current building. This meant going through the entire library to determine which files needed to be transferred to the new library, which files would be sent to storage, and which files needed to be thrown into the garbage can.

This was a massive project. Only a few of us who were managers in the department were really qualified to go through the files because only we knew which ones were worth keeping. I would've loved to delegate this project to someone else, but I had so much invested in this library because of my longevity in the department. This was a form of initiation. I took it upon myself to complete a project that I wasn't asked to do. For an entire week, I worked in that library on my hands and knees and went through every piece of paper from A to Z. It was a dirty job (literally), but someone had to do it. In the end, I was able to discard about forty percent of the files in the library and sent another ten percent to storage. The new library held only the most relevant files. It was also a very organized and clean library, of which I was proud.

I previously mentioned that our studio conducted testing from time to time to gauge viewer reactions to our television programs. This usually required that we hire a focus group moderator who would talk to twelve people in a room and ask them questions about the particular program that was being tested. Every once in a while, we would conduct this testing in Las Vegas, and at one point, I took it upon myself to moderate the focus groups. No one asked me to do it. I felt that rather than try to explain to a moderator what we were trying to find out from the audience, it would be easier for me to speak with the audience directly. As it turned out, we were able to get the information we needed, we saved money because we didn't have to hire an outside moderator, and it was a great experience for me. In this case, initiation was a win-win situation.

Here is one more example of initiation: In the past, there were a couple of times when I was asked to be a guest speaker at a media class at UCLA. I was substituting for my boss, who couldn't make it. I was to give an oral presentation that had already been prepared by my boss and even though the material covered was not my area of expertise, I knew enough to get by. At the end of the presentation, I quickly went through the do's and don'ts of corporate culture. This wasn't in the presentation initially but was something I wanted to cover. I felt that I was educating the class in something that wasn't taught in their classroom, and hopefully they appreciated it. Again, the key is to do things that no one is asking you to do. (By the way, my comments at the end of the class about corporate culture have, in many ways, influenced my desire to write this book!)

Anticipate

One of the key things in business is to be able to anticipate what your bosses, co-workers, and clients want before they ask for it. One of the main criticisms of my employees over the years is that they didn't seem to anticipate my needs as much as I would've liked. Sometimes employees forget that one of their main functions is to make the boss's job easier. One way of doing that is to constantly think of the boss's needs and anticipate what he or she wants before it is asked for. It's very helpful to constantly communicate with your boss and find out what their priority is each day. What are their main concerns? As a boss, I became frustrated many times when I was forced to think of something that I felt my employee should have thought of.

The following is a great example of a time when an employee of mine didn't anticipate my needs and the potential consequences of his lack of anticipation. At one point, one of my former companies was in charge of producing a science fiction drama that was airing on a cable network. We had done some research on the program and we were going to present the results to the producers of the show in Vancouver, Canada, which is where the show was produced. Three of us were going to make the trip from Los Angeles to Vancouver—myself, one of my employees, and a person from the company that had conducted the research and who would do most of the presenting. I had asked my assistant to take care of everything, including booking the flights and the hotel, determining the logistics of how to get to the studio in Vancouver, and how the presentation room would be set up. Ideally, I would've liked everything to have been done without my supervision so I could concentrate on the presentation itself. Yes, it would be great if we all lived in an ideal world.

My assistant booked the flights and the hotel. So far so good. About a day or two before we were to leave, I got an uneasy feeling. There were two things I was worried about. One was the actual presentation room itself. Since we were technically in a foreign country, my question was whether or not we needed an electrical adaptor to convert electricity since we were showing a PowerPoint presentation on our overhead projector. Can you imagine if we traveled all the way to Canada, were about to give our presentation and were unable to hook things up? This would've been very embarrassing. But that scary thought was nothing compared to my other concern. Did we all need passports to fly to Canada? I wasn't concerned about myself because I had a valid passport and was ready to go, but how about my employee and the executive from the other company? Did my assistant anticipate our needs and call ahead regarding the electrical current and did he find out what type of legal documentation was required to enter Canada? *No, he did not.*

I asked him to find out about both issues ASAP (As Soon as Possible) or actually sooner than ASAP since time was running out. As far as the electricity was concerned, it turned out to be a non-issue since Canada uses the same electrical current as we do.

However, the passport issue turned out to be a major one. In order for us to fly to Canada, we were required to have either a passport or birth certificate. As I said, I had a valid passport, and I found out that my employee had a valid passport. That left just one more person to worry about–the woman from the research company who was going to present the findings. I took matters into my own hands and called her myself about a day or two before we were to leave Los Angeles. I explained the situation. She told me that she didn't have a passport. At this point, I was getting very nervous, but we still had some hope. Did she have a copy of her birth certificate? She told me that she wasn't sure and that she would look for it in her house. A few hours later she called me with the bad news–she couldn't find one. No passport, no birth certificate, no trip to Vancouver for her.

Time was now running out and Plan B was called into action. We needed someone else from her company to present the research. Fortunately, her boss had been involved with this project and not only was available to go to Canada but had a valid passport, too. I breathed a big sigh of relief. The three of us flew to Vancouver. The next morning we met the producers, gave our presentation, and took a tour of the set. The presentation went very well, and we flew back to Los Angeles that afternoon.

The point of the story is that if my assistant had properly anticipated all of our needs, it would've been a much less stressful trip for all of us. Thankfully, things worked out well, but it could have been a disaster.

Perhaps I should have thought of the passport situation as soon as we knew we were going to Canada, but I delegated this responsibility to my assistant and felt it was his job to take care of things. When I gave my assistant his review, this example was mentioned to him so that he would know in the future what was expected of him.

One more thing about anticipation. When I was in high school, I was on the chess team (it's not as glamorous as it sounds!). When you play chess, you learn to not only anticipate your opponent's next move but also their next three moves. The same applies to work. When you go to work on any particular day, yes, you need to focus on what projects are due that day but you also need to look ahead. What is needed for next week, the next month, or even the next few months? You can't approach work with blinders on so if you're able to look into the future you will be more successful at anticipating everyone's needs.

Reciprocate

If you look up the word "reciprocate" in a dictionary, it says "to give and take mutually" and "to return in kind or degree." In other words, if someone gives you a compliment or takes you out to lunch, you should do the same for them. If someone thanks you for something, you should thank them for something in the future. However, if someone treats you in a negative way, it's best not to reciprocate, as hard as that may be. Also, don't always expect others to reciprocate when you treat them in a positive manner. Of course, it would be nice if they did, but unfortunately it doesn't always work out that way. I think the best rule is simply to treat others the way you would want them to treat you.

Cooperate

In order to get what you need, it's essential that you cooperate not only with your co-workers but also with employees in other departments. Over the years, I have seen friction between different departments because of the conflicting personalities involved. Sometimes, the friction begins with the department heads and works its way down to the employees. Don't get caught up in this. The best thing that you can do to help yourself is to be friendly and cooperative with members of other departments. It'll make your job so much easier. When I worked in the research department at the television studio, our department would always work very closely with the marketing department. Fortunately, we all genuinely liked each other and enjoyed working with each other, but without the cooperation of both departments none of us would have been as productive and efficient as we were.

RUNG V SUMMARY

- Your work attitude is just as important as your work aptitude.
- Be prepared to work late and volunteer to do so.
- Strive to be a perfectionist.
- Multitask and keep a list of both work and personal projects.
- Follow up with people. You may not be their first priority.
- It's great to have a work/life balance but don't let it get in the way of having a great work reputation.
- Be a team player: Ask your supervisor if you can work as part of a group.
- "Just do it": Bosses don't want to hear excuses.
- Initiate: Come up with new and better ways of doing things.
- Anticipate: Think about your supervisor's needs as well as your client's needs.
- Reciprocate: When someone does something nice for you or thanks you, try to do the same for them.
- Cooperate: It's important to work well with supervisors, co-workers, and employees from other departments.

RUNG VI – THINGS THEY DON'T TEACH YOU IN SCHOOL

WHAT DEFINES SUCCESS?

Sometimes I wished I was on a sports team because it's so easy to determine if you're successful or not. Your team gets a win or a loss each time you play the game. Sometimes you get small victories along the way, but ultimately you are judged on whether or not you have a winning record. Beyond that, you are considered even more successful if your team makes the playoffs. Of course, the ultimate success is if your team wins the World Series or Super Bowl.

In the corporate world, it's a little more difficult to determine success. There's no win or loss column. In fact, every day you'll probably experience wins and losses, but what constitutes winning the Super Bowl in the corporate world? I suppose that in some industries it's landing a new client or making a sale for a lot of money. In the legal field, it is easy to determine success or failure because-if you go to court-you either win or lose. When I worked at the television studio, I think our big victories came when we sold a television program for a considerable sum. It was always a team effort with the salespeople ultimately making the sale. In some cases, hundreds of millions of dollars of revenue was earned for top television programs.

Hopefully, you'll be fortunate enough to work for a company that will do something extra for its employees to reward them for their hard work and success. At the television studio, we'd have quarterly breakfasts for the whole division. The top executives in the company would speak to us and inform us of what was going on within the company. At other times, executives would host an ice cream party to thank employees for their help during a very intense period of time. Our salespeople would sometimes take us out to lunch or dinner to thank us for our help in making a sale. During the holidays, the company would host two parties, one for our division and one for the company as a whole. It is this type of extra effort by the company that employees really appreciate.

HOW TO ACT IN MEETINGS

In any company, there are usually different types of meetings. Some meetings are small with only two or three people. Other meetings can be larger with ten people or more. I used to attend a weekly meeting with many of the top executives of the company, and I was proud to be the sole representative of my department. It showed that my supervisors trusted me to not only attend but also to contribute to these meetings. The weekly meeting was attended by up to fifty executives so sometimes it was standing room only. The meetings were informative, however, many times some of us felt like outsiders because, when certain issues came up, it seemed like the people involved were starting mid-sentence. We didn't have the backstory so we felt a little lost.

One of my former bosses always said that if you have more than just a few people in a meeting, it's not going to be very productive. When there are a lot of people in the room, you really have to watch what you're saying and it may be hard to go into a lot of detail. There were people there like myself who would be called upon to answer questions. If no one asked me a question, I'd volunteer information that I thought would be helpful. There were other people in that meeting who never said a word. If the leaders of that meeting were to ever cut the number of attendees, who do you think would be cut first–the people who participated or the ones who just sat there? That's why you need to participate in some manner in any meeting you're invited to.

Some meetings will be attended only by people who work in your department. Sometimes meetings will be with members of a different department or with representatives of several departments. When you first start out with a company and you are at a lower-level position, you may only be asked to attend intra-department meetings. However, after you've proven yourself, you'll hopefully be asked to attend meetings outside your department. If you feel that you're ready to do so and your boss hasn't asked you, then you should ask them if you can attend these meetings in the future. Attending meetings with people from other departments is a great way to learn about the dynamics of the company and to build stronger work relationships. It also gives you a great opportunity to show others how competent and skillful you are at your job.

When you're in a meeting, always listen carefully to what people are saying. If you have a question because you don't understand something, it's important to ask the question to get clarification. However, ask yourself if this question may sound stupid to people, and if so, wait until after the meeting to ask it.

If you're asked a question and you don't know the answer, don't just say, "I don't know." A better answer is, "That's a great question–let me confirm the facts and I'll get back to you as soon as possible." Of course, you need to keep your word, and as soon as the meeting ends, you need to do your research and get back to that person with the answer.

Meetings are a great way of exchanging information, but too many meetings can be counterproductive. If you're always in a meeting, it means you aren't in your office working. Most meetings will create more work, so usually after you have a meeting, you'll need to go back to your office and handle new requests. Some departments have daily meetings, while others have weekly meetings. It all just depends on what the department head wants to do.

As an executive, having regular meetings with my staff was important to me for two reasons. First, I knew that if my staff and I met and discussed a particular project or projects, everyone would be on the same page and they'd have an opportunity to ask me any questions they might have. I wanted my staff to feel like we were a team, and therefore, we needed to meet as a team. Second, it helped me personally by alleviating my anxiety and any feelings of being overwhelmed. I frequently would be working on multiple projects and was concerned about their progress, but after I met with my staff, I felt more in control of what was going on and felt more comfortable about the progress that was being made. If you have a boss who likes to have regular meetings, try to understand that they may help your boss feel more organized. If your boss is more organized, they can help you stay more organized, too.

One more piece of advice: Never storm out of a meeting if you're upset at something that someone has said. I only observed this once in my career. I was in a meeting with four or five other executives. One executive didn't like what another executive said. This executive got up and stormed out of the meeting. It made all of us uncomfortable. Guess who we spent the next five minutes talking about? If someone upsets you during a meeting, don't let it get to you. Just keep your cool and try to speak with the person in private after the meeting to discuss your concerns.

Here are a few key points to remember about meetings:

✓ Know the agenda ahead of time. Hopefully, you'll be aware of the purpose of the meeting beforehand, and if not, please ask.

✓ Always arrive early or on time. I'd always get to a meeting before most people. If you arrive late, it means you're keeping people waiting and that's rude.

✓ If you arrive at a meeting early and there are other people in the room, don't just sit there in eerie silence; strike up a conversation with them about work, the movies, the weather, or anything non-controversial.

✓ As in an interview, keep your cell phone, pager, and BlackBerry® off. If you're speaking to a group, how would you like it if someone's cell phone went off and it interrupted what you were saying?

✓ If you accidentally leave your device on, do not answer the phone during the meeting or respond to an email or text message.

✓ Bring a writing implement, paper, and most importantly, any notes or reports that will be discussed.

✓ Give your complete attention to the person speaking, even if you're bored or uninterested in what they're saying. Again, how would you like it if you were speaking and everyone in the room was looking out the window or at someone else?

✓ Be careful with profanity. Never be the first one in a meeting to use profanity. If you're in a meeting with people you feel comfortable with and they feel comfortable with you, profanity may be acceptable within that group. However, don't use profanity with people you don't know or in a large meeting. You're always better off being safe than sorry.

✓ This is your time to shine. Meetings can be great brainstorming sessions and a golden opportunity to share your ideas with the rest of the group.

✓ Before the meeting is over, know the action plan. Who'll be responsible for doing what and what's the timeline for completing the plan? If you're not sure, ask during the meeting.

HOW TO BE A GOOD PRESENTER

Once you've been with a company for a while, hopefully you'll be asked to make a presentation to a group of people. Good public speaking skills are necessary for success in the corporate world. While some people enjoy speaking in public, others do not. Personally, I always enjoyed giving presentations, but at least one of my former bosses did not. There's something empowering when you can give useful information to a group of people in a room. The presenter is seen as an expert in some ways, which is a positive thing.

If you don't enjoy speaking in public, you need to figure out a way to motivate yourself so that you'll look forward to and actually volunteer to give presentations. This can only help your career. Why do some people fear giving public presentations? Perhaps they are afraid of being evaluated by their peers or supervisors. Perhaps they feel that they don't know the material well enough or that the people in the audience will be bored or will ask tough questions. Get over it. If you want to move up the corporate ladder, start practicing. Consider joining an organization like Toastmasters International, which helps people become more comfortable and competent in front of an audience. You can practice your communication skills in front of people you don't know so that you'll eventually become successful speaking in front of people you do know.

Many people, myself included, get nervous before they give a presentation. However, I see the nervousness as a good thing. It means I care about what I'm doing and about how my presentation will be received. I was told the story of a very high-level executive who used to get so nervous when he was presenting to a group, that he would sweat profusely. Rather than let his nervousness overwhelm him, he did something about it. This executive went to a speech coach and went on to become a great speaker . . . without the sweat. He could have done nothing, but he took action and it paid off.

I think the best way to defeat nervousness is to be really prepared. Whenever I gave a presentation, I practiced it several times so that I knew the material inside and out. I also tried to anticipate what questions the audience would ask and find out the answers if I didn't know them. There's no reason to be nervous if you're well educated on the subject matter.

Usually, giving a presentation involves utilizing Microsoft® Word or PowerPoint. This means that you will have some sort of audio-visual presentation to give (keep the number of bullet points and the number of words for each bullet to a minimum). This also means that you don't just show up a minute before you give the presentation to see if everything is working properly.

✓ ALWAYS check ahead of time to make sure that everything is hooked up properly and that all of your required materials are where you need them.

✓ DON'T leave anything to chance. Have the phone number of the company's AV (Audio-Visual) or IT (Information Technology) department handy in case there's a problem with a computer, projector, or screen.

✓ ALWAYS bring hard copies of your presentation as a backup in case there are technical problems with your equipment.

✓ ALWAYS proof your presentation and have others proof your presentation well ahead of time so if something needs to be changed, you have the time to do so.

✓ ALWAYS conduct a run-through the day before with the equipment you need if it's possible to set it up that far in advance. Either way, do a run-through about an hour ahead of time just to make sure everything is in place. It alleviates some of the anxiety and stress you may be suffering. I've seen other people give presentations that had technical problems... and let's just say it wasn't pretty. I can tell you from personal experience that being prepared is essential to giving a worry-free presentation.

There is one more important thing to consider when giving a presentation. When you do your run-through, please make sure that whatever material you use (PowerPoint presentation, DVD), it's the right material. One of my former colleagues was responsible for giving a presentation at a big sales meeting. He had asked his boss what he needed to bring to the meeting, and his boss basically told him not to worry because the DVD would be there. His boss had only asked him to make sure that the DVD was going to start in the proper place. The presenter then asked the AV guy if he had the DVD, and if it was the right one. The AV guy said "yes," and the presenter took his word for it. My former colleague nodded to the AV guy to begin the presentation, but the DVD that was being shown turned out to be the wrong version! Let's just say that my colleague's boss was not very happy. While his boss told him not to worry about the DVD, the mistake that my former colleague made was not checking the DVD during a run-through to make sure it was the correct one. Never leave anything to chance, and always do more than what your boss expects.

DON'T GIVE THE BOSS BAD NEWS FIRST THING IN THE MORNING

One of the things that would upset me was when one of my employees would come into my office first thing in the morning and give me some bad news. I would barely have gotten my suit jacket off and had just sat down when someone would knock on my door and ask, "Can I talk with you for a minute?" That was the sign that I was about to get some news that I wouldn't be happy with. Usually, it was an employee telling me that they either had to take vacation during a busy time of year or that they were quitting. They'd probably spent all night thinking about how they'd present the news to me and were likely obsessing over it and wanted to get it off their chest first thing in the morning. What they didn't consider is that most people like to have a few minutes in the morning to hang their jacket, get their cup of coffee, and turn on their computer before facing the day.

The only thing worse than being told bad news first thing in the morning is to be told bad news first thing on Monday morning. Most likely, the employee had been thinking all weekend about what they'd tell me and, again, wanted to do it first thing to relieve their stress. My message is simple: If you have big news to tell your boss, don't do it the second your boss gets to work. Give them a few minutes to settle down. While they may not like what you're about to tell them, at least you have given them the courtesy of letting them get into the swing of things first.

DON'T STAND OUTSIDE YOUR BOSS'S OFFICE

There'll be many times that you'll be very anxious to speak with your boss in order to get something done. You're about to walk into your boss's office when you see or hear that they're on the phone. You're very impatient, so your first inclination is to wait by their office door until they get off the phone. This is generally not a good idea. If you stand there waiting, you'll become a distraction to your boss and they may feel like they have to rush their conversation in order to accommodate you. You shouldn't put them in this position; some bosses may even consider this annoying.

You basically have two choices: You can stand there until your boss sees you and they'll either ignore you (which means you should go back to your office and try again in ten minutes) or they'll motion you to sit down in front of them, which means it's okay to come into their office. The second choice, which is something I always did, is to stand outside my boss's office within hearing distance but without them seeing me. This way they wouldn't feel like they'd have to rush their conversation, and at the same time, I wasn't being annoying. As soon as I heard my boss hang up the phone, I'd just walk into their office and get things taken care of.

However, please be careful and don't eavesdrop on the boss's conversation. If the conversation sounds like it's personal or confidential, go back to your office and try again in a few minutes. Also, if it sounds like the conversation will go on for a while, again, go back to your office. You can ask the boss's assistant to inform you when the boss is off the phone or you can just try again later.

LOYALTY – HONOR YOUR COMMITMENTS

As evidenced by the fact that I stayed with one company for twenty-three years, there's no disputing that I was a loyal employee. However, I am in no way recommending that anyone stay with one company for twenty-three years. It worked for me, but staying with one company for that long is increasingly becoming a rarity in today's world. I joke in my college lectures that if you're a Millennial, you probably won't stay with one company for twenty-three months, let alone twenty-three years. My Baby-Boomer generation has proven our company loyalty time and time again, but today's generation is different. Millennials (and Gen Xers) are less loyal to the company than we are, and to be honest with you, I can't blame them. After hearing stories of widespread company firings, some with no notice at all, it's hard to expect employees to be loyal. That's why I tell people that they can be loyal to people and not necessarily to companies. If you find a group of people that you really enjoy working with, be loyal to them. If it looks like you're being loyal to the company in the process, then so be it.

I think the goal of any company should be to encourage workers to be loyal. This ultimately means making their jobs so enjoyable that they won't want to leave the company. Of course, it only benefits the company if the loyal employee is also an excellent employee. If employees aren't loyal, it means high turnover, which can really hurt a company because it's forced to spend a lot of time and money constantly recruiting and training employees.

Loyalty can come into play even before you begin the job. I met a corporate recruiter from one of the utility companies in Southern California. He told me the story of an intern he had hired who hadn't started the internship yet. The intern then called him to say that he was offered an internship at another company with slightly higher pay. The recruiter explained to him that his company offered a lot of great benefits and experience, but the young man decided to accept this other internship anyway. A few days later, the second company rescinded its job offer. The young man called the utility company recruiter to try to get his internship back, but the answer was "no." I was not sympathetic toward this intern. He was disloyal, and he paid the price. I hope he learned a very valuable lesson about loyalty and the risk of burning bridges while chasing a higher salary. Fortunately for him, this occurred very early in his career. I'm sure that he will be wiser in the future.

When it came to my staff, loyalty meant different things depending on one's title. For example, I would expect an assistant to stay with me for a least a year, hopefully for a year-and-a-half. Many assistants got to the point where they wanted to do more than be an assistant, so they'd generally move on if they couldn't move up the ladder any more with me. For higher-level employees, I expected them to stay on longer, perhaps three to five years. I had one employee who worked for me for about nine years and I did appreciate his loyalty.

For interns and temps (temporary assistants), I had lower expectations, but sometimes these employees couldn't even meet these lower expectations. As I've mentioned, we had a six-month internship program in my department. In this program, it was expected that once the intern accepted the job they'd work for the full six-month period before leaving. During the interview process, I couldn't stress enough how important it was for them to stay and work the entire six months. I explained to the potential candidates that if someone left before the six months, we would have to start all over again to recruit, interview, and train a new person, which hurt our department's ability to perform at an optimum level. If an intern left prematurely, someone else had to pick up the slack. I'd ask the candidate to give me their word that if they were hired, they'd serve the full six months of their internship. I even told them that they could stay longer than the six months and could leave once they found a permanent job elsewhere.

Keep in mind that this internship had no benefits, although it was a paying job. What it gave employees was experience, so once they completed the six-month internship, they were highly desired as a research analyst (which was the next step up). Well, let's just say some interns were overly anxious to move up the ladder. Some of them quit after just two or three months, leaving us short-handed. To make matters worse, they'd only give us a couple of days notice instead of the customary and professional two weeks' notice. Their reasons for leaving were usually that they had found their "dream job" and their new boss needed them to start right away or they wouldn't get the job, or that they found a permanent job which provided full benefits and they needed to take the job for financial reasons.

In virtually all of these cases, the interns were younger employees. They were impatient and wanted to move up the ladder as soon as possible. Unfortunately, their word meant little, whereas my word meant everything to me. While I didn't necessarily expect new employees to be loyal, I did expect them to honor their commitments.

All these people could think about was themselves. They didn't consider the consequences that my department would have to face when they left prematurely. While it certainly wasn't a crushing blow, it did mean extra work for my other employees. It also meant more work for me since I now had to contact HR, write up an ad that would be posted on various websites, read dozens of résumés, conduct many interviews, and spend weeks training a new person. This whole process could take months and could've been done in a much more orderly and less time consuming manner had the employee kept their word.

The ironic thing is that some of these younger employees who left for their "dream job" got fired a few months after they took their new job. I don't think it was worth it for them to burn their bridges with my department as well as losing valuable experience in the process. Gaining the necessary experience for a particular job is extremely important. I've seen younger people move up the ladder quickly, much quicker than I ever did. They were able to get promotions and raises, but the problem was that they reached their new position too quickly. They went from being qualified in their present position to being underqualified in their new position because of their lack of experience. Without that experience, they lacked some of the knowledge that was necessary for the job. I know it's tempting to move up the ladder as fast as possible, but there's no substitute for experience.

Every once in a while an intern was asked to leave. I remember many years ago I had an intern working for me who I thought was doing a decent job. However, she started to complain about her job and at one point got so upset that she started crying and hyperventilating. I walked into her office and closed the door to try to calm her down. I didn't know if I should try to put a paper bag over her mouth to make her stop hyperventilating, but eventually she calmed down. Soon after that, she made the fatal mistake of complaining about our boss, who found out about her criticisms. He decided to terminate her, and even though he was one of the nicest guys you'd ever meet, he was so upset at her that after he terminated her he escorted her down to the parking garage to make sure that she had no time to cause any more trouble. That was the last we ever saw of her.

Temps are another example of employees who aren't expected to have a lot of loyalty, but even some of them didn't understand the ramifications of being unprofessional. I had one temp who was doing a pretty good job. One day, he told me that when he left he would give me two weeks' notice. It was literally the next morning as we rode up in the elevator together that he proceeded to tell me that he had just gotten a job working for a friend and that he would leave in two days. That's right–two days, not two weeks. I was extremely disappointed because, once again, an employee violated the two-week notice rule. What really upset me was that there was only one thing worse than giving me bad news first thing in the morning in my office–it's giving me bad news first thing in the morning before I even get to my office!

Okay, one more temp story: I had a woman working for me as a temp who wanted to be considered for the assistant position on a permanent basis. When we decided not to hire her full-time, I could tell that she was disappointed. Later, she went on vacation and was due back in just a few days. She never made it back. She had sent an email to HR saying that she wouldn't be returning. The only thing worse than two days' notice is no days' notice!

I give you these examples because I think it was very shortsighted of these employees not to give their supervisor proper notice. If you leave a job quickly, you're basically burning your bridges. The question is–can you afford to do that? What if these employees needed a reference from me down the line? Do you think I'd go out of my way to help them when they failed to demonstrate professionalism and failed to honor their commitment? Why risk upsetting someone who may be in a position to help you in the future?

Sometimes a supervisor will try to be loyal to an employee and it can backfire. We had an employee at one of my former companies who had just gotten a promotion and raise a couple of months before their yearly review because their supervisors really wanted to keep them. This was unheard of in our department. I personally thought that it set a bad precedent since any promotions or raises for all employees at that level came at the yearly review. As I said, they wanted to reward the employee for their good work and wanted to make sure that they would stay, so they got the promotion and raise early. Unfortunately, about two months later the employee quit, giving two weeks' notice. The employee did have a legitimate reason for leaving. They were moving to another state, but if I was their supervisor and went out of my way to help them and then they told me that they were leaving, I wouldn't be happy.

My question is this: how much in advance did the employee know that they'd be moving? If they knew that this was going to happen, they should have sat down and told their supervisors so that they didn't have to spend so much time writing up the review and going through the approval process with HR. Their supervisors could have used that time to start looking for a replacement. (Granted, the employee might not have known that their supervisors were going to give them an early review. Also, if the possibility of moving came up after they got the promotion, then the situation was certainly understandable.)

THE DRESS CODE – WEAR YOUR UNIFORM PROUDLY

Working in a corporate environment is in some ways no different than being a member of the military. Sometimes you dress the same as everyone else by wearing the same "uniform"–e.g., a business suit. Some of your individualism may be taken away from you. Fortunately, you do have much more freedom in the corporate world than you would in the military regarding what you can wear. In fact, there are many companies that don't have a strict dress code. Business casual is becoming more acceptable in the corporate world, although this type of dress code may have its limits.

An article by Stephanie Armour in *USA Today*[6] about dress codes in the workplace reports: "Business casual has become a staple of the office, but more companies are trying to enforce rules that set at least a minimum standard of dress, and an increasing number are also enforcing more formal attire–especially at meetings or on days when clients may visit the office." The article goes on to state that the number of employers allowing casual dress days has declined substantially. As one CEO stated, "The pendulum has swung. We went through a too-casual period. . . . In the aftermath of the dot-com bubble, we tightened things up a little. When we were very casual, the quality of the work wasn't as good."

The good news for those of you who don't like to dress up in formal business attire is that major corporations such as IBM, General Motors, Ford, and Procter & Gamble have loosened their dress code requirements in recent years, according to the article. However, keep in mind that how you look can affect how you're perceived. The article goes on to say that in a survey conducted by the online job service TheLadders.com, thirty-six percent of respondents said those who dress casually are perceived as being more creative, yet forty-nine percent said they run the risk of being taken less seriously.

As you might imagine, workplace dress codes can create some confusion. If you're a Millennial, you might prefer to dress more casually at work. Realize, though, that your supervisor may be part of the suit-and-tie generation. They might expect you to dress the way they dress at work. This is just another example of the difference in expectations that I mentioned at the beginning of the book between the younger and older generations.

You dressed up nicely for your interview and you got the job. Why change things now? You're now working in a corporate environment, so you need to look the part. I don't care what the assistants are wearing or what your co-workers are wearing. Look at what management is wearing. If you strive to become a vice-president or head of a department, then look at what the vice-presidents and department heads are wearing. If you're a man, most likely you'll need to wear a suit and tie every day. If you're a woman, you'll probably wear a business suit or long skirt.

You may need to buy new clothes. Nice clothes are expensive, but you must look at this as a long-term investment. Don't buy cheap clothes. In my opinion, you're better off buying well-made clothes on sale at major, well-known department stores such as Macy's, Bloomingdales, Dillard's, or Nordstrom. Also, don't buy all of your clothes at once because styles change and your size may change over time. Accessories are important, too. Buy nice belts, ties, and especially shoes. You should have more than one pair of shoes with different colors. Also, you should make sure the pair you wear to work is polished.

Over the years, I'd usually wear a suit and tie, but it wasn't always easy for me. When I first started my corporate career, I was a little anti-establishment, but I felt that "in order to beat the establishment, you first must become a part of it." My feeling was that I could change things from the inside. What I didn't realize was that over time, I was becoming the establishment—and I actually enjoyed being a member!

At first my boss would ask me to wear a suit and tie to work, which I did for a while. I then got into the bad habit of not wearing a tie. My boss noticed this and asked me again to wear a tie. I did for a while, but my old habit came back and the tie disappeared. The next time my boss spoke with me about it, he was very adamant about my wearing a tie. This time, I was smart enough to listen to him, and from that point on, I always wore one. In fact, many years later, during the dot-com era, many companies, even those with corporate cultures like my company at the time, became a little looser with the dress code and you would see some executives lose their ties. Despite this relaxing of the dress code, I continued to wear a tie because, by this point in my life, I was used to it. I also enjoyed wearing one because I truly believed that "clothes make the man (and woman)."

If you don't dress properly, you may miss out on some great opportunities at work. More than once I've seen some of my employees get a last-minute invite to a luncheon featuring some very interesting speakers from the entertainment industry. However, when these employees weren't wearing suits and ties on those particular days, they didn't feel comfortable going to the luncheon underdressed. If they had worn the corporate uniform to work every day, they wouldn't have missed out on these great opportunities.

Casual Friday

Many companies have a casual Friday policy that allows their employees "to let their hair down" and perhaps wear jeans, sneakers, and even a T-shirt. My advice is not to dress too casually unless everyone, from the president to the guy in the mailroom, dresses casually.

For a long time, I would wear jeans on Fridays. Looking back, I don't think this was a good decision on my part. A better look (which is called "business casual") was when I wore khakis and a nice dress shirt, along with my dress shoes. Why is it a bad idea to dress too casually at work? My experience is that an employee's attitude and production are different (meaning, not as good) in an overly casual atmosphere than in a corporate atmosphere. Why should you take it easier on a Friday than on any other day of the week? Are you getting paid any less? Is the impression you make on your boss any less important? My advice, as a corporate veteran, is to try not to do anything different on a Friday than you would do on any other day.

Earrings and Ponytails Are for Women and Pirates

When it comes to earrings and even ponytails, these are strictly for women and pirates. Chances are that very few of your co-workers are pirates, so if you are a man, leave the earrings at home. Some men wear earrings to make a statement–perhaps they think it's cool, but they just seem out of place in a corporate environment. (Of course, if you work in a creative atmosphere where others dress this way, you'll fit in.)

Furthermore, if I see a man with a ponytail, I can't take him seriously as a potential executive. A ponytail in some ways represents to me someone who is aloof and anti-authority. It doesn't matter if this is true or not. The point is some people may draw negative conclusions about you and your reputation, which means that perhaps your ability to move up the ladder could be threatened. The corporate workplace isn't a place to try to be cool or to make a fashion statement—it's a place of work. If you want to make a statement, do it at home on your own time. Otherwise, people will be focused on your jewelry and hairstyle, not on your ideas and work ethic.

Tattoos

It seems that more and more people, especially younger people, are getting tattoos. Personally, I don't mind if someone has a small tattoo and it's covered up, but some people overdo it and they look like walking comic books. When possible, I would recommend covering up your tattoos. While you might think tattoos are cool, your supervisor might not.

No Facial Hair

In the corporate world, being conservative is usually the way to go. This usually means no facial hair. If you wear a beard or moustache, it may appear that you're trying to hide your face, and if you're trying to hide your face, what else are you trying to hide? Yes, that may be a stretch, but just take a look at the executives at any company and, most of the time, they are clean-shaven. Of course, there are exceptions, but it's always safer to go with the flow.

Having said this, there was one time in my career when I wore facial hair. I had traveled to Antarctica and grew a moustache, beard, and goatee. Since I was roughing it and no one really cared what I looked like there, it was no big deal. When I got back to civilization and went to work, I kept the facial hair for a few months. I didn't really care too much what people thought about it because it was my badge of honor for going on such an adventure. However, there's one thing I should have taken into consideration—I looked terrible! There are some men who aren't meant to have facial hair. I'm one of them. Thankfully, I finally shaved it off . . . and kept it off.

Makeup - When in Doubt, Leave Some Out

Fortunately, most women who wear makeup know when too much is too much. However, there are some women who simply don't know when to stop. I remember one woman at work who had so much eye makeup on, I thought someone had punched her in the nose and had given her two black eyes. Whenever I'd see her, I didn't think of her in terms of her job function. I thought of her as the woman who wore too much eye makeup. Again, always think about how others view you. Don't give other employees reasons to make fun of you based on how you're dressed or how much makeup you have on. You're always safer to put on less makeup than more.

DRUGS AND ALCOHOL

I know that in college some people major in partying. There are fraternity parties, sorority parties, and other opportunities to party. You need to leave that life behind you. Nothing can ruin a person's career faster than drug and alcohol abuse. Unfortunately, I've seen it firsthand.

I knew an executive who worked at another company. I didn't know him well but had met him once or twice. I started to hear rumors about him being addicted to cocaine, and before you know it, he no longer had his job, which was a very well-paid position. I also heard he had gotten a divorce. After some time went by, he got a job working in the entertainment industry. I had heard that he stopped his cocaine abuse at that point.

I later worked with him on a project and got to know him better during the week we spent working together. He was a nice guy, and he did a great job. However, I heard later that he might have suffered a relapse and started using cocaine again. I also heard that he had moved to another city. I hope he was able to beat his demons, but this is how serious drug abuse is—you can lose a career and a family. For what? Cocaine is an addictive drug and the best advice is to *never* try it or any other drug. If you currently use drugs, *stop*—unless, of course, you want to throw your life away.

While drugs are obviously a major problem for some, I've probably seen more people get in trouble because of alcohol abuse, especially at work functions, than for anything else. Regarding alcohol abuse, there have been a few instances that hit close to home for me. The first one involved a former colleague of mine. One night on the way home from a work function, they were arrested for drunk driving and spent a night in jail. For the next several months, they weren't able to drive to work because their driver's license was taken away so they had to depend on others to get them to work. Hopefully, they learned their lesson to not drink and drive. Their supervisors took this all very seriously because it not only reflected badly on the employee, it reflected badly on them. Fortunately for this employee, they were able to continue their career, but what would have happened if one night they or anyone else in that situation was driving drunk and severely injured someone? Think about that the next time you're drinking before you get into your vehicle.

Another serious example occurred when an employee from one of my former companies had a drinking problem. The supervisors of this particular employee were being told by others that they smelled alcohol on the employee's breath during the day. Eventually the supervisors sat down with this employee and confronted them. The employee told their supervisors that they drank at night but not during the day. The supervisors weren't sure if the employee was telling the truth, but the supervisors and the company were nice enough and were caring enough to send the employee to an alcohol rehabilitation center to sober up. The company didn't have to do this, and in fact, it probably would have been justified in terminating the employee if it so desired. Unfortunately, the employee seemed to have a defeatist attitude and told their bosses that they had heard that it usually took more than one visit to the clinic to overcome alcohol addiction. In other words, they were subtly telling their supervisors that they didn't think this would solve the problem. After they returned from the clinic, at a major cost to the company and the inconvenience to their bosses of having to get a temp to fill their position, the employee didn't exactly give their supervisors the confidence that they had conquered their addiction.

To make a long story short, this employee continued to have a drinking problem and their work suffered. Soon after, the company decided to cut back one of its divisions because that division was not as successful as it used to be. There were going to be some layoffs in the company. Unfortunately, this person was one of the employees who got laid off because they worked in the affected division. While their termination was not directly related to their drinking problem, this example illustrates the negative consequences of alcohol abuse.

At one of my former companies, we had a sales meeting at a beautiful resort in Southern California. We had finished our business earlier in the day. A group of us had gathered at the hotel bar in the evening. Since various employees would initially pick up the bar tab (for which they were later reimbursed by the company), there was a lot of drinking going on. A lounge singer in the bar was playing the piano. One of our employees who had been drinking was walking back toward the bar. He put his finger in his mouth and let out a shrieking whistle that was so high-pitched I thought that only dogs could hear it. Unfortunately, everyone in the lounge, including the singer, heard it. She stopped singing and told him point-blank how rude he was. All of the conversation at the bar stopped suddenly as we were all deeply embarrassed. One of the top executives in our company had to tell him to cool it. Oh, and did I mention that the owner of the multi-million dollar hotel was in the lounge at the time to witness this?

Later on in the evening, a co-worker and I walked over to the whirlpool to see what was happening. Some of our employees, who obviously had a few drinks, were diving into the whirlpool. This was not the smartest or safest thing to do. A waitress from the hotel was a witness to it, which was embarrassing. A couple of these inebriated employees decided they were going to take a midnight ocean swim. I was half expecting their bodies to wash up on shore the next morning, which of course would have meant that there'd be two new job openings at my company. Fortunately, they showed up for breakfast the next morning. They were lucky.

Another employee was not so lucky. It was about 1 a.m. when I ran into one of my colleagues on the way back to my room. When I asked him how he was doing, he told me that one of our executives had gotten so drunk that he had fallen down the stairs and cracked his head open. An ambulance came, but this executive refused to go to the hospital and, in his drunken state, signed a waiver form refusing medical treatment.

We subsequently discussed the welfare of this person with a hotel employee who used to be a paramedic. He was worried that if our employee had a concussion and fell asleep, it could have serious consequences. We decided to enlist the aid of a co-worker who was a friend of ours and who just happened to be staying in the room next to the injured executive. Our plan was to keep him up throughout the night to make sure he was okay. After we knocked on his door, he answered, but he was plastered. When we took a look at the gash on his forehead, we told him he needed to get to a hospital to get stitches. He refused. Our friend did the next best thing and put a butterfly bandage on the wound. After a while the hotel manager told us he would be okay, so we left him to fall asleep and awake with what would most likely be a very bad hangover.

After we left his room we followed the hotel employee, who received a call that someone in the hotel had called room service but then didn't answer their door. The person turned out to be a co-worker, so we followed the hotel employee to our co-worker's room. We waited in the hallway until the hotel employee went inside. He told us that our co-worker was passed out, half-naked, on the balcony. The hotel employee woke up our co-worker. The co-worker decided he was still hungry, so I guess he ended up eating his food after all.

Anyway, it ended up being quite an interesting night. The three of us who tried to help the injured co-worker agreed to keep things quiet so as not to embarrass anyone, but the nature of the injury became common knowledge. The message is clear: if you're concerned about your work reputation and if you're concerned about your health, you must limit your alcohol intake, especially at a work function. You may even consider not drinking at all. Observe your fellow employees making fools of themselves, and the next day you'll be thankful that all of the gossip about the previous evening's festivities isn't about you.

GETTING HELP

There are many organizations dedicated to helping people overcome drug and alcohol addiction. You can search on the Internet for drug rehabilitation facilities or organizations such as Alcoholics Anonymous (AA). Many companies have an EAP (Employment Assistance Program) that can also help you get through tough times. If you do have a drug or alcohol problem, you can usually call a phone number. Any interaction with the EAP program will be kept confidential.

CIGARETTE SMOKING

I mentioned previously that I worked for a small advertising agency in New York City back in the early 1980s. I worked in the same room for a year with about ten other people, most of whom smoked cigarettes all day. The windows in that office were closed all the time. I don't want to think about how much second-hand smoke went into my lungs. Thankfully, things have changed. Most offices have a no-smoking policy, so what was acceptable back then is no longer acceptable.

Today, if someone wants to smoke a cigarette, they usually have to go outside. In my most recent job, I'd always see the smokers congregated outside in a designated area. In a way, they're being ostracized, which in my opinion they should be. Nothing good comes out of cigarette smoking. Cigarette smokers take more sick days off than non-cigarette smokers, and if there's one way to get on the boss's bad side, it's to always be out sick. Cigarette smokers have a physical addiction that is hard to break. If you smoke cigarettes, you must try to quit.

My parents used to smoke cigarettes, but thankfully they quit when they were in their thirties. Both are in good health now. My only aunt was not so lucky. She was a heavy smoker, and one day the doctor told her that she had inoperable lung cancer. She died at the age of fifty-four. If you smoke cigarettes, don't just think about yourself. Think about your family and friends as well because they're the ones who'll have to go to your funeral one day.

BREAKING THE LAW

Years ago, I had just returned from a vacation in the Canadian Rockies when my boss told me that one of our friends and co-workers was being accused of embezzling millions of dollars from the company. I was shocked. Apparently, this employee had created some dummy (fake) vendor companies, and she falsified documents to make it appear that these bogus firms were doing marketing work for our company. Our company paid these dummy companies for their "services," which of course didn't exist. This employee was arrested and went to prison.

This woman was very nice, always dressed well, drove a nice car, and would frequently take my boss and I out for lunch. Little did we know where she got the money to pay for these things! She not only threw away a great career and her reputation, but she lost some friends in the process, too.

It's absolutely important to have the highest ethical standards and to not break the law. Your credibility and reputation are your most important assets. Remember this whenever you're in an ethical dilemma at work: are you really willing to potentially damage the one thing (your reputation) that should matter the most to you and that will affect your ability to continue with your career? Fortunately, only a very small percentage of employees break the law and most are caught and must face serious consequences. Don't ruin your career and life like my colleague did.

HYGIENE/BATHROOM ETIQUETTE

Most people don't need to be told that it's important to follow the basics of good hygiene. Most people will take a shower in the morning before they go to work, brush their teeth, and wear clean clothes. Most people don't have a problem with smelling bad, but unfortunately there's a minority of people who do have body odor or bad breath. So what do you do if you come in contact with one of these people? Someone needs to tell the person directly. I'm not saying that you're the one to do it. Perhaps it could be the person's supervisor or a friend from work. Chances are the person doesn't even know that they have a problem. Telling them will be difficult, but it needs to be done.

Years ago we had an employee in our department who had a bad case of body odor. It was very noticeable by a number of us. Our boss called her into his office and closed the door. I don't know exactly what he said to her, but he let her know as discreetly as possible that she had a body odor problem. I was told that she cried in his office when she was told of this. I think she got the message as things improved after that. I know it was difficult for my boss to have this conversation with her, and it was certainly nothing that he was looking forward to doing even though it was necessary. Keep in mind that sometimes we have to get physically close to people we work with, so you should always be cognizant of the fact that personal hygiene is important.

Many people use cologne or perfume at work. However, I think employees should keep usage of cologne and perfume to a minimum. What smells good to you may not smell good to someone else. It's more of a distraction than anything else. Remember, you're not on a date, you're at work, so don't overdo it. Breath mints or spray, on the other hand, are always a good thing to carry in your pocket. Any person you're speaking with will appreciate it.

When it comes to using the restroom, you should use common sense. Always flush the toilet when you're done doing your business. Clean the toilet seat if necessary before and after you are done. Word once got out about a female employee who once left urine on the toilet seat. Whenever I saw her in the hallway, that image always came to mind. Believe me—in no way do you want people to associate you with a restroom.

Always wash your hands with soap and hot water after using the restroom. If you don't wash your hands, not only are you increasing your odds of getting some disease, but think about the person who may be shaking your hand later on in the day. Would you want to be that person? What about if someone sees you in the bathroom and notices that you don't wash your hands? That person will probably tell others, and now you have an unwanted reputation for being unclean.

Never talk too much in the restroom. You never know who's in the stall listening or if someone in the other gender's restroom next door can hear you since voices usually echo in a bathroom.

If the sink faucet is broken or if a toilet is broken or backed up, report it immediately to building services. I was very surprised that things remained broken for a long time before someone reported a problem. Don't assume someone else will do it; just take on the responsibility yourself.

Here's one example of bad bathroom etiquette which, fortunately, isn't too common (I hope). I remember many years ago walking into the men's room at work and one of our executives was standing in front of the mirror with his shirt off. He was washing his face and chest. I found this behavior to be strange, to say the least, and a little bizarre. Couldn't he have gone to the gym to take a shower? It only takes one time in your career to do something a little weird, and you will carry that reputation for a long time.

HOW TO ACT IN AN ELEVATOR

If you work in an office building, you'll most likely be getting on an elevator every day. While the elevator ride usually lasts just a few seconds, how you act during those few seconds can influence what people think about you.

Don't Stand Too Close to Another Person

An elevator is a confined space and claustrophobic to some. If you have the room to move around, position yourself far enough away from other people so that they have some space to breathe.

Don't Stare

This occurs more often with a male staring at a female. First of all, it'll make the other person feel uncomfortable. Second, you will start to get a reputation as a stalker (I'm only half-joking). While it may be human nature to look and observe other people, it's best on an elevator just to give a quick glance and leave it at that.

Don't Talk Loudly

I hate it when I'm in an elevator and two or more people are carrying on a loud conversation. Don't they realize that the person they're speaking with can hear them in a much quieter voice? I always kept the tone of my voice low when I was speaking to someone else in an elevator.

Don't Talk on a Cell Phone in an Elevator

This is a pet peeve of mine. I find it extremely rude and annoying when someone is talking on their cell phone in the elevator. It makes me feel uncomfortable because not only are they usually speaking loudly, but I'm being forced to listen to a conversation that I don't want to listen to. Please wait the ten seconds it will take to get to your floor or the lobby and then you can talk away.

Watch What You Say

Obviously, it's very easy for someone to overhear your conversation in an elevator. If you must have a conversation, keep it on the up-and-up, and if you want to be discreet, then forget about having your conversation in an elevator. And remember that being discreet also applies to using the telephone. If you're on your cell phone in your office or outside your building or pretty much anywhere, you can be overheard. This is especially true in an elevator, which is another reason not to use your cell phone there.

Don't Sing in the Elevator

I remember always getting into the elevator with a guy whom I think was a temp. He'd be listening to his iPod with the earphones in his ear and would sing out loud. My first and only impression was that this person was strange. I thought it was unprofessional of him to sing aloud, and if he ever applied for a job with me, my decision would have already been made before he walked into my office. Again, the key here is to remember what type of impression you might be making on people you don't even know.

If the Elevator Gets Stuck, Don't Panic

I've been stuck in an elevator a few times. Most of the time I acted professionally, but one time I did not. It was a very busy and stressful week for me. I had just returned from lunch and got in the elevator to go to my office. I was the only one in the elevator at the time, but as the doors were about to close, someone stuck their hand in between the doors and forced the elevator to open temporarily. Unfortunately, this action also caused our predicament. This person got in the elevator and hit the button of the floor he wanted. The door closed ... and the elevator didn't move. We hit the "door open" button but to no avail. It was apparent that the two of us would be in that elevator for a few minutes. As I said, I was very stressed out at the time, and I just lost it. I started to yell (well, actually, I just raised my voice) at the other person, blaming him for our predicament. While it was his fault, I should have kept my cool. My yelling sort of paralyzed him, and so I took control of the situation by calling security. I kept yelling at the guy in the elevator, "Why did you have to do that? This could not have come at a worse time!" I was obviously very frustrated at the situation, and a few minutes later the doors opened. Afterwards I would see this person occasionally, but we never discussed what happened. I think I was too embarrassed by my behavior. Also, he was the assistant to a high-level executive. Again, the lesson here is you never know who you're talking to or who you're with . . . until it's too late!

Another time I got stuck in an elevator that was full of people. One of the women in the elevator was very claustrophobic, so she started to panic a bit. There was a man in the elevator who wasn't an employee, and he started to have quite an attitude. Some of the others told him to be quiet, but he persisted. It was a very uncomfortable situation, and obviously if everyone had stayed calm, it would have been easier for all of us. About twenty minutes later, the doors opened and the paramedics appeared. I was a little sweaty from the experience, but I shrugged it off. Thankfully, being stuck in an elevator was a rare occurrence for me.

If you do get stuck in an elevator, just stay cool. This is the one time that it's encouraged to use a cell phone in an elevator. Help will be on the way shortly. If other people get nervous or anxious, try to calm them down. Tell them that everything will be alright. Before you know it, help will arrive and you can go back to work.

RUNG VI SUMMARY

- Meetings are your time to shine. Know the agenda and know the plan of action after the meeting is over.

- To be a great presenter, you must know your audience, practice, anticipate questions, and leave nothing to chance.

- Don't give the boss bad news first thing in the morning.

- Your supervisors value loyalty. If you give your word, keep your word.

- Dress for the position you want, not the one you have. Look at what management is wearing, not at what your peers are wearing.

- Drug and alcohol abuse can ruin your reputation and your career.

- If you smoke cigarettes, try to quit.

- Practice good hygiene and bathroom etiquette.

- When you're in an elevator, don't stare and don't talk loudly, especially on a cell phone.

RUNG VII – STAYING ORGANIZED IN YOUR ORGANIZATION

YOUR OFFICE/CUBICLE

It's possible that you'll start out in a cubicle if you have an entry-level position. If you're lucky, you may get an office. Keep your work area neat and organized at all times. A disorganized workspace is a bad reflection on you. Your supervisors and co-workers will assume that if your workspace is disorganized, you're probably not working efficiently. I worked every day at keeping my desk as clean and organized as possible by throwing out any unnecessary papers and deleting emails daily. Don't wait until your desk is a mess to organize it. I always found that if I had papers all over the place, it made me feel a bit overwhelmed and it affected my attitude toward work. When everything was in neat little piles, I felt that I had a handle on things and I enjoyed doing my work more.

I've had very highly educated and very intelligent employees working for me whose desks and offices were always a mess. They were probably smarter than me, but we'd always butt heads because they were slow in performing their tasks. Perhaps they overanalyzed things, which slowed them down. I think their disorganized offices and slow work pace were tied together somehow. The bottom line is we all have deadlines to meet, and missing a deadline was never an option for me. Another example of being disorganized was that some of the assistants in our department would always have a messy cubicle. Their desks were disorganized all the time and, guess what, so were they. It wasn't a coincidence. On the other extreme, you don't want your desk to be too clean because then people will assume you don't have a lot of work to do and aren't working as hard as they are. I've known people whose desks were spotless, and I knew why–they didn't do a lot of work and that's the reputation they had.

Regardless of whether you have a cubicle or office, you need to make some decisions as to what décor you'll have. On the one hand,

you want to feel at home and may want to add some personal touc
such as family photos or vacation pictures. Always keep in mind
thing—this is an office and you need to keep things professional. You
definitely should not exhibit anything that is potentially inappropriate
or that could be misinterpreted, especially in light of today's strong
sexual harassment laws. Ask (or look) around to see what's accepted
and what's not.

One of my former bosses went so far as to insist that I couldn't
put up a bulletin board on my wall because it would not appear "vice-
presidential." I previously had one on my wall with work memos and
reminders on it, but apparently this was a no-no. Once we moved to a
new building, I didn't put up the bulletin board in my new office. You
might have room to put up a bulletin board on your wall. A bulletin
board can be useful when you're starting out since you can pin up
important and timely reminders for the projects for which you're
responsible. You can also put up materials that you might need to
reference frequently. If you do use a bulletin board, keep everything
you post on it very neat and orderly.

This boss also demanded that I couldn't have a paper calendar on
my desk to write down my appointments. He wanted me to use my
Lotus Notes (or Outlook) calendar instead so that everything would be
on my computer. (Okay, I agree with him on this one.) An electronic
or computer-based calendar can send you an email to remind you
of important meetings. You can also attach documents or emails to
the calendar entry to help you stay organized. I liked using the paper
calendar because, as soon as I sat down, I could see what my schedule
was. However, since my boss insisted, I started to use the Lotus Notes
calendar, and I eventually got used to it.

One of my passions is travel. I almost filled up an entire wall with
my vacation photos. Many people who came into my office really
enjoyed looking at them and were impressed, but my boss didn't seem
to think it was a good idea to have them on my wall. Because it was
so important to me, I left them up on the wall. The important thing
is that your office space represents you, which can add to or subtract
from your reputation as a professional. While I want to say your office
is a "home away from home," the reality is, looking back, my boss
was probably correct about one thing—while it's okay to put personal
pictures up, it's another thing possibly to go too far. Remember, you

want to feel comfortable at work, but at the end of the day, work is work.

YOUR FILING SYSTEM IS THE KEY TO BEING ORGANIZED

There's nothing more frustrating than being on the phone with someone at work and being unable to find the file that will help you answer their question. You'll most likely have two different types of files: hard copies that can go into a file cabinet and email files that are on your computer.

As far as organizing your hard copies, put all paper memos into a folder and either type or handwrite neatly the name of the project that you're working on. Simply arrange all files alphabetically in your file cabinet or drawer. You may want to keep the most recent project files that you're working on in front of you on your desk so if someone calls with a question, you can get the file out easily.

For computer files and emails, you have some choices. If you're using Microsoft® Word or PowerPoint, your documents will be arranged alphabetically, chronologically, or they can be organized by isolating your most recent documents. If they're emails, you can arrange them alphabetically by subject name or by the name of the person who sent the email to you. You can also organize them chronologically or reverse chronologically. Use whichever method you feel most comfortable with.

It's important to constantly delete files. As I've said, don't wait for your desk to be full of so many papers and files that you can't find what you're looking for. You should go through your paper and electronic files at least once a week and delete or throw out the ones that you'll no longer need. Realize, though, that in some companies you may need to keep some documents for legal or other purposes, so be certain to familiarize yourself with your company's document-retention policies. Also, as a practical matter, always remember to keep memos or emails that reflect important decisions you were involved with and the reasons for them in case someone later questions you.

HOW TO PRIORITIZE YOUR PROJECTS

Now that you know how to organize your files, it's perhaps even more important to learn how to organize your projects by properly prioritizing them. You'll be expected to work on multiple projects simultaneously, so what's the best way to prioritize them? First consider the due dates for all of your projects. You can simply prioritize chronologically and work on the projects due first, but this doesn't mean that you can afford to ignore the projects that are due later on. In fact, sometimes you have to work first on the projects that are due last because they will take the longest to complete, which means you need to get a head start on them. If you're just starting out at a company and you're not sure how long a certain project will take to complete, it's best to allow yourself some extra time.

Another method of prioritizing is to work on the projects requested by the most upper-level executives first. If the president of the company requests a project, there's no need to prioritize because their project *is* your top priority! If you can make the head honcho happy, then your boss will be happy and you'll be happy.

Let's say that all project requests go through your boss and the boss then assigns projects directly to you. What do you do when a client or top executive tries to circumvent the process by going around your boss and contacts you directly to get a project done? You could complete the project without telling your boss, but the client may get in the habit of contacting you directly, which could interfere with your boss's delegation process. You're better off telling your boss because one almost foolproof method of prioritizing is to let your boss prioritize for you. Your boss will hopefully know how to prioritize your projects in the most efficient manner. However, please keep in mind that the people who are requesting projects from you all want to be considered your first priority. Try not to tell any of them that you may need more time because you're working on someone else's project. No one wants to hear that. The only time that excuse may work is if you're working on a project for the president of the company. There's not too much anyone can say about that. If you do find yourself in the unenviable position of having multiple projects all due at the same time, well, can you say "overtime?"

TELEPHONE ETIQUETTE

This sounds like it is quite simple, but, actually, the way you answer the phone says a lot about you. It's not just what you say, but how you say it. When you answer the phone, say your name. I would always answer the phone by saying strongly, "Andy Teach." Some people choose to say, "Hi, this is Leslie" or something similar to that (which is fine as well). The important thing is to answer the phone by stating your name.

I once had a younger employee who would answer the phone by just saying "Hello." I felt this was unprofessional. When you're at home, it's obviously okay to answer the phone by saying "Hello" because, among other reasons, there is more of a privacy concern since you don't know whom you're talking to (you don't necessarily want a telemarketer to know your name). However, in a place of business where your calls are typically coming from your co-workers or from outside vendors, you should let the person know right away they've reached the correct person.

Your voicemail message is equally important. Don't leave a long greeting on your voicemail. Also, give the impression that you'll return the caller's phone call promptly. My voicemail would always say in an upbeat manner, "Hi, this is Andy. I can't get to the phone right now, but please leave a message and I'll get back to you as soon as possible. Thank you."

Also, it's important to never leave an angry voicemail message on someone's phone. It can be saved and used against you at a later time. If you're angry at someone, try to calm down first and leave them a message in a normal tone of voice. If you want to curse them out, wait until you hang up, close your door, and then vent your frustrations to yourself. No harm, no foul.

Return Phone Calls Promptly

I'd always try and return a phone call as soon as I got the message that someone called me. When you call someone for information, you probably want them to call you back as soon as possible, so your philosophy should be to do the same for them.

Not returning phone calls can have very detrimental consequences. There was an executive who worked at one of my former companies for many years. He was one of the nicest guys you could meet. I was shocked to learn that the company wasn't going to renew his contract. When I asked other people why, many of them said the same thing—he didn't get back to people in a timely manner. I don't believe this was the main reason why his contract was not renewed, but it does show how important it is to get back to people as soon as possible. Every impression counts.

So, what if you need some information and you need to call someone? If you get a voicemail, should you leave a message? It depends on a couple of different factors. First, if you need to make sure that you cover yourself and are able to say that you left a message at a particular time on a particular day, you should leave a message. This is true especially when you start out and are on a lower rung in the organization and don't want to appear too impatient.

As I rose in the organization and needed information more quickly (and since I knew who was slow to return calls), I always tried to avoid leaving a message because then I'd anxiously await their return call, which never came fast enough for my taste. If I left a message, I'd be just one of several people on a call list, and who knows when I'd get that return call. What I would do is keep calling them periodically until I got them on the phone. If the person has caller ID and sees that you've called them ten times, they may think that you're a psycho, so don't overdo it.

If you have to call an executive, you might try calling them first thing in the morning or during lunchtime since there's a good chance their assistant may not be in the office and, therefore, it's more likely that the person you're calling will answer their own phone. Calling after business hours can work too, since it's more likely that their assistant has gone home for the day.

Keep Your Voicemail Message Up-To-Date
Every once in a while I'd get someone's voicemail message, which was clearly out-of-date. It would state that this person was going to be out of the office during a certain time period, but in fact those dates had already passed. If you're going to be out of the office, make a note to yourself to change your voicemail when you return. Otherwise, it may give someone the impression that you aren't detail-oriented because, if you were, you would have changed your voicemail message promptly.

Don't Make Too Many Personal Phone Calls
Every employee sometimes needs to use the company phone to make personal phone calls, but (in spite of what you might think is common practice) this is not a habit I would get into. Find out your company's policy on personal phone calls. If your company allows it, don't abuse the privilege. Also, when you do make personal phone calls, try not to stay on the phone for too long. You do not want to get

a reputation for always being on the phone and for talking too much. Nothing frustrated me more than seeing and hearing an employee talk on the phone when they should have been working!

In one of my former departments, we used to receive logs of everyone's phone calls. It told us on a monthly basis how many minutes an employee was on the phone and how much money their phone calls cost the company. This phone bill didn't differentiate between work calls and personal calls, but it was pretty easy to figure out which was which. If your company and your boss are strict regarding making personal phone calls, consider getting a calling card or using your personal cell phone. This way, your personal calls won't show up on any logs that are kept by your department.

One of my former employees was originally from another country, so he'd make international phone calls to his family. When we started to see the phone bill, we needed to take some action. While most of the employees in the department had phone bills of maybe $50 to $100 a month, we were astounded that his company phone bill was about $2,000 a month! Once I saw this, I had a talk with the employee and made it clear that this was an abuse of company policy. I'm not sure, but we may have even prevented him from making international phone calls on his company phone at that point. Again, it's accepted that you'll sometimes need to make personal phone calls, but if you abuse the privilege, there may be consequences.

The Speakerphone

Throughout my career, I always tried to avoid putting someone on the speakerphone. Why? I never liked to be put on the speakerphone by someone on the other end because it's a bit impersonal and often it's hard to hear them. However, there are times when it's necessary to put someone on the speakerphone, especially when there's more than one person in the room. As a courtesy, always let the people on the other end of the line know that you'll be placing them on the speakerphone. You should also let them know in advance who'll be on the line with them.

The Conference Call

When you participate in a conference call, some parties may be on speakerphone. Sometimes these calls can be long and monotonous and a little silliness will creep in. Once in a while, one of my former bosses would hit the mute button so that the people on the other end of the call couldn't hear us talking about them. Nothing cruel but we were just having a little fun. However, what if my boss had thought he hit the mute button when he really didn't? Obviously, this could have led to some uncomfortable moments. It's better to be on the safe side and take the conference call seriously. If you feel the need to have some fun with the people on the other end of the line, wait until the conference call is over.

THE INTERNET

The Internet is an amazing tool that can make your job so much easier. You can look things up in an instant. However, the use of the Internet can be easily abused and in some instances can lead to your dismissal. I frequently would walk by employees and see them on the Internet and, of course, wondered why they weren't working. If you're a new employee, you should definitely limit your personal time on the Internet. You don't want to get a reputation for being on the computer for non-work reasons, because if your supervisor starts to question what you're doing, you're doomed.

It's also important to realize that your IT department has the ability to track what sites you visit on the Internet. In fact, about two-thirds of companies track their employees' Internet usage. They know exactly what sites you're on and for how long. Never visit a porn site at work, or any other controversial site for that matter. I knew two executives at other companies who allegedly spent time on the job looking at porn sites. Both of them were fired. I don't know for sure that this was the sole reason they were terminated since I never asked them directly, but when it comes to the Internet, "Big Brother" is watching over you.

EMAIL

Email has revolutionized the workforce. In my early days, we had no email, no Internet, no computers, and no fax machines. Believe it or not, when a document was typed up, you had to use a typewriter, and if the typist made a mistake, they'd put a white liquid called Wite-Out® over the typo, wait for it to dry, and then type over it. The assistant would then hand-deliver any documents that had to go out. Some people take email for granted, but I'm not one of them.

Email has made things so much more efficient. It's unbelievable that you can simultaneously send out an email to a hundred people.

This was unheard of years ago. However, with the good there's some bad. Emails can be very dangerous.

Even When You Delete an Email, It Isn't Truly Deleted

Remember that your IT department can retrieve any email, even if you've deleted it from your computer. Their computers are backed up every day, so it's important to consider carefully the wording of any email you're composing. One of the dangers of email is that sometimes it's difficult to know the tone of the email or the intent of the person who is sending it. Are they being sarcastic and funny or are they really upset? It's not always easy to tell. When you send out an email, consider how others will view it. Is it open to interpretation? If so, change the wording before you send it or you risk having it come back to haunt you at a later date, even if you've deleted it.

Always Check Your Email for Typos

There's one school of thought regarding emails that says it's okay to misspell words and abbreviate words in an email since the objective is to be quick and to the point. I disagree with this. An email represents you and your work. I always treated emails like a business letter. Spell out all words completely and check for typos. Don't use abbreviations like LOL or OMG when emailing someone in your company. I know we live in the world of text messaging, but this is still the business world.

It's important to reread your email a few times before sending it, not only to catch typos but also to find a better way of presenting your objective. I have always found that I could find a better way of saying things after rereading my email a couple of times. The best emails are the ones that go through the self-editing process. Also, you should always utilize spell check but don't rely on it since it's not always 100% accurate because it doesn't account for grammatical errors.

Don't Forget to Attach the Attachments

It can be a little embarrassing if your email starts out with "Attached, please find," but you've forgotten to include the attachment. You're then forced to resend the email with an apology stating that your previous email left out the attachment. While it's not the end of the world if you do so, it can make you look a little forgetful. Attention to detail is important. I've received many emails over the years that left out the attachment or attached the wrong document. Whenever I send out an email with an attachment, I attach the attachment first before typing the body of the email. Even though there are some email services that remind you (with a pop-up message) to add an attachment if the word "attached" is found in the body of your email, this is still a good habit to get into. Furthermore, I always double-click and open the attachment to make sure it contains the correct document (and the correct version) before I send it out.

Don't Type Long Paragraphs

When you write an email, get to the point. Long paragraphs can be overwhelming. Make your emails as easy to read as possible since the point of an email is to convey information efficiently.

Is It Really High Priority?

Whenever you send an email, you typically have the option of clicking a "High Priority" icon (or something similar). This feature commonly shows up as an exclamation mark in red next to the subject line of the email. You should not overuse the high-priority function or people will think that you don't know how to prioritize your requests or manage your time. (This same complaint is often made against people who always want something "ASAP.") Use the high-priority feature only when your email is truly important. For example, if you're sending an email to someone who requested urgent information from you, it's obviously okay to send it high priority because when the requestor receives it, it will stand out from their other emails. If it's an email that you're initiating, ask yourself if it's important enough to shine a spotlight on it. If your email contains great news that helps the company, especially if it's timely information, then by all means click the high priority icon.

Think About Who Needs to Be Carbon Copied ("cc'd") on Your Emails

Sometimes I got in trouble for copying someone on an email and other times I got in trouble for not copying someone on an email. It's important to think about the recipient of your email. It's possible that for whatever reason, your boss doesn't want certain people to see your email so when in doubt it's always a good thing to check with your boss ahead of time and get their approval on the "cc" list. There were many times when my boss and I disagreed about who should be listed on an email. If I firmly believed that I was right, I'd state my case. Many times I'd win, so don't just give in to your boss all the time.

I remember one time our studio had just merged with another studio. I was a bit unclear about the job responsibilities of the new executives. The new president of the company had asked me for some information, which I sent to him in an email. I assumed he didn't want anyone else to see the information or he would have mentioned it. I got a phone call from one of the new executives who worked directly under the new president. She gave me an earful! How could I omit her from this document? As I told her, I didn't know the protocol at the time and didn't feel like I had the authority to copy anyone else on a memo to the president. I felt she overreacted, but regardless, this was just one example of how important it is to send an email to the right people. Rather than making assumptions, you should confirm who should be cc'd.

One last thing: the order of the recipients on the "to" and "cc" lines can be important. It depends on the organization and the personalities of the people you work with. There are two options: you can arrange the names in order of importance from highest to lowest (though the person or persons to whom you are addressing the email should be listed first on the "to" line), or you can list the recipients in alphabetical order. Keep this in mind when sending your emails and, if you need to, consult with your boss or other knowledgeable co-workers.

Don't Send an Email If You Are Upset

Sometimes we get angry at someone who has just sent us an email. It can be from your boss or a co-worker or someone you don't even know. Your first inclination may be to fire off an angry email back to them, which may make you feel better, but in the long run, it's a mistake. If you do write a nasty email, wait a few minutes and read it again. Edit out the comments that will make the reader angry. Show the email to a co-worker you trust and get their opinion. If the person sending you the email is blaming you for something, respond to them in a professional manner, even though you're really ticked off at them. Remember, once you hit that "send" button, you're at the point of no return.

I had a friend at work who would frequently get upset at their boss or others in the company and would write some angry emails, but my friend was smart enough to get someone else (me) to read the emails first and edit them before they were sent. Fortunately, by the time my friend did send each email, it was a watered-down and better version of the original because it got the point across without creating as much conflict.

Over the years, I received several emails from my bosses that bothered me. They'd usually accuse me of doing something or not doing enough of something. It always put me on the defensive, and because I really cared about my reputation, I wasn't the type to just lie down and take it. Usually I'd respond with the facts. Sometimes this would make my bosses even angrier, but because I was angry, I didn't care about their feelings. Looking back, this was probably not the best way to respond to my bosses. At other times, I wouldn't respond with an email, but I'd go into their office and respond in person. Sometimes that would diffuse the situation, sometimes not.

Type in Your Subject First, the Email Address Last

You never want to send out an email without something in the subject line. The recipient might think its spam. For this reason, it's always best to type in the subject of your email first before you start typing the email itself. It is also wise to type in the recipient's email address last. Why? I've accidentally hit the "send" button before my email was complete and I had to follow up with another email apologizing for sending the incomplete email. This can be a little embarrassing so wait until the body of the email is complete before typing in the email address.

If You Access Your Personal Email Account at Work, It's No Longer Personal

I used to check my personal email account at work all the time. While I could control the emails I sent, I couldn't control the emails I received. Sometimes my friends would jokingly send me emails with profanity or attachments with pornography. What if the IT department saw this? I'd like to think my personal email account is private, but if you access it on an office computer, then it's likely no longer private given today's security and monitoring software. Your best bet is to wait until you get home to check your personal email account.

Don't Hit the "Reply All" Button

I can't tell you how many times a "good news" email would go out from an executive to a mass email list, and then someone on the receiving end would send a congratulatory email back to the sender copying everyone on the original email list. If I want to congratulate the executive who sent out the email, I'll congratulate just them. I don't need to let the entire company know that I'm congratulating them. You might think you look good to others when you do things like that, but in reality it tends to make you look insecure.

Here's a good example of when *not* to send a "reply all" response to an email. A few years ago the president of one of my former companies sent out an email to all employees, perhaps to as many as a thousand of them. The intent of the email was not to have the employees respond to it, but one employee did and hurt their reputation in the process. It was perhaps the only time in my career when I did a "triple cringe." The first cringe occurred when the employee replied to the email to begin with. The second cringe occurred due to the content of the email. I can't remember the details, but I do remember I was embarrassed when I read it. The third cringe occurred when I saw that the employee hit the "reply all" button and all one thousand employees saw the embarrassing email. This email hurt not only the employee's reputation, but their supervisor's reputation as well. Again, please think before hitting the "reply all" button.

Don't Forward Non-Work Emails

Over the years, I've received numerous emails from people that were forwarded from others. Sometimes they want you to forward them to other people for good luck. Sometimes they want you to sign up for a cause. Sometimes they are joke emails. Don't forward these emails if you receive them and definitely don't be the person who gets a reputation for initiating or forwarding these types of emails. This is a place of work. If you have the time to send these types of emails, perhaps you aren't busy enough at work.

One Email Can Get You Fired

One of my former employees was terminated, due in large part to various emails he had sent out, including one in particular. He was one of my favorite employees because, once you gave him a project, he ran with it without a lot of supervision. However, while his work was stellar, he had some non-work issues to deal with, which made him feel a little ostracized at work. At one point, he had sent out an email within our department that was interpreted as being "threatening." Keep in mind, this email was now a matter of record. Once he hit the "send" button, there was nothing he could do. The damage was done.

We were all concerned about this email. As it turned out, he wasn't serious about his alleged threats, but stress caused an intelligent person to do something that wasn't intelligent. This email led in part to his departure from the company. I'm happy to say that after he left, he became very successful at another company.

RUNG VII SUMMARY

- Keep your cubicle/office neat and organized. The appearance of being organized matters. It's also (obviously) important to be able to find papers and files at a moment's notice.

- If you're not sure about which project is top priority, ask your supervisor.

- Regarding telephone etiquette, have a professional sounding voicemail message, return phone calls in a timely manner, and limit personal phone calls.

- Be very careful about which websites you frequent on the Internet and how much time you spend on them. Your company and supervisor are watching.

- Email etiquette is very important:

  - Check for typos.

  - Attach attachments first.

  - Don't type long paragraphs.

  - Make sure it's high priority before you send it high priority.

  - Double check the cc list and ask your supervisor if the list is correct.

  - Never send an email when you're upset.

  - Put the subject in the subject line first and the email address in last.

  - Your personal email is no longer personal at work.

  - Be very careful about hitting the "Reply All" button.

  - Don't forward non-work emails.

RUNG VIII – BEING OUT OF THE OFFICE

SICK DAYS

Many companies give their workers ten sick days a year to take off for–guess what?–being sick. Don't take advantage of these sick days. They're not called "lazy days" or "I don't feel like coming to work today" days. They're called sick days for a reason. Only use them when you're either too sick to get out of bed or if you have something that might be contagious. Another acceptable situation is a "personal day" involving a personal or family crisis. But if all you have is a headache or an upset stomach, you obviously should try and come into work. I know it's difficult to work under these conditions, but your co-workers and supervisors will appreciate the effort.

I can't tell you how many times I've come into work with a near-migraine headache. In fact, for years I would get a near-migraine headache every Monday morning. It was extremely difficult for me to work, but I didn't let it stop me. I took pride in the fact that there were two or three years in my career that I didn't take a single sick day. There would always be Pepto-Bismol® pills and aspirin in my desk, and believe me, I always used them.

Unfortunately for me, my career at the television studio didn't start out too well as far as being sick was concerned. I started my career during Thanksgiving week. The company gave us that Thursday and Friday off, so my first week was only going to be a three-day week. I finished my first day on that Monday. I don't know if it was the stress of starting a new job, but I caught the flu and called in sick for the next two days. Fortunately, it was a short week or I would've taken four sick days in my first week. I found out much later that my bosses were worried that they had perhaps made a mistake in hiring me. After all, they hired this new person, and he's already taking sick days in his first week. They were asking themselves if this would be a sign of things to come. Thankfully, it was just an anomaly. Twenty-three years later, I hope my bosses realized that they had made the right hiring decision!

On the other hand, I've had employees who would take all of their sick days each year. These employees were looked upon in a negative way at times because we're all responsible for our health. Yes, sometimes things are out of our control, but keep this in mind: When you're out sick, someone else has to pitch in. They not only do their own work, but they have to do your work, too. How would you feel if one of your co-workers always called in sick and you had to constantly step in and do their work in addition to your own? You probably wouldn't like it either.

You should consider your co-workers regardless of whether you stay home or come in. For example, when I came in feeling slightly under the weather, I'd try not to have any of my employees come into my office. Instead, I would communicate with them by phone. Likewise, if one of my employees had a really bad cold, I would tell them that they should stay home for the first day or two when the cold is the worst and most contagious. There's no point coming into work sick and infecting everyone in your department. Believe me, if you get others sick, they won't appreciate it. In short, do all you can to stay healthy. That means exercising, not eating junk food, not smoking or taking drugs, drinking in moderation, and maintaining some balance in your life.

Let me address a sensitive issue. I know that I won't be politically correct, but I'm being honest. If you're considered overweight, you should make an effort to try to lose some weight. Why? First and foremost, your health is at risk. People who are overweight usually have more health issues than those who aren't. In fact, overweight people usually take more sick days than those who aren't.

Second, there'll be people who may not hire you because of the way you look. They might assume that if you're overweight you'll be out sick a lot and that you might lack the energy required to get the job done in a fast-paced environment.

In fact, there's evidence to suggest that weight discrimination, especially among women, may be just as common as racial discrimination in the workplace. A *USA Today*[7] article written by Svetlana Shkolnikova reported that weight discrimination is increasing in U.S. society. The article, referring to a study in the *International Journal of Obesity*, reported that in some cases weight discrimination "is even more prevalent than rates of discrimination based on gender and race." The article stated that, among severely obese people, "about 28% of men and 45% of women said they've experienced discrimination because of their weight." The article also stated that weight discrimination involved cases in which people say they were fired or denied a job or a promotion because of their weight and that some of these people also suffered interpersonal discrimination focused on insults, abuse, and harassment from others.

Again, it doesn't matter if what people think about overweight people is true or not. What matters, unfortunately, is that this is their perception and it might affect the extent to which you advance in the organization. When people talk about you at work, you want them to talk about how great a worker you are, not about the fact that you are overweight.

INJURIES, ACCIDENTS, AND NATURAL DISASTERS

It's important to know when you should take sick days and when you shouldn't. Sometimes, there are employees who need to take sick days due to injuries. You may feel well enough to go to work despite your injury. It's your decision.

I remember a few years ago I was driving with a friend to Auto Club Speedway in Fontana, California to see a NASCAR race. My car was stopped on the 10 Freeway because of bumper-to-bumper traffic. Unfortunately, the driver in back of me wasn't looking and smacked into my car, which then hit the car in front of me. My car was totaled, and I had to go to physical therapy for six weeks. When I called my dad later that day, he asked me if I had seen any crashes (at the race). I replied, "Yeah, mine!"

The timing couldn't have been worse for me because my company was having a very big sales meeting the next day. Our sales force was flying in from all over the country for a three-day meeting regarding a CBS television show that our studio produced. I was an integral part of that meeting because I had contributed to the writing of the research pitch that would help our sales force sell the show in reruns to local television stations around the nation.

By the next morning, my whiplash had set in. The last thing I wanted to do while injured was to attend an important meeting like this one. So, did I stay home and nurse my injuries, which would have been totally understandable, or did I go to work in pain and attend the meeting? I went to work the next day, in pain, and in fact attended the entire three-day meeting. The meeting went very well, and our company eventually was very successful in selling the program around the U.S. Why did I make the decision I did? It's pretty simple. I felt I had a responsibility and obligation to my colleagues to give them as much information as possible in order to help them sell the show. If I had stayed home, the results might have been the same. However, because I had worked so closely with this project, I knew some of the details better than my supervisors, and every little detail helps. I felt an obligation to go to work and help out as best I could. No one told me to come in. In fact, I didn't even tell anyone until after the meeting started that I had been in an accident. It's not that I wanted any sympathy; it's just that I didn't want any of the salespeople to welcome me with a slap on my aching back!

One of my former employees was in a similar, yet different situation. Many years ago, there was a sales meeting coming up on a Monday and our sales force had flown in from all over the country. My employee, like me, had some health-related issues that had to do with his car. Unlike me, he didn't have a car accident. If he did, he would have had a pretty good excuse as to why he missed the three-day sales meeting. He had driven up the California coast the weekend before the sales meeting in a convertible. Unfortunately, he decided that not only would his car have its top down, but he would have his top down too, as he drove for hours in the sun without a shirt on. Not surprisingly, he ended up with sun poisoning and called in sick for the entire sales meeting. Obviously, he wasn't thinking about what he was doing, but I do remember that my bosses weren't too happy about the situation. Today, I still see this employee once in a while and we laugh about what happened, but at the time, it wasn't too funny.

There was one time when I missed a day of work, and I had a pretty good excuse. It was January 1994. It was the day before the Martin Luther King holiday. I had gone to the Northridge Mall in Northridge, California to look for furniture for a new condo I'd just bought in Sherman Oaks, California. I was at the mall until closing time and then, at about 4:32 a.m. the next morning, the Northridge Earthquake hit. I was staying in Valencia at the time, which is near Northridge. After the earthquake hit, the power in the area went out for about twenty-four hours. There was smoke from fires in the distance, as well as several aftershocks. I'd learned that the freeway I had taken to get to

Valencia just a couple of days prior had been destroyed in some areas, so I couldn't get home right away.

When I reached Sherman Oaks (my apartment was located there as well as my new condo), I really began to see the devastation. There were many cracks in my apartment, and down the block from me there was an apartment building that was literally split in half. The guy in the apartment next to mine had his apartment condemned by the city. The building where I had bought my new condo was damaged beyond repair, and I never even got to move in. Thankfully, my escrow hadn't closed yet (closing date was only a few days away) so I didn't lose any money! My grocery store suffered major damage, so I had to buy groceries from the back of a refrigerated truck in the parking lot. The National Guard was patrolling some of the streets. It looked like a scene from a disaster movie. I eventually made it to work and was surprised to find out that our office was open the day after the earthquake. Some people didn't experience firsthand the devastation that was caused by the quake because certain areas were hit harder than others. The earthquake certainly put things in perspective for me. Hopefully, you'll never have to experience a natural disaster, but unfortunately earthquakes, tornados, and hurricanes are a reality for most of the country.

LEAVE OF ABSENCE/STRESS LEAVE

Many companies allow you to take time off from work for extenuating circumstances. This would include a death in the family, a medical emergency, an extended illness, or some other life crisis. Some employees take what's called "stress leave" and take an extended amount of time off–anywhere from a few weeks to a few months. The reason that they take stress leave is that their job has caused them to get so stressed out that they're having physical and mental problems and are just not able to work anymore under their present circumstances. They've usually gone to their doctor and have gotten a note excusing them from work, which makes it very difficult for their employer to do anything about it.

I knew one former colleague who was so stressed out that he forgot how to get to his office as he was driving to work despite the fact that he had the same commute for years. He had a difficult job and a difficult boss and the stress caused him to just shut down. He went on stress leave and never came back.

Unfortunately, I've seen some people use stress leave as an excuse. They may actually believe that they are stressed out, but that doctor's note makes it much easier for them to collect a paycheck without going to work. I believe that sometimes the stress that they're feeling is directly related to the fact that they aren't a good fit for the job, and if you're having difficulties in your job because you don't have the necessary skills to succeed, you'll feel a lot of stress.

One thing I've noticed is that much of the time those employees who take stress leave never return. I can tell you that if an employee takes stress leave, their co-workers and bosses won't appreciate it because they will now all have to pitch in and do the work of the person on stress leave, which creates more stress for them. Try to avoid taking stress leave if you can unless you really are on the verge of some sort of breakdown.

ERRANDS/DOCTOR APPOINTMENTS

Sometimes I'd get in trouble with one of my former bosses for "always being out of the office." While this wasn't exactly true, it was true that I'd be late or have to leave early for various personal errands or doctor's appointments. These errands caused me great anxiety because I knew my boss wouldn't be happy with my absence. Everyone has to run errands or go to a doctor's appointment at one time or another during work hours. It's inevitable. The best thing you can do is try to schedule things first thing in the morning before work or on your lunch hour. Of course, many times you're at the mercy of someone else's schedule, but just try and give your boss as much notice as possible that you'll be in late or you'll be back late from lunch. If you'll be out, try to get the work done ahead of time or have someone pitch in for you if you can. Most importantly, don't be the person in your department who has the reputation for "always being out of the office."

VACATION

One of the great benefits of working in the corporate world is vacation. There are two schools of thought regarding vacation. Some people think the purpose of a vacation is to proactively relieve stress by getting away from work. These people usually take most of their vacation days. The other school thinks that you should save most of your vacation days either because you don't have time for a vacation or because you can get paid for any unused vacation days (up to a point) when you leave the company. My view is that you should use most of your vacation days each year. If you notice, this view is different than my attitude toward sick days. I feel this way because vacations are planned, whereas sick days often come at inopportune times and create scheduling problems.

The purpose of having vacation days is to take time off to rejuvenate, not to be an added source of income. As for the group that feels they don't have time for a vacation, my response is that because you're building a career, you should think of vacation as a means of pacing yourself for the long run.

Going on vacation means different things to different people. Some people take the time off to stay home to get things done. Other people travel somewhere. My dad always said that you should get away from home when you're on vacation, and I totally agree.

Unfortunately, you may have a boss like I once did who made you pay (not literally) before, during, and after you took a vacation. Before I would go away on vacation, my boss would get nervous, so I had to make sure I told him about the status of everything I was working on and who would handle my responsibilities while I was gone. This was fine, but he made me feel almost guilty that I was taking my well-earned vacation. In fact, many times during the year, he would remind me how I'm "allowed" to take time off. I always replied that I earned that vacation.

Sometimes when I was on vacation, one of my former bosses would ask me to call in. I remember once calling the office from a beautiful farmhouse in Iceland. The fact that I had to call in ruined the moment for me, but that's what the boss wanted. Of course, if something did come up at work, there wasn't much I could do. Another time I had flown ten hours and had just checked into my hotel in Madrid, Spain when I got a call from one of my employees. The boss had asked him to call me regarding something that was very trivial. In other words, it was totally unnecessary for them to call me, but it was my boss's way of making sure that I knew that work came first. He only succeeded in ticking me off and reinforcing my opinion that he could really be a difficult boss sometimes. Personally, I would never purposely try to ruin someone's vacation and would almost never call or email an employee on vacation unless it was absolutely necessary.

I remember the time many years ago when I had asked for two-and-a-half weeks off to go to Australia. I knew I was asking for a lot because that's a long time to be away from work, but travel has always been a passion of mine. I submitted my vacation form to my boss and nervously awaited his response. He approved it, but sent me a handwritten note, something to the effect that next time I request so much time off, I need to be going somewhere really far, like Europe. I had to laugh because Australia is farther away than Europe. My boss didn't share the same love of international travel as myself, but at least he did approve all of my vacations over the years.

Of course, there are times when you can't communicate from a foreign country. Sometimes communication devices won't work overseas. When I went to Antarctica, I basically told everyone not to even bother trying to get in touch with me because there aren't even any towns or cities (only research stations) there. There wasn't much anyone could say about that one.

When you do go on vacation, keep in mind that your co-workers have to pitch in for you when you're gone. Upon your return, you should thank them for helping you out. I once had an employee who wasn't an American citizen and was in the process of trying to get his Green Card. He went to Europe with his fiancée for two weeks to get married but became entangled in a post 9-11 bureaucratic snafu. He was out of the country for three months. From his point of view, I'm sure it was very stressful to not know when he'd be allowed to enter the country, but he was in Europe after all with his new bride so things could be worse. I wasn't happy with the situation because another employee and I had to pitch in for those three months and take over his responsibilities as well as our own. He got a nice three-month vacation while my employee and I had to do double duty. When he finally returned, he did thank us. The company was nice enough to pay him for the three months that he was gone. My other employee and I were team players under the circumstances, but it was a rough three months.

Here's one last piece of advice: Try to schedule your time off during less busy times of the year. If the summer is slower in terms of workload, try to take your vacation then. Submit your vacation request as far as ahead as possible so your bosses can plan ahead. They'll appreciate that. Of course, sometimes there are personal events that may fall during a very busy time of year for you. If you give your boss enough notice and explain why you need the time off, you have a much better chance of having your vacation approved and of not upsetting your boss. You can calm your boss's nerves before you leave by informing him or her who'll be pitching in for you while you're gone and sending the boss an email detailing the status of all of your projects. You should also provide your boss with your cell phone number so you can be reached if necessary.

RUNG VIII SUMMARY

- Use sick days only when you are sick. Your supervisors and co-workers will appreciate it.

- If you need to take a leave of absence or stress leave, do it for legitimate reasons. Keep in mind that your supervisors and co-workers will have to pick up the slack. Thank them individually when you get back.

- Try to schedule your errands and doctor's appointments before work, during lunch, after work, and on weekends as much as possible.

- Use your vacation days each year. Try to take a trip somewhere. Remember that their purpose is to help relieve stress and to help you recharge your batteries.

RUNG IX – SOCIALIZING
IN THE WORKPLACE

DATING A CO-WORKER

Some companies have strict rules or guidelines regarding dating other people at work. Some companies do not. It's certainly understandable why you'd want to date someone from work. After all, you probably spend more time at work than anywhere else, so it's much more convenient to meet someone with similar interests as yourself at work than anywhere else. You see these people every day and really get to know them well. Having an office crush on someone is nothing new. The question is what do you do about it?

My advice is to never date anyone in your department, anyone on your floor, or anyone in your building that you'll frequently see walking around or on the elevator or in the lobby. I know from personal experience that if you date someone from work and break up with them, it can be very uncomfortable when you see them again. You also may run the risk of the other person bringing a sexual harassment suit against you if they want revenge against you. Furthermore, there is now someone at work who knows intimate details about you, and they may share those details with co-workers.

I dated someone from work for a while, and then we broke up. She was very upset about the breakup. Fortunately for me, she didn't work on my floor (I took my own advice) but was a floor up. Unfortunately for me, every Tuesday morning my boss had a staff meeting on her floor and I had to deliver copies of reports to him at the staff meeting. My ex-girlfriend's desk was right by the conference room of the staff meeting, which meant I had to pass by her every Tuesday morning. When she saw me, I'd get the cold shoulder, so it was very uncomfortable for me. Can you imagine if she worked in my department and I had to see her every day? It would probably affect my work since it would've been hard to focus. It could've also affected my co-workers who might have been uncomfortable given the situation.

Over the years, many of my co-workers didn't take my advice. There have been a few instances of people in my department who have dated each other, and in some cases they ended up getting married! One of those cases ended in divorce, though neither person was still working in our department at the time. Coincidentally or not, for many of these relationships, it seemed that while the parties were dating, the woman in the relationship would leave the department while the man stayed. Perhaps this was because dating someone you work with, even in "the best of times," can still be stressful because you are always around each other. Regardless, I would definitely avoid it.

There are two sides to these stories. On the one hand, it's understandable why someone would want to date someone else within their department. At first, most of them keep their relationship a secret, but if the relationship becomes serious, they eventually go public with it. On the other hand, I think that they're all taking a big risk. Let's say both of these people are working for me and one of them needs to improve in a few areas. If I criticize one of them, the other one will hear about it and may treat me differently as a result. Do I now need to tiptoe around the issue because they're dating? I shouldn't have to. What if this couple has a nasty breakup? This will certainly affect the other people in the department who might be forced to take sides. This isn't fair to them. It'll be more difficult to concentrate on work when they see this former couple being forced to interact with each other, potentially making it uncomfortable for everyone else. This is selfish and shortsighted on the part of the dating couple.

I once asked a co-worker who dated, and eventually married, someone else from our department, "What would have happened if you broke up while you still worked together? How would you have handled this?" His response was that he knew it would work out and if there was an issue, one of them would've gotten a job somewhere else. My response is: Why would you put yourself in a position where you might be forced to leave a great job and career because you had made a bad dating choice? Most romantic relationships don't work out in the end, so please keep that in mind when you're thinking of dating someone at work.

DATING THE BOSS

No, no, and no! This is a terrible idea. First, it's a very foolish act because if you date the boss and become the boss's favorite, this obviously won't go over too well with your co-workers. Moreover, even if your boss treats you the same as your colleagues (and you have genuine feelings toward one another), you still run the risk of being perceived as taking advantage of the situation, which will harm your credibility.

At worst, if you are using the relationship to succeed and the only way you can move up the ladder is by sleeping with the boss, then you've chosen the wrong career. If you have any self-respect, you would want to advance based on your accomplishments and brain power, not based on what happens in the bedroom.

In more cases than not, it's usually a male boss who dates a female employee. I've seen examples of this over the years at various companies. In some cases, the female employee gets a big promotion, sometimes even skipping a step when moving up. When this happens, the rumors start to fly.

One example comes to mind. The woman involved was in her mid-twenties, and she was very attractive. Her boss was probably in his forties, and he wasn't attractive. He was in a power position and probably was able to date a woman who normally wouldn't go for his type. She possibly saw an opportunity to move up the ladder quickly, gaining a higher title and an increase in salary. What neither person considered was the effect this relationship would have on their reputations and on the other people who worked in this department. What if you were in this department and worked harder and were smarter than this woman? How would you feel if you saw her move up the ladder because you heard she slept with the boss? It could hurt your morale and could affect the quality of your work. Basically, it's not fair. I met this woman once or twice, and let's just say I was not impressed. Her boss, on the other hand, was a very smart guy. At one point, I heard that she had left that department. I don't see how anything good came out of this situation since both of their reputations had suffered.

Another example involves a person who allegedly had slept with several executives, including some very high-level ones. None of these executives worked in this person's department, but the fact that this person was close to the executives gave the appearance of helping that person move up the ladder. Unfortunately, this employee didn't have a good reputation to begin with and, in fact, was disliked by many people. As a result of the rumors, they were probably resented even more. Your reputation is everything. It's important to be proud of your accomplishments at work. It's also important to be well liked by everyone, not just by key people in the company. Sleeping your way to the top won't endear you to too many people.

Years ago, I knew a female boss who liked a male co-worker. At one point, she bought him a birthday gift. Many of the other employees felt left out. Why hadn't they received a gift on their birthday? This boss made the mistake of blatantly picking a favorite in the department. Some of the employees weren't big fans of this boss to begin with, but this incident made things even worse. It was very difficult for them to motivate themselves to do a good job when their boss treated one of their colleagues differently. They just wanted to be treated fairly. (By the way, the employee she liked turned out to be gay, so her efforts were wasted!)

A former colleague of mine once asked me for some career advice. She was having trouble with her boss and wanted to know how she could improve the situation. I gave her some advice and she told me that things were improving between them. I found out later that she was sleeping with the boss! I guess she forgot to mention this "minor detail" to me. I wonder if her sleeping with the boss had anything to do with the difficulties she was having with him???

SEXUAL HARASSMENT

In California, all employees are required to take a sexual harassment class once every two years. Sexual harassment can mean many things, not just the obvious ones. When most people think of sexual harassment, they think of a supervisor who tells their employee that if the employee wants to keep their job or get promoted, they need to sleep with the supervisor. This is the extreme version of sexual harassment, but there are many less obvious examples.

If you have a photo hanging in your workspace that can be deemed sexually offensive, this could be considered a form of sexual harassment. The photo may just have a woman or man in a swimsuit, and even though there's no nudity involved, if someone finds this offensive and mentions this to you, you need to take the photo down. Of course, you should never have a photo like this up on your wall to begin with. You have to take into account that some people are very sensitive. It only takes one person to complain for you to possibly get into serious trouble. When it comes to hanging photos or artwork on your wall, when in doubt, leave it out.

I once had a female employee tell me that one of my male staff members was following her around, which made her feel uncomfortable. I immediately sat him down and told him that this was unacceptable and that this was a form of sexual harassment. If you feel that you're a victim of sexual harassment in any way, you should inform your supervisor or your HR representative immediately. Don't wait and don't feel embarrassed about your situation.

There was one time when I did something that could be interpreted as sexual harassment. Our division was having a sales meeting in Santa Barbara, California. Several members of my department, including myself, were scheduled to give a presentation at the meeting. I wanted to start my portion of the presentation with some humor. At that time, the CBS television series *Survivor* was fairly new, so I wanted to do a tie-in with that show. I had a photograph of myself in a suit and tie standing between two bikini models. In the background of the photo was a thatch hut, similar to one you might see on *Survivor*. This photo was taken at a television convention a couple of years earlier. I did have the foresight to ask some of the women in my office whether they felt the photo was offensive. Some said "yes," others said "no." Since I had it in my head that it would be funny, I decided to use the photo. When I flashed the photo on the screen in front of about seventy-five supervisors and employees, I quipped that here I was with my two friends, Monique and Unique. I heard some nervous laughter and then moved on. A few days later, one of my co-workers told me that two of the women who were in attendance took offense to my presentation. Technically, some could have interpreted this as being sexual harassment. I didn't use good judgment in this situation, and I should've listened to the women who told me beforehand that this might be offensive.

DISCUSSING YOUR DATING

Here's one thing I did wrong, but hopefully you can learn from my mistake. It's very easy to discuss your social life with others at work. Don't do it. At one point, I made the mistake of talking too much about my dating life. Later, it started to get back to me that certain people didn't appreciate this.

I realize that when we make friends at work, we like to tell stories. These stories sometimes allow us to bond better with our peers. What you should realize, though, is that at work you always run the risk of becoming the subject of too much gossip, so in general you're better off keeping your private life to yourself. As I said, your reputation is everything. You want your reputation at work to be about your abilities at work, not about your personal life. If I had to do it all over again, I would keep my personal life to myself and keep things on a more professional level.

THE WORK PARTY

Meeting your co-workers at a work function can be a very positive thing. It's a way to get to know the people you work with. You may also find out that you have a lot more in common with these people than you initially thought. However, a work party can be a trap, and if you fall into the trap, you may never get out.

As I mentioned earlier in the book, one of the biggest dangers of a work party is drinking too much alcohol. I have been to dozens of work parties over the years and have seen many people get drunk at these parties. If you get drunk at a work party, your co-workers might remember this for years to come. People say things when they've had a couple of drinks that they wouldn't ordinarily say.

Many years ago there was a company Christmas party where the assistant to a top executive had been drinking. Her boss was dancing with his wife and he looked innocently at his assistant who was nearby. The assistant blurted out, in front of everyone, "What are *you* looking at?! Can't anyone have some fun around here?" I didn't witness this incident myself (thankfully), but from what I heard, it was true. What a stupid thing to say to your boss in front of other people, including his wife. I was surprised that she still had a job the next day. I don't know what the ramifications were for her, but this happened a long time ago and I'm still talking about it.

Another example from a Christmas party involved a new intern who got drunk. He was singing Madonna songs loudly and, at one point, had to be physically carried out of the party (because he was drunk, not because he was singing Madonna songs!). I still see him once in a while. He's doing well in his career, but unfortunately, I am still talking about this incident years later. I'm sure he'd rather be remembered for something else.

A final example of the consequences of drinking at a work party occurred at the home of one of my co-worker's parents. Again, it was around Christmas time (funny how all this stuff seems to happen over the holidays). My co-worker was hosting a party for our department. Our big boss was there with his girlfriend, and I was there with a girlfriend. The big boss had just hired a new assistant, who was at the party alone. Unfortunately, she had a few too many drinks and was literally hanging all over me (in front of my girlfriend) and was hanging onto another executive. To make matters worse, she was telling our boss that she liked him. At the end of the party, I saw that my girlfriend was upset. When I kind of smiled to let her know that it wasn't a big deal, she slapped me in the face! I didn't do anything to encourage this assistant's behavior, but I paid the price. By the way, this assistant actually ended up working in our department for a long time, so fortunately for her, she wasn't penalized for her behavior. Years later, whenever I'd see her, we would joke about that night. But the message is clear: don't get drunk at a company holiday party.

I do have a few more observations about work parties. One is that I've always noticed that at work parties, people in the same department frequently hang out with each other. This always bothered me. Why? While it's good that they see each other every day and there is camaraderie between them, I felt that they all were missing a great opportunity to meet people in a social setting who work outside their department. It's so important to form strong bonds with people who work in other departments, so if you're at a work function, you should make an effort to introduce yourself to as many people as possible. You'll be glad you did.

Another observation is that sometimes at work parties (or any business function for that matter) the person speaking with you isn't really that interested in the conversation. I've been to several business functions at which my own colleagues would simultaneously talk to me and look around the room for the next person to talk to. They may have been searching for someone in particular that they wanted to speak to that day, but it made me feel a little unimportant. As a result, I never did that to anyone else, and neither should you.

There's one more incident that has bothered me for years. I once had an intern who was in our department for only a few weeks before realizing that the job wasn't for her. She had started right before the Christmas party and, like everyone else, was invited to the party. On the invitation, there was a message indicating that we weren't allowed to bring a guest. Our annual Christmas party probably had about a thousand attendees, so you could imagine how big it would be if everyone came with a guest.

The new intern, as it turned out, showed up at the Christmas party with her husband. Here I was as a twenty-year veteran—and here were many others who had also been with the company for a long time—attending the party without a guest or significant other. Of course, most of us wanted to bring a friend or a loved one but the invitation stated otherwise. By being careless and not paying attention to the invitation or by disregarding the rules, the new intern committed a social blunder. I wasn't happy, but hey, these things happen.

RUNG IX SUMMARY

- If you are going to date someone at work, make sure you rarely see them in the workplace. Keep in mind that intimate details about you may no longer be private.

- Never date the boss.

- If you are being sexually harassed, report it to your supervisors and the HR department as soon as possible.

- Don't discuss your private life with people at work. It can come back to haunt you.

- The work party can be a really great event, but it can be a trap, too. Limit your alcohol intake at work functions or don't drink at all. It just takes one incident to damage your reputation.

RUNG X – THINGS YOU CAN AND CAN'T CONTROL AT WORK

OFFICE GOSSIP

As you can see from some of my previous examples, it's easy to be the subject of gossip. Even if you just mind your own business at work, people will still gossip about you. You'll probably gossip about people at work, too. It's hard to avoid. The key is not to give your co-workers anything to gossip about. However, it isn't always that easy. For example, if you always dress nicely and wear nice jewelry and look like you just came from the beauty parlor, you would think that people would speak nicely about you. Unfortunately, the jealousy factor may come into play, and people may gossip about how rich (or arrogant) you might be.

If you're single and talk about your dating life, this may come back to haunt you, as it did with me. If you discuss your finances at work, people will gossip about that. Keep in mind that if you tell one person at work anything about yourself, you might as well have told everyone at work because there are no secrets.

At one of my former jobs, I was friendly with a female co-worker. We'd go to lunch or hang out once in a while after work. I know that there were some people at work who thought she and I had been intimate. This was untrue and, in fact, nothing sexual had ever happened between us. I told this to several of the people who heard the rumor, but I'm not sure they believed me. There are a couple of lessons to be learned from this. Always be aware that no matter what you do, there will be times when you will be gossiped about. Also, sometimes there's only so much you can do to try to correct a false rumor. Do your best and then move on. Anything more will just make it seem worse . . . and true. The point is that sometimes things are just out of your control. If you let office gossip bother you, it will take your focus off your job. And that's not something you want to let happen.

DISCRIMINATION

I hired many people during my corporate career and was interested only in hiring the best person for the job. I didn't care about their race, gender, age, sexual orientation, religion, national origin, physical handicap, or anything else that doesn't have to do with a person's actual job performance. I think most people have the same philosophy, but unfortunately not everyone does. My position on discrimination is very clear. If you're discriminated against, you should definitely consider filing a discrimination suit. However, the thing that really upsets me is that some people use this as an excuse to get money from a company when their job performance is the real reason for their problems.

Some people who sue companies for discrimination are actually hiding behind the fact that they're incompetent. They refuse to admit their shortcomings and instead want to take it out on the company that gave them a job and a livelihood. They believe they're discriminated against because of the way they look, which in some cases is just ridiculous because their supervisors must have interviewed them for the job and obviously saw with their own eyes what the person looked like. If the company were truly discriminatory, they wouldn't have hired them in the first place.

Furthermore, when these employees were first hired, they were probably happy to have a job and financial security, but now they're willing to turn around and bite the hand that fed them. What I want to say is "be an adult." Take responsibility and admit that you aren't the right person for the job and move on. Don't hide behind something that isn't true. If you do, you'll find that your reputation will be damaged, perhaps permanently. As I said, if you're truly being discriminated against, then by all means you should hold your company responsible.

Unfortunately, many companies will cave in to employees even if they know that the employee isn't being discriminated against. They will settle out of court in many cases because it's simply less expensive for them to do so, even if they know they'll eventually win the case. Personally, I think that this is setting a very bad precedent. If a company has a reputation for paying off employees who are suing them for discrimination regardless of whether it's true, I think more employees will sue that company for discrimination.

I was told of one instance in which a person who allegedly was not the most competent employee sued a company for discrimination. The company settled with the employee on the written condition that the employee would take no further legal action against the company. This is standard procedure for most organizations. The employee signed the document and received a financial settlement from the company. Later, the employee sued the company anyway and won more money! I'm sure this is a rare case, but it illustrates what happens when a company gives in to an employee who shouldn't be suing in the first place.

OFFICE POLITICS

Every office and company has its politics. Unfortunately, your success or failure could be determined by how well you play the game. You may not be the type to suck up to your boss (I wasn't), but it doesn't hurt to do it once in a while. It's important to know what the reputations are of the people with whom you'll be working. It's also important to know who knows whom within and outside the company. It wouldn't be unheard of to speak unkindly about a person to a co-worker, only then to find out that your co-worker is friends with the person you spoke of unkindly. It's a small world, so be very careful of whom you trust.

You may very well find that someone who isn't that competent or well liked gets to keep their job and may even move up the ladder because their family happens to know a high-level executive in the company or perhaps their father is a big shot in the business. It's not always fair, but it is reality.

DON'T DISCUSS YOUR SALARY WITH ANYONE

Discussing your salary with anyone at work (except your boss) is something you should avoid. We had an unofficial rule at work to never discuss our salary. When my bosses found out that some of our employees had discussed their salaries with their co-workers, let's just say that they weren't too happy.

People are compensated at different levels for different reasons. If a co-worker who is at your level finds out that you're making more money than they are, they may go to your mutual boss and ask for a raise, which in turn may tick off your boss if they find out you've been discussing your salary. Having said this, if there's a way for you to discreetly find out what other people at your level are earning (as I mentioned previously in the book, there are websites that give salary ranges), whether it's in your department, your company, or at a competitor, this could help you. This is especially true when you are asking for a promotion or raise (more on this later in the book). However, if you're going to quote to your boss someone else's salary, don't use their name.

I'll never forget a big blunder that I made just a few years ago. I was copying my W-2 form because it was tax time, and of course the W-2 form contains your salary. The copy machine had broken down, and after it was fixed I thought I had brought all of the copies with me. I was wrong. One of my co-workers walked into my office and handed me a copy of my W-2 form. I assumed that he did take a look at my salary. I think I asked him not to tell anyone what my salary was, but I also know it's hard to keep a secret like that one. I was really embarrassed. The lesson here is if you're going to copy confidential information at work, make sure you take *all* of the copies with you. (Another lesson is not to use the office copy machine or other equipment for personal use.)

CONTROL YOUR TEMPER

It's very important to be able to control your temper no matter where you are, but especially at work. If you get a reputation for being a hothead, this can only hurt you. I must admit, I'd get upset very easily at work, but I never let anyone see me get upset. I have punched and broken a computer mouse or two in my time and have kicked my computer more than once if it wasn't working fast enough for me. Of course, kicking the computer didn't make it go any faster, but at least I felt better by getting my aggression out. (And I never broke the computer, which would have been very hard to explain to our IT department!)

My blood pressure would soar at times because of the actions or inactions of my employees. I'd usually go home and then think about how I'd sit down with them the next day to discuss the problem. I'd play out the scenario several times in my head, and sometimes I'd get up in the middle of the night thinking about it. To say that I was obsessed with my upcoming employee meeting was an understatement. When I thought about what I'd say, I'd always picture myself speaking to the employee while I was mad and upset. Basically, I was telling them off, and I could feel my heart race. I felt angry because I took things too personally. The good news is that by the time I actually met with my employee the next day, I had gotten so much of my hostility out by role playing the conversation in my head that I wasn't nearly as upset when I finally spoke with them in person as I was the day before. The lesson is that you should never speak with a boss or employee while you're upset because you may say things that you will regret later. Take some time to think about it.

RUNG X SUMMARY

- **Office gossip hurts reputations. Don't spread it.**

- **If you are truly discriminated against at work because of your background, you should take action—but don't use it as an excuse if it's not true.**

- **Office politics can be hard to avoid. It's important to understand it and play the game if necessary.**

- **Be very careful when discussing salary with co-workers. Many supervisors frown upon this, so do it discreetly or utilize websites to get salary information.**

- **Control your temper at work. You don't want to be seen as being unprofessional.**

RUNG XI – TRAVELING ON THE COMPANY

THE BUSINESS TRIP

One of the great perks of the corporate world is the business trip. However, some executives find them to be a necessary evil because, while they're useful from a business point of view, the business trip takes them away from their family. They also have to deal with lines at the airport and have to suffer through long flights and the inconveniences of renting a car. Others, like me, love business trips because you get to travel and have your airfare, hotel, and meals all paid for. An added bonus is racking up points on your corporate card, which eventually you can redeem for free airfare and hotels for your personal vacations (assuming your company allows it). Of course, the purpose of a business trip is to conduct business, which means a lot of preparation is necessary. I've always had successful business trips because I always did my homework. Furthermore, I always remembered that going on a business trip was a privilege, not a right.

Over the years, I've been fortunate enough to travel to Buffalo, Kansas City, Laguna Nigel, Las Vegas, Miami, New Orleans, New York, Orlando, Palm Springs, Phoenix, San Diego, San Francisco, San Jose, Santa Barbara, Tucson, Vancouver (Canada), and Washington, D.C., on the company. I've been to some of these cities several times. My bosses knew how much I enjoyed travel, so they kept sending me places when the opportunity presented itself.

I'd frequently turn my business trip into a personal trip. I'd take some extra time and do some sightseeing, as long as it didn't cost my company any additional money. In fact, sometimes I'd stay over on a weekend after my business was completed. I'd actually save the company money on the airfare because of my Saturday night stay over, which sometimes gets you a discounted rate. If I stayed an extra night or two in a hotel, I'd make sure to pay for the hotel out of my own pocket. The same was true for meals or a rental car. If you can arrange it so you have some free time to sightsee, you should try and take advantage of it.

There is an annual television convention of the National Association of Television Program Executives (NATPE) at which hundreds of millions of dollars in sales transactions of television programs take place over a three-day period. This convention also featured numerous celebrities, and overall, from what I heard, it was an action-packed event. From my department, only my bosses were invited. Myself, and many other people wanted to go, but from a financial standpoint, the company had to limit who went, which I understood. Since the next convention would take place in San Francisco, I decided to go on my own. I'd drive there from Los Angeles and pay for my own hotel room. One of the employees of the company would sneak me into the convention by loaning me someone else's badge, which got me in the door. Basically, my attendance didn't cost the company any money. I figured that if I could be seen helping out, maybe the company would get used to me being there and would officially invite me to go in the future.

My initiation paid off because I was officially invited to go to this annual convention and ended up going for many years to come. Even in the years when I was invited, I never lost sight of the value of taking the initiative. At one point, I asked our cable salespeople if I could attend their meetings with the various cable networks. Even though it wasn't necessary for me to be in these sales meetings, our cable salespeople graciously allowed me to attend and to participate. It was an awesome learning experience, and I never would have been invited if I hadn't asked. It was great to feel that I was learning as much as I could and meeting as many people as I could. It meant a lot to me to be part of a successful team, and it really helped build my morale and made me even more excited about my job. As an added bonus, I'd usually have some time to do a little sightseeing and to experience some great meals.

There was one more perk during the NATPE convention. I had my picture taken with many celebrities over the years, which gave me bragging rights with my family and friends. I had my photo taken with Pamela Anderson (three different times), Katie Holmes, Chuck Norris, William Shatner, David Duchovny, Jane Seymour, Milton Berle, Michael Richards, Donny and Marie Osmond, Pat Sajak and Vanna White, and the casts of *The Nanny, Married…With Children, The King of Queens, Evening Shade, Party of Five, Mad About You,* and *Just Shoot Me.* Did I mention how much I loved working in the corporate world?

There were two types of business trips for me—those on which I was with my bosses or co-workers and those on which I went on my own. I acted the same on either type of trip. I always remembered that I was representing my company and my department, so I never did anything that would be embarrassing to anyone. That's not to say that I didn't have any fun on these trips. After the business part of the trip was over, I would go out and have a couple of drinks. My point here is that if you go on a business trip, especially with co-workers, it's okay to have a drink or two, but don't overdo it. If you meet someone of the opposite (or same) sex, just be discreet. You don't need your co-workers to find out about it because it's probably not a good thing for your boss back at the office to focus on the fact that you were drinking and trying to put the moves on someone. Your boss should be focused only on the fact that you did a great job and he or she won't hesitate to send you again.

For many years, I attended an annual business meeting for researchers. It was usually in Orlando, which is a destination I loved going to. However, much to my surprise, my boss decided that he was going to let someone else go in my place to an upcoming Orlando research meeting. Normally, about three or four of us would attend this meeting from our department. I wasn't happy about this decision. However, I didn't give up. Two factors worked in my favor. First, I sent my boss an email outlining why I should go. This included the fact that this was a great place to network on behalf of our department since there would be representatives from every television studio, broadcast network, and major cable network. Second, the person my boss had chosen to possibly go in my place was an employee who had a history of showing up late to meetings. When my bosses had asked him why he had come late to a recent work function, he didn't have a good answer. Bottom line—I went instead of him.

Leading up to this decision, our boss had questioned what we do at this annual convention. All he seemed to hear about was the partying aspect of the conference. I was very honest with him and told him that during the day we attended the conference and at night we generally hung out by the bar. Personally, I never get drunk, but I have seen others who have and with potentially serious consequences. During one of the more recent conferences, a number of us were at a bar where two people from our industry almost got into a fight. One of them was a former employee of the other. He got really drunk and almost punched his ex-boss after insulting him in front of everyone. Thankfully, no blows were exchanged, but this points out once again the dangers of drinking at a work function. As with all things, moderation is key.

During the last year of my career at the television studio, part of our division had a sales meeting at a five-star hotel in California. We had meetings during the day, and after dinner a colleague and I went to the hotel bar. We arrived before most of my other work colleagues, so I sat next to two women who were at the bar. They turned out to be sisters, and I ended up speaking with them for the next couple of hours. During this time, my boss and other work colleagues sat at a table near the bar. When I got up to escort the ladies to their car, my boss stood up with the other people at his table and gave me a standing ovation. After I walked them to their car, I returned to the bar to hang out with my boss and the others.

A few days later my boss called me into his office and chastised me for speaking with these women. He was upset that I didn't spend enough time with my colleagues at the bar. My response was that I saw my colleagues all the time, and I was only having a nice conversation with these sisters. In fact, I think that I reminded him that he was the one who stood up and led a standing ovation for me, so I was really puzzled as to why now he would criticize me. The point is that you really have to watch your behavior on a business trip, especially if your boss is there with you.

SAVE THE COMPANY MONEY

When you first start out in any job or career, you probably won't be in a decision-making position to spend or to save the company's money. However, I can assure you that if you do save your company money, someone there, probably in the finance department, will be very grateful. How can you save your company money, especially on a business trip?

Try Not to Use the Mini-Bar

Whenever I traveled on the company, I'd try to make sure that when I turned in my expense report, it would be as clean as possible. This meant that when I stayed at a hotel, my charges would be for staying at the hotel only. I tried not to use the mini-bar or laundry and tried to limit room service. I'd never utilize the pay-per-view movie services that hotels offer (and you should never order an X-rated movie). I'd also make all of my phone calls on my company cell phone as opposed to the hotel phone, which always seems to be extremely costly. If I went out to meals, I tried to get my co-workers to use their company credit cards to pay. The bottom line is that I was concerned about the bottom line . . . and you should be, too. The last thing you need is for your bosses to question your expenses on a business trip. If they do, it could be your last business trip.

Check the Hotel Bill

Even if you're traveling on the company, once you get your hotel bill, you should examine it carefully and look for any mistakes or overcharges. Your company will appreciate this. On one of my business trips to Las Vegas, the Venetian Hotel charged me $800 to stay on a Saturday night. Not $800 for a week, but $800 for one night! I had spent the entire week at the Venetian because that's where we were conducting our business meetings. Even though I wasn't paying for it out of my own pocket, I thought the hotel was ripping my company off for charging so much. After all, that same room can go for as low as $200 a night during the week. While I understand why Vegas hotels raise their rates on weekends, I felt that raising the rate that much was ridiculous, and I let the person at the front desk know that's how I felt. Of course, I lost that argument, but at least I tried.

Submit Your Expense Report on Time

It's important to stay off the radar screen as much as possible with your bosses. One way of doing this is to get your expense reports in on time and double-check them so that every penny is accounted for. Don't forget to submit all of your receipts and remember how much your tips were. If your boss suspects you're taking advantage of your expense report by perhaps ordering the most expensive meals or paying for someone else for whom you shouldn't be paying, you run the risk of raising a red flag.

A former colleague of mine was always late submitting his expense reports. It eventually caught up with him because, after repeatedly submitting his expense reports late, the company actually took away his corporate credit card for a while. This was embarrassing for him. If this wasn't an incentive to change his behavior, I don't know what was. I'm guessing that after that he began to submit his expense reports on time. The reality is that some employees do need an incentive to change their behavior. The important thing is that the employee learns from their mistakes and changes their behavior.

Try to Negotiate with Vendors

While negotiating with vendors isn't necessarily business-trip related, it's still an important area that gives you an opportunity to save your company money. Over time, I was entrusted with dealing directly with vendors. These were companies that provided a service to our department and company. Sometimes, the vendor fees or costs were non-negotiable, but at other times the vendors would be willing to negotiate. On occasion, vendors would give me a reduced cost because I had established a long-term relationship with them. This definitely helped to save the company money. I'd sometimes ask if they could provide information to me free of charge that they'd normally charge for, and they'd sometimes oblige. At other times I'd ask if they could waive a penalty charge that would normally cost a few thousand dollars, and sometimes they would. It's important to note that you won't get anything for free or at a reduced charge unless you ask for it.

RUNG XI SUMMARY

- **When you go on a business trip, keep in mind you are representing your company.**
- **If your boss goes on a business trip with you, be on your best behavior and keep him or her informed about what you're doing.**
- **Keep expenses down. For example, try not to use the mini-bar.**
- **Double-check the hotel bill for extra or hidden charges.**
- **Get your expense report in on time and account for every penny.**
- **Try to negotiate with vendors. Your company will appreciate it.**

RUNG XII – THE PEOPLE AT WORK

THE GENERATION GAP AT WORK

While I touched upon generational differences earlier in the book, I'd like to take this opportunity to go into a little more detail and to reiterate a few things. In recent years, it's the first time in history that four different generations are in the workplace at the same time. These generations are working together, or at least trying to work together. As I mentioned earlier, studies indicate that many members of each generation simply don't respect, understand, or communicate with members of other generations. This obviously hurts productivity. I believe one way of overcoming this obstacle is simply to try to understand where each generation is coming from in terms of how they were brought up, the historical events that affected them, and what their priorities are.

Members of the oldest generation, known as the Matures or the Radio Generation (some grew up before television was invented), are about sixty-five years old or older. They comprise approximately 8% of the workforce. They grew up during tough times—the Great Depression and WWII. They vowed never to go through such difficult economic times again, so they developed a very strong work ethic and invented the 9-to-5 day. They are loyal to their employer and expect the same from their employees.

The Baby Boomers (there was a big baby boom right after WWII) range in age from their mid-forties to mid-sixties and grew up during the 1950s Cold War and the turbulent 1960s. They make up approximately 41% of the workforce. They have a very strong work ethic and sometimes judge their success by their title, their salary, and by how many hours they work each week. Baby Boomers are also all about paying their dues and expect the same from their employees. This is one reason why there is conflict between Baby Boomers and Millennials since many Millennials want to move up the ladder quickly while the Boomers want them to pay their dues first. In fact, one of my former Baby Boomer bosses once told me that it took him a certain number of years to get a promotion so therefore it would take me the same amount of time, even though that had nothing to do with my work performance. Baby Boomers are also very loyal to their employer, just like the previous generation. Importantly, they are in charge. Many (if not most) upper-level executive positions are held by Baby Boomers. In fact, because of the bad economy in recent years, many Baby Boomers who had planned to retire at a certain age will be working longer than they had anticipated.

Members of Generation X (also known as the MTV Generation) are between their early thirties and mid-forties and grew up during the Reagan years and the Gulf War. They comprise about 30% of the workforce. They were the first generation to grow up with two working parents and became very independent as a result. Furthermore, many of them witnessed their parents getting terminated, so Gen-X questioned company loyalty and became more loyal to the person and not the employer. This all helps explain why they were the first generation to avoid the do-or-die Baby Boomer work ethic (which may also explain why another nickname they have is the Slacker Generation).

The youngest generation in the workplace is Generation Y (also known as the Millennials). Its members are between ten and thirty years old and their adult members make up about 21% of the workforce. They grew up during the "New Millennium," which included the events of 9/11. As I mentioned earlier in the book, Gen Y is the most technologically advanced generation ever (some of them grew up with cell phones in their cribs!), and they are goal-oriented, well-educated, and optimistic, but some of its members have a reputation for being entitlement focused, switching jobs often, and wanting a balance between work and life.

Speaking of technology, I grew up with slide rulers instead of calculators, big black-and-white television sets instead of sleek high-definition color TVs, AM radio and record players instead of iPods, typewriters instead of computers and iPads, and no fax machines, Internet, cell phones, or Blackberrys®. It's amazing we ever got anything done in those days. Yes, times have changed, and for the better.

HOW TO OVERCOME THE GENERATION GAP AT WORK

As we have seen, every generation is brought up differently and has different ideas and expectations of what their jobs are going to be like. If you are a member of Gen Y or Gen X and you work for a Baby Boomer and they're all about making work their first priority, then you should know that they will most likely expect the same from you. It is equally important for Baby Boomers to understand where Gen Y and Gen X employees are coming from and to try to take their needs into account.

I think the best way for Generation Y to overcome the generation gap is to go along with the flow, at least in the beginning. Don't make the mistake that one of my former employees made. She was very smart but shortly after she was hired, she started criticizing a major project that my bosses and I had been working on. She thought she knew better than we did but my bosses and I had fifty years of work experience combined and she had three. Who do you think knew better? This project ended up making our company hundreds of millions of dollars. The mistake she made was not getting to know the people and the politics first. Get a great work reputation before you start criticizing the way things are done. This may take several weeks, months, or even a year, but at that point your supervisors will listen to you. Unfortunately, all this employee accomplished was to alienate herself from her supervisors.

Even though there is a generation gap in the workplace, there doesn't have to be. Don't let age differences get in the way at work– embrace them instead. Get to know people from other generations by observing them, speaking with them, and learning from them. You'll be glad you did.

LIFE ISN'T FAIR, SO DON'T EXPECT WORK TO BE EITHER

You may be the best employee in the company. You may be the smartest employee in the company. However, this doesn't mean that you'll necessarily be treated fairly or equally. A lot will depend on your relationship with your boss and your co-workers. They might not like your personality or attitude no matter how great you are at your job. You may find yourself doing menial work when your counterparts who've been with the company for the same amount of time or even less time than you are getting the plum projects.

When you're with a company for a while, you may notice that certain people who are in high positions don't seem to know what they're doing. This happens at every company. There are other people who are smarter than their bosses but have trouble moving up the corporate ladder. As I've said, sometimes politics plays a role in these matters, and there's nothing you can do about it. Don't expect the corporate world to be a perfect world. It's not. If you know in advance that you and others may not always be treated fairly, it may be easier to deal with these issues.

Like me, you may find yourself in a position that just isn't fair. It can be very frustrating to be in this position, so you need to find out if there's anything you can do to correct your situation. I'd always complain if I felt I was being treated unfairly. Perhaps I complained too much, but at least I felt like I did all I could to try and correct the situation. Sometimes, that's all you can do.

Often, the hardest thing about work is not the work—it's the people. No matter where you work, you'll be working with people with different backgrounds, experiences, and attitudes. It's inevitable that you'll clash with some of these people at some point in your career. It's amazing to me sometimes that anything gets accomplished in a work environment because you have so many different types of people who are basically forced to work together, and yet, somehow, it all works out in the end.

You never know what frame of mind someone will show up with at work. Will they be cranky because they didn't sleep well? Will they be distracted because they have a headache? Will they be argumentative because they broke up with their girlfriend or boyfriend the night before? Will they be excited about coming to work because they always have a great attitude, no matter what? Every person at work has a different story and motivation for being there. The workplace is a melting pot of different lifestyles and personalities. What can you expect?

For one thing, think of your department as a family. Your bosses are the parents, while you and your co-workers are the children. In every family, there will be a favorite and there'll be the black sheep of the family. Once in a while you argue with your siblings. Sometimes you talk back to your parents. You might get punished for these incidents. A department is very much the same.

THE ASSISTANT

One of the most critical jobs in any company is the assistant job. When you start out, you should realize you might not get an aide. If you do get one, you might have to share this person with a colleague. If you have someone who's very competent, your job will be made much easier. In fact, a reliable assistant who knows the ins and outs of a company is invaluable. On the other hand, if you have someone who isn't that competent, your job could be a living hell. You might have done a great job on a project, but then your assistant gets hold of it and makes a simple mistake, perhaps a typo, and this is the one thing your boss notices. You might have done a lot of hard work on a project, only to have your assistant make some errors that cause you to miss a deadline. There was nothing worse than having an assistant make edits to one section of a document, only to get the document back and discover that they made an error on something that previously had been okay. This is why it's so important to weed out the bad assistants in the interview process so that when you hire one, you have the cream of the crop.

Before I talk more about my various experiences with assistants, let me give some advice based on lessons I've learned, sometimes the hard way: You *must* treat them well. Even if you feel that you have someone who isn't doing what you need, treat them with as much respect as possible. You can always document any problems you have with HR, but in the meantime, you'll get more from a person who likes you than from one who doesn't. Assistants have a tough job and usually they don't get paid a lot of money. Many also work for several different people, so that means they likely are working on several projects at once. If your project is urgent, you need to state that. Otherwise, be patient. The key is to communicate as much as possible about what you need. Finally, on this subject, here's the single best piece of advice I can give: When you appreciate your assistant's work, tell this to him or her. Show it! Compliment your assistant. Treat them to coffee or lunch occasionally. It's the small things that matter.

Whenever we were interviewing for assistants, our HR department would give them Microsoft® Word, Excel, and PowerPoint tests. That was a good way to evaluate some of the basic document skills that were required. However, I found that in our department expert knowledge of PowerPoint was becoming increasingly important, so I developed our own PowerPoint test that simulated some of the exact documents that the assistant would be typing if we hired them. This test was much more difficult than the one that HR administered, and it was more reflective of what the job demanded. It was just a way of increasing our odds of getting a really good assistant.

One of my biggest frustrations over the years was that, although the job title was "assistant," I felt that many assistants were just typists. What's the difference between a typist and an assistant? A typist is someone who can type a Word or PowerPoint document. An assistant is someone who can not only type a Word or PowerPoint document but can also anticipate the needs of the supervisor. An assistant is also someone who can make helpful suggestions on how to make a document better—that is, someone who truly assists rather that someone who merely executes. You usually find a true "assistant" working for very high-level executives. Their function relies less on typing skills and more on skills involving setting up meetings, reading materials, and helping the executive organize their time efficiently. Assistants to high-level executives get higher salaries than those working for lower-level people, so those positions attract better-quality applicants.

What kinds of assistants did we have over the years? Where do I begin? Let's see, we once had a former stripper in our department. I don't know how great her stripping skills were, but her professional office skills were mediocre at best. We had someone who smoked pot every morning before she went to work (unbeknownst to us at the time). There was also someone who dressed up as a hooker for Halloween. Personally, I felt it was a little unprofessional to dress up in costume at work on Halloween, but you don't want to ruin people's fun. Her unwise choice of dressing up as a prostitute reflected our unwise choice in hiring her. Just as she didn't put much thought into how she would be perceived by dressing up that way, she didn't put much thought into her job, either. When she first started with us, I gave her a one-page memo to type. It took her three hours to complete! I knew then that she was the wrong person for the job. (Our boss eventually terminated her.)

There was also the assistant who went on the set of one of our television shows. Later, we received a call that she was "stalking" the star of the show. We had someone who was an actress on the side, so she'd have to leave the job once in a while for auditions or for a shoot, which, of course, put more stress on us. There was an assistant who would always say, "What do you think I am, an imbecile?" (He wasn't.) In a previous chapter, I mentioned the assistant who got drunk at a party and caused me to get slapped in the face. I once told an assistant that I didn't think she was too smart. Her reply was "I got A's in school . . .

some." Do you get the picture? It's not easy to hire a good assistant. By the way, please don't think that I'm picking on females. It just so happens that over the years most of our assistants were female, which is why I have more examples of problems with female assistants. On a positive note, our longest lasting and fastest assistant was female.

Despite the problems we've had in hiring good people, the assistant position is a great entry way into a company in some industries. This is true in the entertainment industry, where sometimes it's important just to get your foot in the door. Perhaps there are no openings in a company for a position for which you are qualified. What can you do? You can apply for an assistant job. You may be overqualified and you may feel it's beneath you, but once you're in, you can eventually move up the ladder. I know of one person who was an assistant to an executive and, years later, became that person's boss. I also know a few people who started out as assistants and moved their way up to president of the division!

As an assistant, you interact with many departments in a company, and if you do a great job, then you'll get noticed. There are some people who are content with being a subordinate for their entire careers. That's great, but if you want to move up the ladder, there are definitely times in some industries when taking an assistant job first can help you break into the industry and learn the ropes. If that's the case, there's one thing you need to do: You *must* excel at your assistant job and not act like this is only temporary for you until you find your ideal job. It's not fair to the people you work for if you don't have a great attitude and if you don't give one hundred percent, and thus make a bad impression. This could hurt your chances of getting promoted later on.

If you're an assistant, you should always work to improve yourself. If you type a lot of presentations and your company gives classes on programs such as Word, PowerPoint, and Excel, take them to improve your worth and your skills.

As an assistant (or any employee for that matter) it's also very important to constantly communicate with your boss or bosses. You need to know ahead of time what meetings they have coming up, what projects are high priority for them, and what you can do to make their job easier. That last point is extremely important. Always ask yourself what you can do to make your boss's job easier. The best way to find out what they expect is to ask them. Always ask what the deadline is on a project. As I've mentioned before, be flexible with your work hours. Be prepared to work overtime if necessary, even if you get a project right before you're supposed to go home. We had an assistant who would leave at 6 p.m. on the dot every day, even if they were in the middle of working on a project for me. They usually didn't even think to ask me when this project was due or how important it was; they just got up and left and didn't even check in with me first. Thankfully, they were very fast, but if you're an assistant, I strongly recommend checking in with the people you're working for before you leave for the day.

One more piece of advice that will help you build your working relationship with your boss. As an assistant, you'll be interacting with your boss a lot. Try to talk with your boss once in a while about non-work-related subjects. Find out what your boss's passions are and talk about them. Remember, it's critical to have a great working relationship with your boss. If you do, you'll enjoy your job a whole lot more.

THE BOSS

This may be the most important section in the entire book. So much of your success or failure can depend on your boss and your relationship with him or her. This person controls your destiny. There are two rules I have regarding the boss. Rule #1 is to develop a strong work relationship with your boss. Rule #2 is to follow Rule #1! If you have a good relationship with your supervisor, your job will be made easier. If you have an antagonistic relationship with your boss, your job will be made that much harder. However, no matter what type of relationship you have with your manager or what type of person you work for, there's one golden rule—always do whatever it takes to make the boss look good. How important is it to have someone that you can work with and get along with? A Gallup Poll[8] of over one million employees found that if a company is losing people, the biggest reason for them leaving is their immediate supervisor.

In my career, I've had many types of bosses, some good, some not so good. The following are examples of different types of bosses and how to handle them.

The Good Boss

I've been fortunate to have had the good boss more than once in my career. This is the type of manager we all want. The good boss is one who's genuinely a nice person. He or she is a mentor to you, constantly teaching you, and guiding you along in your career. They are very patient with you and rarely criticize you. If they do criticize you, it's done in a constructive manner. You look forward to going to work each day to interact with them because they're very supportive and you know you can count on them. The good boss will explain things concisely to you so that you'll know what's expected of you and how to go about working on a project. This person will know when it's necessary to manage you and when it's alright to allow you more independence.

The good boss may take you out to lunch once in a while. He or she may just go out to lunch with you because you are generally liked and are good company. If you're fortunate enough to have the good boss, don't take advantage of his or her kindness. If they give you an inch, don't take a yard.

There was a executive at one of my former jobs who wasn't my boss per se. She'd request projects from me and my staff, and we'd complete them for her. I always enjoyed working with her because she was just a "cool" person. I admired her because she was very intelligent and knew exactly what she wanted, which made my job easier. She'd include me in meetings that she didn't have to. Although she wasn't a direct boss of mine, I still considered her a good boss in a way, and more importantly, I considered her a mentor.

The Tough Boss

The tough boss can be difficult to work for. He or she can be very demanding. I considered myself a tough boss, and I knew that I could be difficult to work for. The tough boss can be highly critical of your work and may not give you as much positive feedback as you desire. The tough boss doesn't want to hear excuses. They just want perfection. This manager may not be the easiest person to get along with, or may not want to be friends with you, but at least is usually fair. You may be cut some slack once in a while, but you shouldn't get used to it. Deep down the boss is "good people," but the stresses and pressures of working in the corporate world often stream down to employees.

If you have a tough boss, then you have to remember that this person is all about work. They can be very businesslike and results-oriented, so you also need to be results-oriented to have a good relationship. With any type of boss, it's important to figure out what motivates this person and what makes him or her happy. Once you figure this out and do what is expected of you, you should be able to develop a good working relationship.

The Incompetent Boss

The incompetent boss is hard to respect because everyone else knows that this person really doesn't know what he or she is doing. It's difficult to work for someone you feel knows less than you do; therefore, it's difficult to respect this person as a supervisor. This lack of respect by you and others can also render the boss powerless, which can hurt your department. You feel that you can't learn because of the lack of knowledge and leadership. If this person is so incompetent, how was a supervisory position obtained?

I remember many years ago my father told me about a high-level executive at a television studio who didn't know what he was doing. Of course, I wondered how such a person was in such a high-level position. As I made my own way in the corporate world, I was able to observe some incompetent bosses. Some move up the ladder simply because of long tenure with the company and have done a decent enough job to warrant a promotion. Others got along really well with their bosses, so even if their supervisors realized the shortcomings, they were willing to overlook those weaknesses because of the personal relationship between them.

Sometimes executives operate by the saying, "The devil you know is better than the devil you don't know." They realize that someone may not be the most competent person, but they are afraid to try someone new out of fear that things could be even worse. Some incompetent bosses delegate their work to their staff, so if they have a great staff and the work gets done, they don't look so incompetent after all.

What do you do if you have an incompetent boss? First of all, I know how frustrating it can be to work for an incompetent boss because I've been in these types of situations during my career. It can be difficult to motivate yourself to do a great job when you see someone above you who has a bigger title and a bigger salary, but doesn't seem to know the job. If you have an incompetent boss, sometimes patience can be used to your advantage. As time goes by, hopefully more people will realize that you're competent and your manager isn't. If you and others do a great job and you overshadow your supervisor enough times, this will be noticed. Eventually, upper management will need to make a decision. Perhaps your boss is feeling the heat and will decide to move on voluntarily. Perhaps he or she will be forced to leave, or perhaps upper management will do nothing. The best thing you can do is to continue giving one hundred percent and to hope for the best. If you truly resent working for this person and you don't feel he or she will be leaving any time soon, it may be time for you to move on. However, if you're patient and stick it out, you may be rewarded with a great opportunity.

The Unreasonable Boss–Aka, "The Boss from Hell"

The unreasonable boss might be the toughest one to work for. This is someone who seems to have it in for you, no matter what you do. He or she will never admit an error and will blame others for their mistakes. This type of boss is the opposite of a mentor and can quickly cause your morale to spiral downward. Whenever you submit a report, the unreasonable manager will tear it apart, as evidenced by the amount of red ink on it. Impossible demands will be made on you. The unreasonable boss is always highly critical of their employees no matter what, and even if your department gets kudos from other departments, your boss won't be satisfied. In other words, this boss will never be happy with your work, always saying that you need to do better. The boss's whole life usually revolves around work.

One of my unreasonable bosses would always say that people in our department were lucky to have a job. This would usually come in response to some complaint we'd have. The unreasonable boss is usually a control freak, and no matter what plan you might have, the unreasonable boss will come in and make it impossible for you to execute your plan.

This story is brief, but it is one of my favorites. This happened several years ago at the television studio before I began my career there. The company Christmas party was coming up, and at that time, the research department was located a few miles from the main studio. The head of the department had told everyone that they needed to come back to work after the Christmas party. Let me repeat that. The boss told everyone in his department that they had to drive back to the office after the Christmas party. This was possibly a first in the corporate world. Can you imagine what a morale deflator that must have been? How could these employees have enjoyed the party when they knew that they would have to go back to work afterwards? One of the employees actually had the guts to speak up and asked the boss a simple question: "Why do you have so much contempt for us?" Unfortunately, the boss didn't change his mind. Why would a supervisor do this? This certainly wasn't a way to get your employees to give you the "Boss of the Year" award. As it turns out, he probably just wanted to look good to his bosses by being able to say his department was working the night of the Christmas party.

Here are few more examples of what it feels like to work for an unreasonable boss. I had a boss who would assign us a project on which we would work for a couple of weeks. We felt that when we presented the project to the boss, we had done a pretty good job and that we had completed the project. Unfortunately, whenever we presented the project to our boss, his response was usually, "This is a good start." Good start? We thought we were done! How's that for making you feel like you don't know anything. Of course, we got used to this, so we always knew what to expect.

There were several times when after I had presented a project to one of my former bosses, he'd say, "This needs a lot of work, a lot of work. Let's meet on this tomorrow morning." I'd come in the next morning expecting the worst–a total rewrite. We'd then go over the project, and he'd only make a couple of minor changes. The day before he said it needed a lot of work, but today it was like I presented it to a completely different person. Why did he say that if he didn't mean it? I think there were two reasons. First, I felt he just wanted to play with my head by making sure that I knew I wasn't good enough and that he was the person who always knew best. Second, it's possible that other priorities might have come up or perhaps we were running out of time, so he made things easier. Regardless, this situation happened enough to make me feel that when you have a boss who seems more interested in making you believe you don't know what you're doing, it certainly hurts your morale and your ego. Keep in mind that so much of what we do is subjective. There's no right or wrong, just someone's opinion of what is right or wrong. How did I survive working for the unreasonable boss? More on that later.

I've worked for all of these types of bosses, including some who were a combination of all of the above. Of course, I preferred to work for the good boss, but they're hard to find. It's amazing what the corporate world can do to some people. The reason you find so many difficult bosses is because, once you're in management, you've got it pretty good as far as salary and perks go, so you'll do almost anything possible to keep the gig going.

When to Stand Up to the Boss

This is an area that always got me into trouble. When I think back to how many times I would disagree with one of my former bosses or debate him on things, it's amazing we were able to work together for twenty-three years. On the one hand, he was tolerant of me talking back to him so often—other bosses may not have put up with it for so long. On the other hand, I felt that he deserved to be talked back to or to be debated at times because he was just plain wrong (at least in my opinion!). My boss used to joke that I must have been on the debate team in school (which I wasn't) because I always had an answer for everything and would always argue with him.

Sometimes it's the right thing to do when you stand up to the boss, but other times it isn't a wise idea. You need to know when to pick your battles. It all depends on what type of relationship you have with your boss. The longer you work for someone, the better you'll know what their tolerance is for you standing up to them. Every once in a while, I'd have an employee talk back to me, but usually they had worked for me for a while and they would apologize to me soon after that.

As you can probably tell, over the years I complained a lot. If I mentioned what I complained about, you'd probably agree with me 90% of the time. Unfortunately, after a while, when my bosses saw me approaching them, they no longer saw Andy the executive coming toward them. Instead, they saw Andy the complainer coming toward them. This was not a good thing. In fact, sometimes I would complain to Boss A about Boss B and then later would complain to Boss B about Boss A. Who knew that they would actually discuss this among themselves and compare notes? I guess you could say this strategy didn't work out too well for me.

So when is it okay to stand up to the boss? I think if your boss blames you for something that isn't your fault and responsibility, you need to defend yourself. If your boss yells at you for any reason, you need to let them know that this is not acceptable. If you feel that you're being treated unfairly, you need to stand up for yourself.

There are different ways to stand up to your boss. Each one will probably get different results. The first way is to simply arrange a meeting to sit down and speak with your boss and outline your concerns in a civil manner. You need to present the facts and propose a reasonable solution. If you do this well, hopefully your manager will understand where you're coming from.

Another way is to argue. This is something I've done many times, and based on my experiences I wouldn't recommend it. While arguing certainly made me feel better because I felt that I had gotten my point across, I don't think my boss appreciated my second guessing him. One thing you should never do is to yell at your boss. For some bosses, the first time you yell at them might be the last time because they might terminate you.

Why did I always argue with one of my former bosses? We just had major philosophical differences about how to go about things. Part of it was cultural because I grew up in the New York metropolitan area, where people are more direct and confrontational. If they have a problem with you, they'll tell you to your face. My boss, on the other hand, had a Midwestern background. Midwesterners are more reserved. If they have a problem with you, they may not confront you directly. He'd sometimes ask me to do things that I didn't feel comfortable doing, so I'd put up a fight.

The downside of all of my arguing over the years was that it strained my relationship with him. I'm sure that many times he probably felt it would be better if I were no longer there. Yes, the work may have suffered if I was gone, but it would have made things go much smoother for him had I not been there. After all, who wants to have an employee who often confronts you and argues with you, even if it's on important business decisions? It can take its toll. Fortunately for me, this person put up with me for twenty-three years, so I must have done something right! I'm living proof that you can get your point across and even argue and still keep your job. However, as I said, you really need to know where you stand before you take an argumentative tone, if at all.

THE CO-WORKER

Throughout my years at the television studio, our department had undergone many personnel changes. There were some years in which many employees in our department were difficult to work with and coming to work was a grind. Fortunately, in recent years, we had a department in which everyone got along and helped each other. Having a department where everyone acts as a team makes corporate life so much more enjoyable and rewarding.

The good news is that in a recent Gallup Poll[9] when American workers were asked to rate their satisfaction with thirteen different aspects of their jobs, one of the characteristics they were most satisfied with was their relations with co-workers. Sixty-nine percent of the respondents were "completely satisfied" with this aspect of the job.

The Supportive Co-Worker

This is the ideal co-worker to have. This co-worker is someone who works with you, not against you. They believe in teamwork and doing what's right for the department as a whole. They'll try to help you when you need help and will expect the same from you. If you do something right, they'll not only compliment you but they'll also speak highly of you in front of your supervisor and other co-workers. If you work with them on a project and it's not what the boss wanted, they will share the blame. They've put their own ego aside to make the team stronger. If you can find a department full of supportive co-workers, you've found a corporate pot of gold.

The Backstabbing Co-Worker

This isn't the ideal co-worker to have. This person will take every opportunity to criticize you behind your back, thinking this elevates them to some extent in the minds of their supervisors. In many cases, the backstabber is extremely ambitious and wants to get to the top as soon as possible. This schemer doesn't care who gets in their way as long as they can get someone out of the way. Sometimes the backstabber is competent at his or her job, but this is not always the case. Teamwork is not a word in the backstabber's vocabulary. This plotter is out for themselves. Beware of the backstabber. They may be standing behind your back as you read this.

If this person is standing behind your back, take the opportunity to ask them to sit down and discuss the problems that exist between both of you. It's very important to get to the heart of the matter as soon as possible. If you're fortunate, the backstabber will respect your attempt to patch things up. If you are not fortunate and nothing changes, you should speak with your supervisor. If that doesn't work, speak to HR.

Personally, I feel that life is too short and your career is too important to have to constantly deal with people who make your job difficult every day. Backstabbers can really hurt morale and productivity in a department, so if they try to take advantage of you, use all of your available resources to fight back.

The Jealous Co-Worker

Everything was going fine for the jealous co-worker until you rode into town. You're a hard worker, you initiate, and you get things done quickly and accurately. You're getting kudos from your bosses and you're respected by most of your co-workers. The jealous co-worker now sees you as a threat, so your relationship with them suffers.

At one of my former jobs, I was the new kid on the block and wanted to make a great impression. That didn't sit well with at least one of my colleagues, who may have felt that I was taking some of the spotlight away from her. This employee felt threatened by me, and I felt she had taken advantage of me more than once by allowing me to work on projects that she should've been working on. Since I was new, I didn't want to stir the pot, so I didn't complain that I was doing more than my share of the work. My feeling was that it was important to complete the project and worry about who does what later on.

At that time, we had a new boss. Many of us in the department were not happy because we had some issues with this new person. She was about to go out of town and instead of putting me in charge, she put the jealous co-worker in charge, despite the fact that the jealous person was about to go on maternity leave and wasn't going to be around much anyway. I thought it was a slap in the face, so I complained to our manager.

Right after I complained, the jealous employee stood outside my office and yelled, "So how does that feel? Now you know how it feels." She was referring to the fact that I was the one who now felt left out. Regardless of whether she was right or wrong, the fact she was yelling at me in front of my office didn't sit too well with me. After I followed her to her office and closed the door, we had it out. We both made our cases. In the end, we both felt better about the situation and made up. After that point, we actually got along well. We had let the tension build to a point where it needed to be released. If you have a problem with a co-worker, you should consider confronting them in a professional manner and discussing it. However, confronting someone at work could have the potential of backfiring and making things worse, so it really depends on your own situation and how well you know your co-workers.

The Incompetent Co-Worker

The incompetent co-worker can make your job much harder because if you work with someone who doesn't know what they're doing you may have to pick up the slack. This means being forced to take on more responsibility (and stress) whether or not you want to. I remember that at my first job at the advertising agency in New York I shared an office with a very nice colleague. We held similar titles, but I didn't think this person was as competent as they needed to be. My work opinion of this co-worker changed my overall opinion of them because I was of the mind that everyone needed to pull his or her own weight equally. Unfortunately, I wasn't as close to this co-worker as I used to be once I decided that I would have to work harder to make up for their shortcomings.

At one point, this person left the company to do something unrelated. This is what happens with many incompetent workers—they (or someone else) realize that this job is just not for them. They then try to find something that is right for them. The danger is that when an incompetent worker stays in a job or career that isn't a good match it ultimately puts more pressure on co-workers.

What should you do if you work with someone who is incompetent? First, you should find out if your other co-workers share the same opinion. If so, you (and one or more of your colleagues) need to speak with your boss. Give specific examples to your supervisor, describing when you've worked with the incompetent person and explain how their part of the job wasn't done properly, thus forcing you to do additional work. When you speak with your boss, you need to do it in a non-backstabbing manner. Just state the facts. Let the manager reach his or her own conclusion about whether this is an employee they want to keep. Hopefully this employee is not politically connected in the company. If so, they might be hard to terminate and you and your colleagues might be stuck working with them for a long time.

When I've worked with incompetent people in the past, it's been very frustrating. I complained about them to my boss, and usually the boss was already aware of the problem. However, sometimes the person wasn't incompetent enough to warrant being fired, so I just had to live with it for the time being. Eventually, an incompetent co-worker, like an incompetent boss, will be found out and, in more cases than not, will leave their department.

When the Boss Is Away, the Co-Workers Will Play . . . Or Fight

I've mentioned that a department is like a family, sometimes like a dysfunctional family. When the parents (the bosses) go out of town, the children (your co-workers) can sometimes act up. Here are a couple of memorable examples that I've experienced.

Years ago, before I started to attend the annual television convention known as NATPE, our bosses had gone out of town as usual to attend the convention. My co-workers and I were left to mind the store. At that time, we had an employee who had become our "computer guy." Even though I didn't know much about computers, I actually was the one who had trained him on computers, but then he took things to the next level. For some reason, we got into an argument about something, and the next thing out of his mouth was, "F--k you Andy!" He said it loudly and in the middle of the hallway for all to hear. Keep in mind that he was a very nice and quiet guy, so we were all a little shocked by his behavior. I'm sure that if our bosses were there, he wouldn't have said that. The next day he apologized to me. (By the way, years later my bosses and I still laughed about it because it was so uncharacteristic of him.)

Another, more serious, incident happened a couple of years later when my bosses were away at that same convention. This time I was with them, so I didn't witness this firsthand. We had an employee in our department who was responsible for overseeing our computers and research presentations. We had another employee who would require the services of the first employee to get some projects completed. I can tell you from personal experience that the first employee could sometimes be slow in completing projects for me, which frustrated me many times. I guess the second employee was also frustrated by the same lack of speed and lack of attention, so that employee proceeded to loudly curse out the first employee in front of everyone, using words that were described as "threatening" and as "gang language." At one point, the employee who lost control had to be restrained by their co-workers because it seemed like this person wanted to physically attack the other employee. Similar to the previous example, this was even more shocking because the employee who made the alleged threats was very quiet and reserved, so when I heard about this, I couldn't believe it. Human Resources became involved, as they should, and things quieted down after that. The employee who lost their temper eventually left our department and went to work at another company, likely in part because the atmosphere was a bit uncomfortable after that blow-up. I think the situation could've been avoided if the first employee was faster in getting back to people and if the second employee had voiced their concerns earlier and had not kept them inside for so long. That is why I always say that communication is key.

RUNG XII SUMMARY

- **Your relationship with the people at work is perhaps the most important key to success.**

- **There is a generation gap at work. Older workers have certain expectations of younger workers, and if these expectations are not met, conflict arises. Try to understand where older workers are coming from in terms of their background and work ethic. Observe them, and most importantly, communicate with them.**

- **Work very closely with your assistant if you have one. A really good assistant can make your job much easier.**

- **There is probably nothing more important than your relationship with your boss. They control your destiny.**

- **It is usually not wise to stand up to your boss, but if they treat you unfairly or yell at you, you need to make your feelings known in a professional manner.**

- **Develop a very strong relationship with your co-workers. Remember you are part of a team, so try to help them as much as possible and hopefully they will help you in return.**

- **If you have any conflicts with supervisors or co-workers, don't wait until the pressure builds. Sit down with them and discuss the issues at hand, even if it's difficult to do.**

RUNG XIII – CLIMBING THE RUNGS OF THE LADDER

MOVING UP THE CORPORATE LADDER

Hopefully, you're ambitious and when you find a job you really enjoy, you'll want to move up the corporate ladder. This means getting promotions and pay raises. What qualities do you need to move up the ladder? There are many of them. However, I'd like to start with one quality that doesn't necessarily mean that you'll move up the corporate ladder–and that's longevity. I think many employees wrongly assume that since they've been with a company for a long time, they're entitled to a promotion. While this may be true in some companies, I feel that it's not the length of service that matters most, but rather it's the quality of service.

I'll never forget being in a company meeting at one of the advertising agencies for whom I worked. When promotions were announced in the company, one woman who had been with the company for twenty-five years was crying because she didn't get a promotion to vice-president. She felt that her length of service alone earned her a promotion, but unfortunately for her, it didn't.

THE "CORPORATE COMMANDMENTS"

So how do you earn a promotion? I've mentioned most of the factors throughout this book, but here's a review of the work rules to live by. These are what I call the "Corporate Commandments" (and there are more than ten, in no particular order). Many of them can help you move up the corporate ladder and get a promotion. At the very least, they are just good advice.

RELATING TO YOU:

1. *ALWAYS THINK ABOUT YOUR WORK REPUTATION.*

2. *HAVE CONFIDENCE IN YOURSELF.*

3. LEARN FROM OBSERVING.

4. YOU CAN'T DEMAND RESPECT; YOU MUST EARN IT.

5. BE ABLE TO TAKE CONSTRUCTIVE CRITICISM.

6. CONTROL YOUR TEMPER.

7. BE AN INITIATOR.

8. NO ONE SHOULD BE HARDER ON YOURSELF THAN YOU.

9. LIMIT ALCOHOL INTAKE AT WORK FUNCTIONS.

10. LEAVE YOUR PERSONAL PROBLEMS AT HOME.

11. DON'T BE AFRAID OF CHANGE–YOU MUST EMBRACE IT INSTEAD.

12. HAVE A POSITIVE ATTITUDE.

13. HAVE A SENSE OF HUMOR AT WORK.

14. TOUT YOUR ACCOMPLISHMENTS IN A PROFESSIONAL MANNER.

15. LEARN FROM YOUR MISTAKES AND FROM THE MISTAKES OF OTHERS.

16. DRESS FOR SUCCESS.

17. DON'T SMOKE CIGARETTES OR TAKE DRUGS.

18. ACT PROFESSIONALLY AT ALL TIMES.

19. GO OUT FOR LUNCH ONCE IN A WHILE–DON'T ALWAYS WORK AT YOUR DESK DURING LUNCH.

20. DON'T LET YOUR EGO GET IN THE WAY OF YOUR SUCCESS.

21. TAKE SICK DAYS ONLY WHEN YOU'RE ACTUALLY SICK.

22. BE PATIENT WHEN IT COMES TO YOUR CAREER ADVANCEMENT.

23 LEARN BY ASKING THE RIGHT QUESTIONS.

24. STAY HEALTHY–WHEN YOU HAVE YOUR HEALTH, YOU HAVE EVERYTHING.

25. MAXIMIZE YOUR 401(k) PLAN CONTRIBUTIONS.

26. TAKE RESPONSIBILITY FOR YOUR ACTIONS.

27. DO WHATEVER IT TAKES TO GET THE JOB DONE.

RELATING TO YOUR WORK:

28. BE COMPETENT AT YOUR JOB.

29. IT DOESN'T MATTER HOW GOOD YOUR WORK IS IF YOU MISS A DEADLINE.

30. ATTENTION TO DETAIL IS EVERYTHING.

31. DEVELOP A ZERO-TOLERANCE POLICY FOR TYPOS.

32. REREAD AND EDIT YOUR EMAILS BEFORE SENDING THEM.

33. KEEP A LIST OF ALL OF YOUR WORK AND PERSONAL PROJECTS.

34. BE WILLING TO WORK OVERTIME AND WEEKENDS WITHOUT COMPLAINT AND WITHOUT EXPECTING TO BE PATTED ON THE BACK.

35. BE AT WORK EARLY OR ON TIME.

36. ARRIVE FOR MEETINGS EARLY OR ON TIME.

37. ALWAYS CHECK TO MAKE SURE YOU ATTACH THE CORRECT ATTACHMENT BEFORE SENDING OUT AN EMAIL.

38. USE YOUR CAR, TRAIN, OR BUS AS A SECOND OFFICE.

39. ALWAYS FOLLOW UP.

40. THERE ARE NO PROBLEMS–ONLY SOLUTIONS.

41. CONDUCT RUN-THROUGHS FOR ANY PRESENTATION THAT YOU'LL BE GIVING.

42. KEEP INFORMED ABOUT WHAT'S GOING ON IN YOUR INDUSTRY.

43. KNOW YOUR COMPANY'S PRODUCT INSIDE AND OUT.

44. KEEP YOUR WORK AREA ORGANIZED AT ALL TIMES.

45. *CONSTANTLY DELETE UNWANTED FILES AND EMAILS.*

46. *RETURN PHONE CALLS AND EMAILS WITHIN 24 HOURS.*

47. *HAVE A PLAN OF ACTION FOR HANDLING YOUR WORKLOAD–USE YOUR TIME IN THE SHOWER, DRIVING TO WORK, AND EVEN WHEN WORKING OUT, TO MAP OUT WHAT YOU'LL BE DOING THE NEXT DAY AND NEXT WEEK.*

48. *ALWAYS ACCEPT INVITATIONS TO WORK FUNCTIONS.*

49. *LEARN AS MANY COMPUTER PROGRAMS AS POSSIBLE.*

50. *IT'S ALWAYS BEST TO HAVE A JOB WHEN LOOKING FOR ANOTHER JOB.*

51. *DON'T JUST WORK HARD, WORK SMART.*

RELATING TO OTHER PEOPLE:

52. *SOMETIMES THE HARDEST THING ABOUT WORK IS NOT THE WORK, IT'S THE PEOPLE.*

53. *REMEMBER THAT YOUR JOB IS TO MAKE THE BOSS'S JOB EASIER.*

54. *DO WHATEVER IT TAKES TO MAKE YOUR BOSS LOOK GOOD.*

55. *DEVELOP A REPUTATION FOR GETTING ALONG WITH PEOPLE, ESPECIALLY YOUR BOSS AND CO-WORKERS.*

56. *DON'T DATE ANYONE AT WORK WHOM YOU MIGHT RUN INTO OCCASIONALLY (AT WORK).*

57. *ANTICIPATE YOUR BOSS'S NEEDS.*

58. *BE A TEAM PLAYER.*

59. *GIVE COMPLIMENTS AND ACCEPT COMPLIMENTS WHEN DESERVED.*

60. *MAKE AN EFFORT TO GET TO KNOW PEOPLE IN OTHER DEPARTMENTS.*

61. *PARTICIPATE IN ANY MEETING YOU'RE INVITED TO.*

62. *CONSTANTLY NETWORK AND HAVE GREAT CONTACTS IN YOUR INDUSTRY.*

63. *IF THE COPY MACHINE RUNS OUT OF PAPER, DON'T WAIT FOR SOMEONE ELSE TO REFILL THE MACHINE–JUST DO IT YOURSELF.*

64. *DEVELOP A STRONG RELATIONSHIP WITH AS MANY ASSISTANTS AS POSSIBLE.*

65. *PAY FULL ATTENTION TO THE PERSON SPEAKING TO YOU.*

66. *DISCUSS NON-WORK ISSUES WITH YOUR BOSSES AND CO-WORKERS EVERY ONCE IN A WHILE.*

67. *IF YOU HAVE A PROBLEM WITH SOMEONE, CONSIDER DISCUSSING IT WITH THEM DIRECTLY.*

68. *TREAT OTHERS WITH RESPECT.*

69. *REMEMBER THAT OTHERS ARE DEPENDING ON YOU.*

70. *OVERCOME THE GENERATION GAP THROUGH COMMUNICATION AND OBSERVATION.*

71. *KEEP YOUR SUPERVISOR INFORMED OF YOUR PROGRESS AT ALL TIMES. THIS WILL PREVENT THEM FROM HAVING TO MICROMANAGE YOU.*

72. *ALWAYS ASK FOR, DON'T DEMAND, A PROMOTION OR RAISE.*

73. *THE DEPARTMENT THAT WORKS TOGETHER HAS THE MOST SUCCESS TOGETHER.*

HOW TO MANAGE YOUR EMPLOYEES

As you move up the corporate ladder, you'll eventually be put in charge of other employees. You're now the teacher, not just the student. If you aren't able to manage your employees properly, your job will become much more difficult.

This is the chapter in which I ask you to do as I say, not as I do. This vital area for success is perhaps the one area that led to my leaving the corporate world. If you ask most managers, they'll tell you that perhaps the toughest thing at work is managing other people. It's sometimes very difficult to motivate people who work for you to do things that they don't want to do. It's very easy to take things personally when your employees don't follow your instructions.

There are different ways of managing employees. One way is to micromanage them, which is to supervise them very closely. I managed up to seven employees at one point. I was a micromanager. I'd constantly be on top of my employees, asking them how much progress they'd made on a particular project. I was always asking them when they'd be done and would walk into their office to make sure they were working on an assignment. I'd chastise them for talking on the phone too much or talking with their co-workers too much when they should've been working. I'd ask them why they had taken such a long lunch when a deadline was approaching. I'd try to proof every report and email they sent out. Would you like to work for a boss like that? Probably not. If you don't want to be micromanaged, keep your boss informed of your progress on projects at all times. This will take away their need for constantly checking in on you.

What were the results of my micromanaging? On the plus side, my work reputation was spotless. People knew that I always got results and that my work and the work of my employees were top-notch. We always went above and beyond what was asked, always met deadlines, and always sent out reports with one hundred percent accuracy. I received many compliments both verbally and in writing throughout the years from executives who utilized our services. However, micromanaging had a price.

As you can imagine, many of my past employees didn't enjoy being micromanaged. Some of them complained about me to my bosses. As I mentioned previously, a couple of them even went so far as to complain to HR without my knowledge. If you have a problem with your boss, you need to speak about it directly with your boss first, before you go over his or her head or behind their back. In my case, going behind my back to HR didn't exactly endear these employees to me, and this certainly didn't help our relationship. Remember, it's important to have a good working relationship with your boss, so if you start complaining about him or her too much or to the wrong people, it could have a detrimental effect on you. I'm not saying you shouldn't complain about your boss. I'm just saying that you should try to work things out first and complain to HR only as a last resort.

One important thing to keep in mind is that no matter how you treat and manage your employees, you'll most likely be seeing them from time to time after one of you leaves the company. Obviously, it's better to have a strong working relationship with them so that when you do see them in the future, it won't be an uncomfortable situation. Even though many of my employees didn't enjoy working for me, we still had a cordial relationship in the years after they left the company. Some of them actually gave me leads in finding a new job after I left the company.

Why were they cordial to me despite the way I managed them? There are a couple of reasons. First, you should try to never burn your bridges with anyone. Who knows, perhaps they might even end up working for me again one day, or more likely, I could end up working for them! Second, although I was tough on them, I never mistreated them. In other words, I never yelled at my employees like a football coach would yell at his players. I also bought all of them holiday/Christmas gift cards every year, so I guess I wasn't totally heartless! Last, I hope that they learned a few things when they worked for me and realized this later.

Why did I micromanage my employees? For starters, I was a perfectionist. I believed that I had more knowledge, experience, and speed than my employees. Of course, I also had less patience than my employees. I felt it was necessary to point things out to them along the way. It was also necessary to be on top of them to make sure they worked fast enough to meet deadlines. It doesn't matter how good your work is if you miss a deadline! I probably managed the employees who were slowest the most. As I mentioned in a previous chapter, some of the smartest employees I ever had were also the slowest. Their work was great, but I never enjoyed the stress of working until the last minute to meet a deadline. When the president of the company says they need a project done by 4 p.m., you better have it done by 4 p.m. or, if possible, earlier. This is why I constantly would ask some of my employees how much progress they had made and when they expected to be done. This was my way of saying, "Hey, we need to work faster because our deadline is approaching." If I didn't manage my employees this way, we would have missed many deadlines. Because I was a part of management and was ultimately responsible for whether the project got done, missing a deadline was unacceptable to me.

What I found over the years is that some employees need to be micromanaged, while others don't. I didn't micromanage every employee, but I did micromanage most of them. At one point, I was fortunate to have had an employee who was self-sufficient. He was smart, knowledgeable, and fast. I would give him a project, leave him alone, and that project would get done quickly and accurately. I didn't need to micromanage him, so I was happy and he was happy. He certainly appreciated my confidence in him. (I've also received many thank-you notes from him over the years, so that's a nice touch as well.)

The moral of the story is that you need to manage each employee differently. If they are new or relatively inexperienced, they may need to be micromanaged. However, at some point, you have to stand back and let them do things on their own. This was hard for me to do because when I attempted to do that, things would fall through the cracks and I was the one who got the blame and who had to take responsibility. When that happened, I would go back to micromanaging.

When it came to my style of micromanaging, I did get some solace from watching Donald Trump's *The Apprentice*. I noticed that in the final show of the first couple of seasons, the ultimate winner was the one who micromanaged their employees. This person knew at all times what their employees were doing, whereas the loser was chastised for not knowing and not controlling what several employees were doing.

One thing is for sure: micromanaging does get results. The key is to do it in a way that motivates your employees and that, ultimately, isn't considered too obtrusive. In my opinion, you can "micromanage" effectively by doing the following. First, always act as a mentor to your employees, letting them know they are always free to ask you questions. When they do ask questions, it is imperative that you are never judgmental. Second, when you meet with an employee to discuss a project, you should be as specific as possible about what you think is necessary. If possible, try to divide the project into specific action steps or tasks. Third, you must always communicate the relative importance of the projects you are assigning. For example, if a particular project is a high priority, you must tell the employee that—and, by all means, let them know the stakes that are involved (for example, the president of the company will not receive a memo that he needs for a meeting with another executive). If it is a low-priority project, let them know that as well. You never want to get the reputation as a manager who always wants everything "ASAP." So, what's the bottom line?–prioritize and communicate. If you do those two things consistently, then micromanaging should take care of itself.

The other extreme to micromanaging is what I call "macromanaging." While I rarely managed my employees this way, I was managed this way by one of my bosses. I'd proven myself from a work perspective, so he gave me complete independence. This was great for me because it really helped me make a name for myself in the company. However, there are hidden disadvantages to macromanaging. For example, by giving newer or unproven employees too much freedom over their projects, ironically they might not be learning as much as they could if they had the benefit of your experience. You need to tailor your management style to the employee. In my case, I had proven myself.

So, if I enjoyed my independence so much, why wouldn't I give that independence to my employees? I think the difference was that I felt that I was much more detail-oriented than most of my staff and really strategized and planned things out ahead of time so that I was prepared for any eventuality. My boss could afford to give me independence because I was more involved in the day-to-day activities than he was. With my own employees, it was a little different. As I said before, I felt that I had a lot more knowledge and experience than they had. I didn't feel comfortable letting them do things on their own because I felt that the quality of work would not be as high. Of course, the goal is to teach them and help them get to a point where they can be independent. I believe that if you follow the steps I outlined above, you can have the best of both worlds.

Another criticism of my management style was that I never got personal with my employees. I rarely asked them how their weekend was or how their wife or husband was doing. I was pretty much all business with my employees, and that can be a negative thing. If you do manage employees, I don't advise you to become close friends with them. As I've seen, it's very possible they'll take advantage of your friendship, which can make it difficult to manage them objectively. On the other hand, it's important to show your employees that you care about them as more than just employees. That's not to say that I never engaged my employees in personal conversations. I just didn't do it enough.

One criticism I received from a former boss was that I never walked the halls with a smile on my face and that my employees were looking to me to set the tone. The main reason I didn't walk around with a smile is because my boss had created so much stress for me. Much of the stress was unnecessary, which translated into me walking around with a serious demeanor all the time. The irony is that I would joke around with my bosses and with the other executives in the company, but unfortunately, I would rarely joke around with my own employees.

HOW TO MANAGE YOURSELF

There's one employee I micromanaged more than any other–*me*! I was always tougher on myself than I was on any of my employees. My motto was "Refuse to Lose." I'd beat myself up if I or one of my employees made a mistake. I think it's very important to be hard on yourself, because if you're not hard on yourself, someone else will be.

The best way to manage yourself is to follow the "Corporate Commandments" I listed earlier. I think it's important to remind yourself once in a while that you do need to manage yourself. Sometimes it's so easy to get caught up trying to figure out how to manage your boss or your employees that you forget to manage the most important person at work–you!

DON'T LET YOUR EGO GET IN THE WAY

It's no surprise that some people in the corporate world have big egos. Some people have earned them, some have not. What's important is to not let your ego get in the way of your success. I've seen examples of top executives who, to their detriment, let their egos get in their way.

I'll never forget what happened to a very high-level executive at one of my former companies a few years ago. He had been extremely successful in his career and was one of the best in the business. The rumor going around was that he was about to get a very big promotion, and it was just a matter of logistics before it was announced. The next thing we knew, he had left the company! It was a shocking revelation for many of us. We all wondered what had happened.

Apparently he had asked for a lot more money and threatened to leave if he didn't get it. His ego probably allowed him to believe that his boss and the company would meet his demands. He was wrong. His terms weren't accepted, and when he said he'd leave the company, the company took him up on his offer. I know that he was very upset with his boss and the company for the way they treated him, especially after so much success. It just goes to show that everyone is expendable.

No matter how good you are at your job, be careful about how you go about trying to get a promotion and raise. Keep in mind that if you threaten to leave, this could easily backfire on you. If you check your ego at the door, you should be okay. Remember, if you do your job well, you'll eventually get what you deserve. I've seen far too many people leave a job prematurely (and hurt their careers) because they felt their ego was bruised by some perceived slight. If they had only stuck it out, they would have eventually gotten what they wanted.

HOW TO ASK FOR A PROMOTION AND RAISE

When you climb the corporate ladder, it means that you're making progress in your career. For most people, this means getting promotions, pay raises, and more responsibility along the way. In an ideal world, your boss would come to you and tell you what a great job you've done and would inform you that you're about to get promoted. Unfortunately, many times you have to ask for a promotion or raise. So what's the best way to go about doing this?

You're going to need to set an appointment with your boss to discuss your wishes. You should try and schedule a time when your boss can give you his or her full attention, so as not to feel rushed because of an impending deadline for some project. Of course, you'll be dressed well as usual and be prepared with the specific points you want to get across.

Asking for a Promotion

A major theme when asking for a promotion is to tell your boss about all of your accomplishments and to explain why these accomplishments have prepared you for more responsibilities and leadership. Before I give you my list of suggestions, remember one thing: Don't ask for a promotion unless you're ready for one. You're better off waiting a bit while you gain more experience and knowledge than rushing things because you feel the pressure to move up. You may have heard the saying, "No wine before its time." Well, no promotion before its time is a good saying, too. First learn it, then earn it.

When you feel you're ready, I recommend the following:

- Tell your boss how much you love your job. I know that "love" is a strong word, but this is one instance where it needs to be utilized.

- Discuss how successful you've been on the various projects your boss has asked you to complete.

- Talk about the projects you've worked on that you weren't asked to do.

- As I said earlier in the book, you should already have a file of thank-you notes, emails, and compliments from executives and co-workers in the company and perhaps from outside of the company. Be prepared to show this file to your boss.

- Tell your boss how much you've enjoyed working with him or her and with others in your department. Tell them how much you've learned and that you look forward to learning a lot more.

- Mention the long hours you've put in and the lunches you've worked through.

- Talk about your increased workload. Don't forget to have a piece of paper that lists your day-to-day responsibilities as well as other responsibilities you have.

- You must remember one important thing—a promotion will always mean taking on more responsibility. Outline the additional responsibilities you'll be taking on in the future to warrant this promotion.

- If there are executives in the company who will step up to the plate for you and will recommend you for a promotion, then mention those executives to your boss.

- Tell your boss that you're one hundred percent confident that you'll excel in this new position.

- Generally, discuss how you've made your boss's job easier and how you'd like to continue accomplishing that.

- If this new position involves managing someone else, tell your boss that you look forward to mentoring this person and that you'd love to take any management courses that are available.

Asking for a Raise

A major theme when asking for a raise is to concentrate on your value to the organization. This obviously involves referring to your accomplishments, but it also means you should have a good idea of what you are worth compared to others.

- Knowledge is power, so you want to come in with an appropriate idea of what someone at your level is paid in your organization and in other organizations. I know I said earlier in the book not to discuss your salary with anyone, but I also said that this can help you when asking for a raise. This is the one time when you should take the risk because it will benefit you financially. You should also check out those salary websites I've mentioned.

- If there's someone you can trust in your department who has knowledge of the salary range for your position, ask them for this information, but swear them to secrecy. As I said, you don't want your boss to find out you've been nosing around.

- Since you've networked and have contacts at competing companies, ask your contacts what a similar position at their company pays. This is an especially good technique if you don't feel you can discreetly find out your position's salary range from people in your company.

- Negotiate your salary. If you truly have done a great job and your bosses really value you, they won't want to see you leave the company. Most likely, they'll have some wiggle room as far as your salary is concerned.

- Never accept the first offer unless you are told upfront that there's no room for negotiation or the offer meets your expectations. In our department, we'd always have a salary range depending on one's experience. I'd always try to give an employee the most

I could, depending on how much we had budgeted for that position.

- Keep in mind that if your boss gives you too high a salary, then they might have to bring other people in your department up to your salary level to keep things equal. A lot depends on your department's budget.

- Ask for, but don't demand, more money. Never threaten your boss as far as salary is concerned. If you tell your boss that you'll leave the company unless you get the salary you want, you must be prepared to leave the company if your wishes aren't granted. Even if you get what you want but it's a result of tough negotiations, or you did it in a threatening manner, your boss won't be too happy with you. You could possibly have done some serious damage to your relationship.

- If you're not happy with the offer, I think the best way to ask for more money is to say something similar to the following: "I really appreciate your offer, but is it possible to get . . ." and then after naming your figure, explain why your performance and increased responsibilities merit more pay. Again, do *not* burn a bridge with your boss. Your common sense and people skills should tell you when you're hitting a wall.

AN EMPLOYMENT CONTRACT – TO SIGN OR NOT TO SIGN?

At some point in your career when you become management material, you may find yourself in the position of being offered a contract to sign. From the time I was a manager through the time I was a vice-president, I signed a series of three-year contracts. The duration of a management contract will differ depending on where you work, assuming your company even uses management contracts. You'll usually have some options. The contract could be three years "firm," which means that you're committing to a full three-year term. You may get a "two-plus-one" contract, which means that you're signing up for two years firm and then the company has the option of extending your contract for the third year. The other option was usually a "one-plus-one-plus-one," which meant that you were signing on for one year firm and the company had the option of extending your contract after year one for another year and after year two for a third year.

There are both advantages and disadvantages to signing a contract.

Advantages:

- You have the peace of mind that you'll have a job and financial security for a certain amount of time.

- You'll most likely have bigger percent raises by signing a contract versus not signing.

- You're showing the company that you're committed to them and believe in them.

- If for any reason the company downsizes and needs to lay you off, you'll be guaranteed some sort of financial settlement for the remainder of your contract.

Disadvantages:

- You've basically tied yourself up at work for an extended period of time, so if things negatively change (perhaps you get a new boss you can't stand), you're stuck.

- If you find a "once-in-a-lifetime opportunity" somewhere else, you can't legally take it.

- Even if you're in your option year and you want to leave, if the company wants to exercise their option to keep you on for another year, they have the legal right to do so.

- Signing a contract makes it easier for the company to avoid a lawsuit should they determine that your services are no longer required. Instead of firing or terminating you, which they would have to do if you don't have a contract, all they have to do is tell you that your contract is not being renewed. This makes it more difficult for you to take any legal action against them.

Despite these disadvantages, many companies will allow you to get out of your contract if you're really unhappy. It takes some legal wrangling, but I've seen it happen more than once. After all, it does no one any good to be in a work relationship if at least one of the parties involved isn't happy. However, you need to think seriously about these things before you sign a long-term contract because, beyond the legal issues, you are in effect giving your word that you'll remain with the company for a certain amount of time.

RUNG XIII SUMMARY

- Be patient in your quest to climb the corporate ladder. There is no rush.

- Read and reread the 73 "Corporate Commandments."

- When you manage a staff, treat them as people, not as employees. Work with them and be sensitive to their needs.

- Take time to manage yourself. Think about what makes you happy.

- No matter how smart or successful you become, check your ego at the door.

- When asking for a promotion and raise, keep in mind that it's not about longevity–it's about performance. You must be able to take on additional responsibilities in your new role.

- If you are offered an employment contract, read it carefully.

RUNG XIV – CLIMBING A NEW LADDER

WHEN IT'S TIME TO GET A NEW JOB

It's funny how excited we get when we find out we've gotten a new job. Then, we start our new jobs and some of us get a taste of reality. For whatever reason, our enthusiasm diminishes and the life is sucked out of us. What do you do? One of the toughest decisions you'll ever have to make is when to leave a job. It's always best to have a job when looking for another one. If you quit a job because things are difficult for you, you may be labeled as a quitter and your next potential employer may have a lot of questions for you. Before you quit a job, you need to ask yourself the following questions:

- What is the main reason or reasons for my unhappiness?

- Do I still enjoy the work that I'm doing?

- Is the work tedious and boring?

- Am I learning new techniques or technologies?

- Do I like the people I work for?

- Do I like the people I work with?

- If I'm having problems with other people at work, is it partly my fault?

- If my boss is the main problem, is there any way to fix the problem?

- Am I being treated unfairly?

- Is the stress of the job too much for me?

- Am I the right person for this job?

- Am I so depressed and miserable because of the job, I don't even want to get up in the morning and go to work?

- Is it a money issue—perhaps I like the job, but I need to make more money?

- Am I being recognized for my accomplishments?

There are many factors to take into account when considering leaving a job. If you're not being considered for a promotion at your present company but another company is willing to give you more responsibility, a bigger title, and more money, then it's a no-brainer. If the work itself doesn't excite you, then it's time to move on. If you're having difficulties with other people in the company and you feel that it's a hopeless situation and that you have done everything in your power to make things better, then it's time to move on. If you're constantly stressed out and you feel overwhelmed all the time, then you're probably not a good fit with the position and should move on. If you *hate* your job, it's time to move on.

It's probably best not to tell anyone that you're looking for another job because once your boss hears that, they may ask you to leave before you have a new job. Some bosses might be understanding and will actually help you find a new job. It all depends on your relationship with your boss. The most important thing is to be honest with the people you work with once you've made your decision to leave. Please remember that if you're miserable, try not to make others miserable. You need to take the high road and give two weeks' notice once you find another job and work hard in those final two weeks. You don't want to tick anyone off because you might need them as a reference sometime in the future. You just never know. In fact, I highly recommend that when you send your resignation email to your supervisors and HR, you should make sure that you thank everyone for giving you such a great opportunity, tell them it was a great learning experience, and offer to help out in any way you can.

Remember the gentleman I had mentioned earlier in the book who left a note on his first day before he went to lunch and never came back? Well, I give him credit for knowing when it was time to leave his job. He certainly didn't waste a lot of his time or his employer's time by leaving on his first day. However, he certainly didn't make any friends by not giving any notice. What would have happened if he had stuck it out a bit more? Maybe he would have changed his opinion of the job, maybe not. As I stated earlier in the book, try not to judge the job based on your first day or first week. It simply takes a little time to get into a comfort zone at any new job. Give it some time before you make the decision to move on.

Sometimes leaving a job is not your choice. How do you know if you're about to get fired or laid off? There are usually a few signs such as people start ignoring you, you're not invited to meetings as much, and some of your responsibilities are being taken away. If you suspect that your job may be in danger, speak with your boss. Of course, there's a good chance your boss may not be honest with you, so you need to look for non-verbal cues, too. If your boss can't look you straight in the eye or seems nervous about speaking with you, it may be time to beat him or her to the punch and start looking for a new job.

RUNG XIV SUMMARY

- **If you are unhappy at your job, write down all the positives and negatives. How can YOU change the negatives?**

- **If you have done all you can do to improve the situation but you still are unhappy, it's time to get a new job.**

- **If you do leave your job, leave on a high note. Offer to help out with the transition and think about the positives you've experienced at the job. Keep in contact with your former supervisors and co-workers if possible.**

RUNG XV – LEARNING FROM PAST MISTAKES

After you leave a job to "climb a new ladder," even if you're happy with your new job or career, my advice and experience is that you take some much-needed time to reflect on what you did right and what you did wrong in your previous jobs. That's the reason I wrote this book!

The following is a summary of all the things I feel I did right in my corporate career, as well as those things I did wrong (or at least could have improved upon). It's important to learn from both.

WHAT I DID RIGHT

- ✓ Had a great work ethic–worked long hours and weekends if necessary without complaining

- ✓ Made great contacts at my company and other companies

- ✓ Dressed well–always wore a suit and tie

- ✓ Remembered I represented the company when attending off-site meetings or conventions

- ✓ Tried to use humor as much as possible

- ✓ Never yelled at anyone

- ✓ Had integrity

- ✓ Was very detail-oriented

- ✓ Was always honest with people

- ✓ Read trade magazines and Internet articles about my industry

- ✓ Was conscientious

- ✓ Tried to go above and beyond what was expected

- ✓ Initiated projects and ideas

✓ Never drank alcohol during a work day or took drugs

✓ Never smoked cigarettes

✓ Gave my employees holiday gift cards to show my appreciation for them

✓ Spoke up and participated in meetings

✓ Was always fiscally responsible–tried to save the department and company money

✓ Never took sick days unless I was sick

✓ Took credit for my ideas, but didn't take credit for other people's ideas

✓ Had meetings with employees to let them know what was going on

✓ Would frequently go out to lunch with my direct boss

✓ Took the job seriously

✓ Maintained my self-respect

✓ Was never late to a meeting or presentation

✓ Worked through lunch many times

✓ Returned phone calls and emails on the same day I received them, if possible

✓ Practiced oral presentations several times and anticipated questions

✓ Kept a list of projects and personal things to do at all times

✓ Looked ahead to the next day and next week, trying to anticipate what would be needed

✓ Thought things through several times so I could come up with the best way of attacking a problem

✓ Micromanaged my employees to insure minimal mistakes

WHAT I DID WRONG

- ✓ Complained too much

- ✓ Didn't take my employees out to lunch

- ✓ Thought that my way was always the best way (which of course, it was!)

- ✓ Put projects before people

- ✓ Too critical of my employees

- ✓ Not nearly as computer proficient as I should've been

- ✓ Not patient

- ✓ Always let myself be on the defensive

- ✓ Had difficulty giving compliments to employees

- ✓ Stayed too long in a bad environment

- ✓ Talked too much about my social life

- ✓ Got used to coming in late each morning

- ✓ Never brought in donuts or bagels in the morning

- ✓ Got upset at the little things

- ✓ Let stress get the better of me at times

- ✓ Criticized my bosses too much

- ✓ Micromanaged my employees to insure minimal mistakes

By the way, you'll notice I put micromanaging on both the "What I Did Right" and "What I Did Wrong" lists. As I said before, when properly done with effective communication and prioritization, "micromanaging" can be effective. When done in an insensitive or undiplomatic manner, it can be a negative.

THE BEGINNING OF THE END (AKA, THE WRITING ON THE WALL)

At the beginning of this book, I mentioned that my television studio career had ended prematurely. However, it wasn't a total shock to me because I had seen the signs up to a year before that. My final year was a very difficult one. Looking back, I probably should have left on my own, but since I still enjoyed what I did, I decided to tough it out for as long as I could.

It's funny how things can change on a dime. In the year prior to my contract not getting renewed, I was somewhat optimistic that I'd get a promotion to senior vice-president. I had talked to both of my bosses about this possibility, and while neither of them said "yes," they didn't say "no" either. In fact, both of them said that they weren't against it. While I knew that getting a promotion was a long shot, at least I had some hope.

One of the things that gave me hope was that my big boss had told me that if we had a good pilot season, this would bode well for me. Let me explain what that means. Pilot season in the television industry runs from about January to May each year. It's a very intense time for us because, as a production company, this is the time of the year when we produce pilots. As I mentioned earlier in the book, a pilot is the first episode of a new television show and is used to sell that show to the networks. If a network likes the pilot episode, they will "greenlight" it as a series and will order usually at least six episodes that you'll see on television anywhere from a few weeks to a few months later. If the network doesn't like the pilot episode, the program never makes it to your television set.

My job was to test these pilots by showing them to potential viewers. Based on viewer opinions, we'd edit the pilots to make them better. Our studio would then submit the tested and edited pilots to the networks. Later, I would go to New York City for the "upfronts." These were presentations made by the networks to their advertisers heralding their new shows and announcing what their new fall prime time (8-11 p.m.) schedules would be. It was during upfront week that I'd assist our production and development executives with any research or scheduling questions before the networks announced their final schedules. It was a very tense and nerve-racking week for everyone in the company.

As it turned out, everyone's hard work paid off as our company had its best pilot season in many years. I was very proud of the work I had done to organize and oversee all of the testing on these pilots and to provide support to our executives during upfront week.

When I returned to L.A., I reminded my boss of what he'd said about us having a good pilot season and how that would bode well for me in terms of possibly getting a promotion. I was shocked and disheartened to hear from him that the results we got were a team effort from the research department and not based on any individual. I reminded him that it was me who was one hundred percent responsible for organizing the testing of these pilots, who had attended all of the pilot tests, and who had written up the analyses on half of these pilots and who had provided input and proofed the analyses of the other half of the pilots. Furthermore, I was also the only member of the research department to have attended the New York upfronts, and it was me who worked in our New York office to 1 a.m. to finish an analysis of the newly announced prime time television schedule. In this particular case, I didn't feel that it was a team effort since I'd done most of the work. When my boss downplayed my contributions, I should've known that things weren't going to go well for me in the future.

Soon after that, my contract was about to expire. My direct boss was going to take me out to lunch to discuss my future. I was hoping to hear about a promotion but, if not, at least another three-year contract with the company. Now, I wasn't thrilled about discussing something so important over a meal. Since my boss suggested we talk over lunch, I went along with it. I was a little nervous, and after we ordered food the discussion began. My boss proceeded to tell me that not only was I not getting a promotion, but to keep my job I had to get a personal coach to help me with my attitude toward the big boss as well as to improve my management skills. I was shocked and disappointed. Needless to say, I wasn't too hungry after that.

One of the reasons I was asked to get a personal coach was because, as I mentioned earlier, I've sometimes had a difficult relationship with the big boss, even though I'd worked for him for almost twenty-five years. We just didn't see eye to eye on many things. Furthermore, he felt that he was always right, no matter what (I wonder whether he got that attitude from me or was it vice versa?). Even when I proved that he was wrong, he'd never admit it. He even told me on more than one occasion, "You need to kiss my ass more." Now, I would never tell my employees to do that to me. My boss would also tell me that I needed to respect him more, but I firmly believe that you can't just demand respect, you have to earn it. To put another nail in the coffin, he'd say something to me like, "Now, you probably think that working here for twenty-three years means something, but. . . ." In other words, what he was saying–as many executives like to say and ask–is, "What have you done for me lately?" It's so sad that being a loyal and productive employee for so many years just didn't mean too much at that point.

As I've mentioned, for the past several years, I had signed a series of three-year contracts. However, this time I was only offered a one-year extension on my contract and that was only with the provisions that I accepted a personal coach and improve in ten different areas. Now, some people would have left then and there and gotten another job, but I still enjoyed the work despite the obstacles, so I decided to stick it out. I thought that having a personal coach could be beneficial to me for many reasons. One of them was that it would be nice to have someone objective whom I could tell my side of the story to. I accepted the terms and signed a one-year extension.

To add insult to injury, I had asked my boss at that lunch if one of my employees was going to be promoted to my level, which at the time was vice-president. My feeling was that although this employee was smart and a good worker, there were still a few areas in which he needed improvement. I felt he needed an incentive to get a promotion, which would be to improve in those areas. If you reward an employee with a promotion without first asking them to improve in certain areas, there's no longer any incentive for them to change their behavior. My boss told me at the lunch that there had been no discussions about promoting this employee to vice-president. Well, a few weeks later, I found out that this employee had threatened to leave the company and get another job unless he was promoted and would no longer report to me. My bosses obliged him without consulting me, despite the fact that he was my employee at the time and had been for many years. Now this employee was no longer reporting to me, and to make matters worse, one of our lower-level employees who had previously reported to me was now going to report to him. Furthermore, *my* assistant was now also *his* assistant, and he had equal say in the hiring of any assistant in the future. Once again, my stomach turned as the bad news just kept coming in. My research empire was crumbling.

When it came to getting a personal coach, I was trying to figure out if this was good news or bad news. On the plus side, I was told by others that if the company is paying for a personal coach, it usually means that they're investing in you because they feel that you're worth keeping as an employee. On the negative side, I felt that one of the reasons they brought in a personal coach was so they could say they did everything they could to help me improve, which would help them avert any potential lawsuit. Obviously, I was a little suspicious of their motives.

I ended up interviewing three potential personal coaches and chose one whom I felt I could work with the best. We agreed on either meeting in person or talking over the phone at least once a week. I was very honest with her and told her about the difficulties I'd faced and would continue to face. In fact, I told her that a year from now, no matter how much I had improved, my boss would say that I hadn't improved enough. Was I pessimistic or realistic?

As I said, my big boss had given me ten areas to improve in, which I felt was an insult given my track record at the company and given my most recent accomplishments. Nevertheless, I was determined to make as much progress as possible. The ten areas were as follows:

1. **INITIATION:** Send out ideas, thoughts, and articles; be more predictive and less reactive.

2. **INNOVATION:** Create new ways of doing things; increase computer literacy.

3. **MOTIVATION:** Convey more passion and a stronger work ethic.

4. **COMMUNICATION:** Inform management of what you are doing.

5. **LEADERSHIP:** Be a cheerleader and teacher; promote teamwork; lead by example.

6. **MEETING DECORUM:** Approach meetings with a positive attitude; don't be a naysayer or criticizer.

7. **STYLE:** Display proper business etiquette; be respectful of others.

8. **PRODUCTION COVERAGE:** Be more of a production executive.

9. **CABLE COVERAGE:** Improve relationships; be accountable for movie database (explained below).

10. **CORPORATE PROJECTS:** Be more involved in new ventures.

Overall, these ten areas were a good place to start for any employee, but I felt that I was being picked on. Some of these things I'd already been doing, but others I indeed did need some improvement in. About eight months after I was informed about the ten areas and about four months before my contract was to expire, I sent an email to my bosses that detailed the progress I'd made in each of the ten areas. Granted, it would be hard to show extreme improvement in all ten areas for any employee, but I did document where I'd made progress and felt that I was on the right path. I was waiting for a response from the big boss, but he never even replied to my email! I couldn't believe it. After all, he was the one who came up with the ten areas of improvement, and now he wasn't even giving me any feedback on my progress or lack of progress. How was I supposed to know how I was doing?

My other boss had poked his head in the door and told me that my email was a positive thing and that he'd be sending me a response. Based on our conversation, I was expecting a nice, long, complimentary email. Instead, all I received was an email stating, "I appreciate your review of ways you have made progress and I look forward to discussing this further." My first impression was that the big boss had told him not to send me anything in writing that could be misconstrued as being too positive. They were being extremely careful about what they'd tell me. The fact that the big boss didn't even comment on my email was a sign—a warning sign that I was in trouble.

Another warning sign was related to the movie database project mentioned in number nine in the ten areas of improvement. Without getting into much detail, I'd basically been utilizing the computer and pulling movie information myself, which was a big accomplishment for me considering my lack of hands-on computer experience. For many years my staff would pull most of the data for me, which meant now I had to learn a new trade to get this information. I was proud to have been able to do this. However, my direct boss commented to me that, although I had promised to learn this system, I still hadn't learned it. This, of course, was totally untrue. I had even told my boss that I had learned the system and was using it, so it was another punch in the stomach to not even be recognized for what I was doing. It reinforced my contention that my direct boss simply didn't know what I did every day, which was unfortunate.

Believe it or not, as I was getting closer to my contract renewal or non-renewal, the situation was actually looking positive for me. I was less antagonistic toward my big boss in meetings, and my bosses did recognize that I was showing some improvement overall. When I spoke with my immediate supervisor, he gave me the impression that they were working on a contract renewal for me. He couldn't tell me exactly what was happening, but I was at least encouraged by our conversation. Everything seemed to be pointing toward a contract renewal . . . and then the unexpected happened.

One of my employees had been working for me for three years. He was a great worker but was also very quiet. If you gave him a project, he would get it done without complaint. My main criticism of him was that he was more of an executor than an initiator, and that he didn't speak up enough in meetings. When my personal coach first started, she came to our department and spoke with my bosses and employees about me. This particular employee told her he appreciated that I gave him independence to work on his projects.

The end of my contract was approaching, but about a month before it expired and before I knew about my future, this particular employee's contract was also expiring. My bosses and I had approved a promotion and big raise for him. I presented this to him and was surprised when he told me that he might move further away from the office. He didn't want to be locked up in a long-term contract in case he did move and he decided to get another job. I sent my big boss an email about this, and in his typical manner, he criticized me for being nonchalant in reporting this information to him. As usual, I couldn't figure out why I was the one being criticized. After all, this was a life choice by one of my employees.

My boss was suspicious about my employee's reason for rejecting the long-term contract and decided that he and my other boss would speak directly to this staff member. I was quite surprised and shocked to learn that this employee didn't enjoy working for me and would stay only if he no longer reported to me (sound familiar?). I was shocked because, in the three years he had worked for me, not once did I hear one complaint from him about me. As far as I'm aware, not once did my bosses hear a complaint about me from this employee. As I mentioned, he had told my personal coach that he appreciated the independence that I had given him. However, if I had to sum up his complaints, it mostly had to do with me micromanaging him as well as the way I treated him. He felt that I was condescending to him at times (I probably was when I felt he had missed obvious things) and that I didn't give him enough credit for his work (I totally disagreed with this complaint since many times I'd come up with an idea but the email would go out under his name, meaning that he'd get the credit, and I would compliment him verbally in front of others or in emails). The bottom line was that this was one employee in a long line of employees who had complained about the way I managed them. It was the final straw that broke the camel's back.

Soon after my bosses spoke with the employee, I went on vacation to Alaska (at least I got to go to some great places before I left the company!). When I got back, I was informed that this former subordinate was promoted and that he'd no longer report to me. Here I was, a vice-president, who always had six or seven employees reporting to me, and now I had no one reporting to me. Since a large part of being a vice-president was managing others, it would now be difficult for my bosses to justify keeping me around as a "solo" vice-president. My direct boss came to me and asked that I come up with any ideas on how I saw my job going forward. I came up with a couple of ideas, but they were rejected. This was the end of the line for me.

This was a very difficult and stressful time. I was afraid that my boss would soon call me into his office and tell me that this would be my last day. I discreetly started to pack things up and started to delete emails from my computer just in case I was given no notice to clean out my office. When my boss called me into his office, I was expecting our HR representative to be present to give me the bad news (a word to the wise—when the HR representative is present in a meeting with your boss, it's not a good sign). Fortunately, the HR rep was not there. It was just my direct boss and I. He told me what a difficult decision it was to not renew my contract, and he started to tear up a bit. After all, we had worked together for twenty-three years.

Was I bitter toward the employee who was the final nail in my coffin? Let me put it this way: I wasn't upset at him for complaining about me; I was upset at him for not complaining about me sooner! Perhaps his quiet demeanor prevented him from complaining, but how was I supposed to know there was an issue if no one told me about it? So after twenty-three years with the company, my management style and antagonistic relationship with my boss finally caught up with me. It just goes to show that performance alone is not enough to guarantee you're safe in your job. You have to be a good manager of people, and you have to have a good working relationship with your boss. I truly believe that I managed employees the way I was managed by my big boss. Had my boss not been so critical of me throughout the years and had he not put so much pressure on me, perhaps I could've managed my employees in a better manner. In some ways, it was a miracle that I lasted that long.

What I could never understand about my big boss was why he felt compelled to constantly criticize his employees, especially me. Many times a tough or unreasonable boss might feel insecure because he or she might not be smart enough or competent enough to handle their job, so they criticize others to make themselves look or feel better. This was definitely not the case with my boss. He was exceptionally smart and really knew his stuff, which made his management style even more puzzling to me.

I now had to come to terms with the fact that my long career at the television studio was about to end. We all agreed that I'd stay for about another three months and would do whatever work was necessary. Unfortunately, without a staff and being on my way out, there wasn't much work given to me at all. My bosses and I had a meeting shortly thereafter, and the big boss told me that he thought I'd be doing more work than I was (of course, no one was giving me any work). What really hurt me was that the big boss told me that if he had to do it all over again, he'd have made the day they told me my contract wasn't being renewed my last day. He even went so far as to ask me if I could leave sooner than we agreed, so now instead of leaving in three months I was going to leave in two months.

Furthermore, my boss was going to be out of the office for a few days, and he asked me to have all of my photos taken off the walls by the time he got back. It was bad enough that my twenty-three year career was about to end, but my boss had to rub salt in the wound by treating me like some short-term, lower-level employee. I guess he felt somewhat uncomfortable about the whole situation. Unfortunately, after working for him for twenty-three years, I wasn't too surprised by his reaction. I guess this was one of the realities of the corporate world.

I think that my experience brings up an important question. How should you act when you know that you will be leaving your job in a few days or in a couple of weeks, especially if it wasn't your decision? Your final days could be an awkward time, but it doesn't have to be that way. You should be as professional as possible, even if you dislike your job or the people you work with (which I didn't). Volunteer to help make the transition for your co-workers and bosses as easy as possible. I've been fortunate to have some employees write an entire manual before they left their job that explained step-by-step how to perform their job functions. This was much appreciated by me as a boss. Be proud of the time you've spent at the job and be happy that you will eventually be moving on to something bigger and better. As I've said before, don't forget to thank everyone at work for helping you along the way.

I was hoping my bosses would at least throw me a farewell party. After all, I had worked for them for twenty-three years, so it was the least they could do. Well, I guess I was hoping for too much because they told me that they didn't feel comfortable with this. As I said, they felt a little awkward about the situation and probably didn't want people asking a lot of questions. As usual, I took matters into my own hands and threw my own farewell party at a local restaurant. I invited about one hundred people and about ten attended. No, the small turnout wasn't because I was disliked by my peers. My party fell on a Jewish religious holiday. On top of that, one of our television shows was being filmed that night so many executives either went home early for the holiday or went to the taping. I didn't take it personally. Oh, by the way, my bosses did end up coming to my farewell party after all. While they felt awkward about being the hosts of the party given the circumstances, they were fine with attending it and even paid for it. I'm glad they came.

On my last day with the company, I met with our HR representative and filled out some paperwork. She then took away my BlackBerry® and I.D. cards. I felt like a convicted felon who, upon arriving at prison, must empty his pockets and hand everything over to the guards.

After that, I went around to everyone I knew in the building and said goodbye. I took the high road and even said goodbye to the employee who hastened my exit. After I said my goodbyes, I gathered up a few belongings in my office, and like Elvis, I left the building. There were still many executives I hadn't said goodbye to because they were located in another building a few miles away. The following week, my first week of unemployment, I went over there and said my goodbyes to them and wished them good luck, as they did to me. That was it–the end of my long career at the television studio. Even though I was sad to leave, I was very proud of my distinguished career and felt very fortunate to have had the opportunity to work there.

As far as my bosses were concerned, I actually had dinner with them the week after I left the company. In the weeks following my departure, I stayed in contact with them by phone, by email, or in person. Despite the difficulties I endured working for them, especially the big boss, I did owe them a lot. Without them, I wouldn't have had such a great career. I compared our parting of the ways to a divorce–after spending so much time with your "spouse," sometimes it just doesn't work out and you have to split up, and that's what we did. Thankfully, I didn't have to pay them any alimony!

So, given all of the difficulties I had with my bosses, given all the difficulties I had with my co-workers, and given all the difficulties I had with my employees over the years, *why did I stay so long?*

Well, my pain threshold was pretty high, so I was able to withstand a lot of adversity. For me personally, the advantages outweighed the disadvantages. Yes, there was plenty of stress, but you'd be hard pressed to find any corporate executive position without stress. Yes, I worked for a very difficult boss at times, but who's to say that if I had changed jobs, my new boss would be any better? Besides, he wasn't difficult all of the time. We actually had many enjoyable times together during my career.

Furthermore, I was in a comfort zone because I knew a lot of the people at work and they knew me. Our department and the company had a lot of great people working there, some of whom I had worked with for fifteen or twenty years. I still loved what I did–meaning that I enjoyed the work itself and the challenges I faced every day. That's key. I was also getting rewarded financially, and we had some great perks like our 401(k) plan and profit participation.

I think that another important reason why I stayed so long is that the people I worked for and with became my West Coast "family." I mentioned before that sometimes your bosses feel like parents and your co-workers seem like siblings. Since my real family lives on the East Coast, my bosses and co-workers were like a substitute family for me. Because of the relationships I developed over twenty-three years, maybe it didn't seem like I was just going to work every day. Maybe it seemed like I was seeing my family every day . . . and there's a lot to be said for that.

In the end, I decided to stay until they kicked me out. I had a good thing going and wanted to max it out. I had learned from television stars–who had ruined their careers by leaving very successful shows prematurely to go out on their own, only to be never heard from again– that quitting a good thing has many disadvantages, especially if there's a chance you can make it better. I didn't want to be like them.

My story doesn't necessarily mean that I recommend you hang on to your career for dear life if things are going badly for you. As I said, it all depends on your individual pain threshold and what's important to you. No matter where you work, you'll always have obstacles to overcome. It's up to you whether or not you want (or are able) to overcome them. As long as you still enjoy going to work and feel that you're making a difference, you should stay. If you aren't happy and don't feel that things will improve, well, change can be a good thing.

THE UNEMPLOYMENT LINE

One of the first things I found out when I lost my job is that there's no longer such a thing as an unemployment line, at least in California. I was looking forward to driving to the nearest unemployment office and hanging out with my fellow unemployed brethren. However, everything is now done on the phone or on the Internet. Unemployment benefits don't necessarily come anywhere close to equaling your salary, but it's nice to at least have some money coming in. However, it was extremely frustrating to call the California unemployment hotline about twenty times without getting through. In fact, they won't even allow you to wait on hold. The message just tells you to call back at another time. This alone was enough motivation for me to look for another job.

Unemployment has its advantages and disadvantages. On the plus side, it's nice to be able to sleep late and get up whenever you want. You now have time to catch up on all the things you haven't had time to do, like fixing up the house, going to a lawyer and writing a will, turning a vacation video into a documentary, etc. In fact, I started out with twenty-five things to do, and quickly got down to a very few manageable things to do. Being unemployed can also help your mental and physical health. I definitely felt less stressed out. I also felt better physically because I exercised a lot more since I had the luxury of working out whenever I wanted to. My dry cleaning bills were next to nothing, and I saved money by eating out a lot less. Also, I saved a lot of money on gas because I no longer had to commute.

On the negative side (and this is a big negative), I no longer had any money coming in. Many of the things on my to-do list cost money. Fortunately, working in the corporate world had been very good to me financially. I had saved and invested well and always maxed out my 401(k) contributions every year.

Another negative regarding unemployment is that after a while it just got boring. I missed the camaraderie of the workplace. During the day, when I went out to the mall, the supermarket, or the beach, there were very few people around because they were all at work! There's only so much television you can watch or so much time you can spend on the Internet before you get bored.

One sad reality about being unemployed is that some people who were your work friends don't call you once you leave the business. When you work with them, you go out to lunch or have drinks and everything's great, but once you leave, those invitations (and opportunities) sometimes stop. There were a select few who stayed in touch with me, but you would think that some of the other people whom I've worked with for ten to twenty years would at least call or email me once in a while. Perhaps they're waiting for me to call or email them?

A NEW BEGINNING

After working in the corporate world for almost thirty years, I certainly have a lot of great memories. As I look back at my corporate career, I think about how I climbed up the corporate ladder, but I sometimes wonder if I made it to the top rung. After all, how do you know if you've risen as far as you can? Obviously, the answer is different for everyone. Most people won't become president of the company, but that doesn't mean that they're not successful. I believe you can make it to the top of your ladder and never have any regrets as long as you've given one hundred percent of yourself to your career and if you're proud of your accomplishments. More than anything, at the end of the day, I believe that if you have a great reputation at work, then you've truly climbed to the "top" of the corporate ladder.

I think about all of the projects I've worked on, all of the presentations I've given, all of the people I've met, all of the places I've been to, all of the headaches (both literally and figuratively) I've suffered, all of the commuting miles I've logged, all of the stress I've endured, all of the meals I've gone out to, and all of the meetings I've participated in. One thing is for sure—I wouldn't trade my corporate career for anything!

I now understand why multi-millionaire executives continue to work. It's not about the money. It's about having a sense of accomplishment. It's about working with a team to solve a problem and getting satisfaction from doing it. It's about the excitement that comes with helping to make the big sale. It's about having a purpose. With a career, a person has a sense of purpose. Without a career, many people have a void in their lives. Now I have some idea about what retirement might be like, and it might not be all it's cracked up to be.

I had previously mentioned some of the advantages of being unemployed, but there's one more big advantage to being unemployed that I forgot to mention—it gave me the time to write this book! I hope that you've learned a few things that will help you in your career. You have a lot to look forward to.

I WISH YOU THE BEST OF LUCK WORKING IN THE CORPORATE WORLD, AND I HOPE THAT YOU CLIMB EVERY RUNG OF THE CORPORATE LADDER UNTIL YOU GET TO THE TOP AND STAY THERE!

Best always,

Andy Teach

NOTES

[1]Stephanie Armour, "Generation Y: They've Arrived at Work with a New Attitude," *USA Today*, November 6, 2005.

[2] Harris Interactive poll conducted online on behalf of CareerBuilder.com among 3,147 hiring managers and human resource professionals (employed full-time; not self-employed; with at least significant involvement in hiring decisions) ages 18 and over between February 11–March 13, 2008.

[3]"College Class of 2010: Use of Career Center Linked to Job Offers." NACE 2010 Student Survey. 31,470 students representing more than 400 colleges and universities nationwide took part; more than 13,000 of those were graduating seniors. Survey conducted February 9–April 30, 2010.

[4]"CareerBuilder's Annual College Job Forecast Finds New College Graduates Will Have To Compete Much Harder For Jobs," April 15, 2009. Survey was conducted online by Harris Interactive on behalf of CareerBuilder.com among 2,543 hiring managers and human resource professionals ages 18 and over between February 20–March 11, 2009.

[5]Sarah E. Needleman, "Young Job Candidates Find Too-Casual Tone of TextSpeak Turns Off Hiring Managers," online.wsj.com, July 29, 2008.

[6]Stephanie Armour, "'Business Casual' Causes Confusion," *USA Today*, July 9, 2007.

[7]Svetlana Shkolnikova, "Weight Discrimination Could Be As Common As Racial Bias," *USA Today*, May 21, 2008.

[8]"Reason for Leaving Job is Immediate Supervisor," gallup.com, Gallup Poll, Date Unknown.

[9]"U.S. Workers Remain Largely Satisfied With Their Jobs," gallup.com, Gallop Poll, August, 2009.

INDEX

GPA requirements, 19

H

"happiness-related" criteria (*see Qualitative Criteria*)

Harris Interactive Poll
    GPA requirements, 19
    job interview mistakes, 30-31

Harrison, Lee Hecht
    survey on generation gap, xvii

health insurance (*see benefits*)

HMO (Health Maintenance Organization), 59

Human Resources
    asking questions of, 14, 31, 36, 50
    calling references, 20, 40-41
    department explained, 49-50
    file on me, 52
    interfacing with, 65
    involved after argument, 184
    involving termination, 41, 51-52
    sending resumes to, 15

hygiene, 119-120

I

Indeed.com, 22

initiation
    examples of, 90-94, 161

International Journal of Obesity
    article, 139-140

international students, 13-14

Internet, the
    growing up with, xvii
    job listings on, 21-22
    researching companies, 31-32
    using caution on, 131
    utilizing to network, 6

interns
    expectations of, 45, 106-108

internships
    getting foot in door, 56
    including on resume, 17-18
    six-month, 40, 56, 107-108

interview
    do's and don'ts, 30-42

informational, 5-6, 15, 17, 23, 31, 72
    lunch/dinner, 48-49
    mock, 42-47
    mistakes, 30-31
    questions, 35-37
    telephone, 47-48

iPod
    listening to at work, 87-88
    listening to in elevator, 121

IT(Information Technology) department
    having phone number of, 103
    retrieving deleted emails, 132
    setting up ID and password, 65
    tracking Internet usage, 131

J

job, the
    decision process before accepting, 54-63
    first day, 66-67
    sleeping on, 82-83
    staying late, 83-84
    time to get new one, 201-203
    where to find out about, 21-29

job fairs, 24

"Just do it," 84-85

L

leave of absence/stress leave, 142-143

life insurance (*see benefits*)

LinkedIn.com, 6, 22, 26-29

list
    keep a project, 87

Los Angeles
    first job, 9-10
    moving to, 8-9
    West Coast career, xv

Lotus Notes (Outlook) calendar, 125

loyalty, 75, 105-110, 167

lunch
    as networking tool, 7
    interview, 48-49
    scheduling appointments during, 143
    sleeping at, 82-83
    when to go to, 67, 83
    with co-workers, 55, 155, 170

Made in the USA
San Bernardino, CA
23 August 2014